The Political Economy of Pension Financialisation

The Political Economy of Pension Financialisation addresses – for numerous countries – how and why pension reforms have come to rely more on financial markets, how public policy reacted to financial crises, and regulatory variation.

The book demonstrates how the process of pension financialisation reveals that pension policy is not only a social policy that affects retirement income, but also a financial policy that impacts savings rates, corporate finance and the economy. The chapters shed light on pre-funded private pensions as one key component of financialisation, as they turn savings into investments via financial services providers. Readers will also see how pension financialisation and the broader financialisation of the economy are here to stay, despite negative developments during and after the financial crisis.

A systematic and comparative overview of the financialisation of pensions, *The Political Economy of Pension Financialisation* is ideal for scholars and postgraduates working on Political Economy, Public Policy and Finance.

This book was originally published as a special issue of the *Journal of European Public Policy*.

Anke Hassel is Professor of Public Policy at the Hertie School of Governance, Berlin, Germany. Her research centres on public policy and comparative political economy as well as on the institutional foundations of business systems, labour rights and corporate social responsibility.

Tobias Wiß is Assistant Professor in Political Science at the Institute of Politics and Social Policy, Johannes Kepler University, Linz, Austria. His research areas include comparative welfare state analysis and comparative political economy with a focus on pensions and family policy.

Journal of European Public Policy Series
Series Editors
Jeremy Richardson is Emeritus Fellow at Nuffield College, Oxford University, UK, and Adjunct Professor in the National Centre for Research on Europe, University of Canterbury, New Zealand.
Berthold Rittberger is Professor and Chair of International Relations at the Geschwister-Scholl-Institute of Political Science at the University of Munich, Germany.

This series seeks to bring together some of the finest edited works on European Public Policy. Reprinting from Special Issues of the *Journal of European Public Policy*, the focus is on using a wide range of social sciences approaches, both qualitative and quantitative, to gain a comprehensive and definitive understanding of Public Policy in Europe.

Innovative Approaches to EU Multilevel Implementation
Moving Beyond Legal Compliance
Edited by Eva Thomann and Fritz Sager

Transforming Food and Agricultural Policy
Post-exceptionalism in Public Policy
Edited by Carsten Daugbjerg and Peter Feindt

EU Socio-Economic Governance since the Crisis
The European Semester in Theory and Practice
Edited by Jonathan Zeitlin and Amy Verdun

The Future of the Social Investment State
Policies, Outcomes and Politics
Edited by Marius R. Busemeyer, Caroline de la Porte, Julian L. Garritzmann and Emmanuele Pavolini

The Politics and Economics of Brexit
Edited by Simon Bulmer and Lucia Quaglia

Free Movement and Non-discrimination in an Unequal Union
Edited by Susanne K. Schmidt, Michael Blauberger and Dorte Sindbjerg Martinsen

The Political Economy of Pension Financialisation
Edited by Anke Hassel and Tobias Wiß

For more information about this series, please visit: https://www.routledge.com/Journal-of-European-Public-Policy-Special-Issues-as-Books/book-series/JEPPSPIBS

The Political Economy of Pension Financialisation

Edited by
Anke Hassel and Tobias Wiß

LONDON AND NEW YORK

First published 2020
by Routledge
2 Park Square, Milton Park, Abingdon, Oxon, OX14 4RN

and by Routledge
52 Vanderbilt Avenue, New York, NY 10017

Routledge is an imprint of the Taylor & Francis Group, an informa business

© 2020 Taylor & Francis

All rights reserved. No part of this book may be reprinted or reproduced or utilised in any form or by any electronic, mechanical, or other means, now known or hereafter invented, including photocopying and recording, or in any information storage or retrieval system, without permission in writing from the publishers.

Trademark notice: Product or corporate names may be trademarks or registered trademarks, and are used only for identification and explanation without intent to infringe.

British Library Cataloguing-in-Publication Data
A catalogue record for this book is available from the British Library

ISBN 13: 978-0-367-36835-7

Typeset in Myriad Pro
by codeMantra

Publisher's Note
The publisher accepts responsibility for any inconsistencies that may have arisen during the conversion of this book from journal articles to book chapters, namely the inclusion of journal terminology.

Disclaimer
Every effort has been made to contact copyright holders for their permission to reprint material in this book. The publishers would be grateful to hear from any copyright holder who is not here acknowledged and will undertake to rectify any errors or omissions in future editions of this book.

Printed in the United Kingdom
by Henry Ling Limited

Contents

   Citation Information   vii
   Notes on Contributors   ix

1   The political economy of pension financialisation: public policy
    responses to the crisis   1
    Anke Hassel, Marek Naczyk and Tobias Wiß

2   Reinforcement of pension financialisation as a response
    to financial crises in Germany, the Netherlands and the
    United Kingdom   19
    Tobias Wiß

3   Multipillarisation remodelled: the role of interest organizations
    in British and German pension reforms   39
    Bernhard Ebbinghaus

4   Re-assessing the role of financial professionals in pension fund
    investment strategies   58
    Margarita Gelepithis

5   Countering financial interests for social purposes: what
    drives state intervention in pension markets in the context of
    financialisation?   78
    Pieter Tuytens

6   Insuring individuals … and politicians: financial services
    providers, stock market risk and the politics of private pension
    guarantees in Germany   97
    Marek Naczyk and Anke Hassel

7 EU pension policy and financialisation: purpose without powers? 117
   Waltraud Schelkle

8 Financialisation meets collectivisation: occupational pensions
   in Denmark, the Netherlands and Sweden 135
   Karen M. Anderson

   Index 155

Citation Information

The chapters in this book were originally published in the *Journal of European Public Policy*, volume 26, issue 4 (2019). When citing this material, please use the original page numbering for each article, as follows:

Chapter 1
The political economy of pension financialisation: public policy responses to the crisis
Anke Hassel, Marek Naczyk and Tobias Wiß
Journal of European Public Policy, volume 26, issue 4 (2019) pp. 483–500

Chapter 2
Reinforcement of pension financialisation as a response to financial crises in Germany, the Netherlands and the United Kingdom
Tobias Wiß
Journal of European Public Policy, volume 26, issue 4 (2019) pp. 501–520

Chapter 3
Multipillarisation remodelled: the role of interest organizations in British and German pension reforms
Bernhard Ebbinghaus
Journal of European Public Policy, volume 26, issue 4 (2019) pp. 521–539

Chapter 4
Re-assessing the role of financial professionals in pension fund investment strategies
Margarita Gelepithis
Journal of European Public Policy, volume 26, issue 4 (2019) pp. 540–559

Chapter 5
Countering financial interests for social purposes: what drives state intervention in pension markets in the context of financialisation?
Pieter Tuytens
Journal of European Public Policy, volume 26, issue 4 (2019) pp. 560–578

Chapter 6
Insuring individuals ... and politicians: financial services providers, stock market risk and the politics of private pension guarantees in Germany
Marek Naczyk and Anke Hassel
Journal of European Public Policy, volume 26, issue 4 (2019) pp. 579–598

Chapter 7
EU Pension policy and financialisation: purpose without powers?
Waltraud Schelkle
Journal of European Public Policy, volume 26, issue 4 (2019) pp. 599–616

Chapter 8
Financialisation meets collectivisation: occupational pensions in Denmark, the Netherlands and Sweden
Karen M. Anderson
Journal of European Public Policy, volume 26, issue 4 (2019) pp. 617–636

For any permission-related enquiries please visit:
http://www.tandfonline.com/page/help/permissions

Contributors

Karen M. Anderson is Associate Professor of Social Policy at University College Dublin, Ireland. She received her PhD in political science from the University of Washington (Seattle, USA) and has held positions at Radboud University Nijmegen (The Netherlands), Leiden University (The Netherlands) and the University of Twente (The Netherlands). Her research focuses on comparative social policy development, the interaction of labour market policy and social policy, and the impact of Europeanization on national welfare states.

Bernhard Ebbinghaus is Professor of Social Policy at the Department of Social Policy and Intervention and Senior Research Fellow, Green Templeton College at University of Oxford, UK. In addition, he is Associate Member of Nuffield College, University of Oxford, UK, as well as visiting Mercator Fellow at the Collaborative Research Centre, Political Economy of Reform and MZES External Fellow, University of Mannheim, Germany. Since October 2017, Professor Ebbinghaus has been Head of Department of Social Policy and Intervention.

Margarita Gelepithis is Assistant Professor of Public Policy at the University of Warwick, UK. Previously she taught public policy at University College London, UK, and at the University of East London, UK, and comparative social policy at the London School of Economics, UK, where she is currently a visiting fellow (at the European Institute). Her research interests lie in the comparative study of how rich democracies deal with prevalent forms of labour market inequality.

Anke Hassel is Professor of Public Policy at the Hertie School of Governance, Berlin, Germany. Her research centres on public policy and comparative political economy as well as on the institutional foundations of business systems, labour rights and corporate social responsibility.

Marek Naczyk is Associate Professor in Comparative Social Policy and Director of Graduate Studies at the University of Oxford, UK. His research is at the crossroads of social policy, comparative political economy and international political economy. He is a graduate of Sciences Po Paris and received his DPhil in politics from the University of Oxford in 2013. He is also Research Associate at the Centre d'etudes europeennes, Sciences Po Paris.

Waltraud Schelkle is Professor of Political Economy at the European Institute and has been at London School of Economics, UK, since autumn 2001, teaching courses on the political economy of European integration at MSc and PhD level. She is Adjunct Professor of Economics at the Economics Department of the Free University of Berlin, Germany. She has previously worked as Development Economist, from 1989 to 2002 as Staff Member of the German Institute of Development in Berlin. Her research interests are the evolving economic governance of EMU and social policy reforms directed at financial markets.

Pieter Tuytens is LSE Fellow in the Political Economy of Europe, at the London School of Economics, UK. Previously he worked as Policy Consultant (Technopolis Group and IDEA Consult) and completed a traineeship at the European Commission (DG ENTR). His research focuses on the political economy of welfare states. Other work focuses on the welfare-finance nexus, especially regarding the allocation of pension fund assets.

Tobias Wiß is Assistant Professor of Political Science at the Institute of Politics and Social Policy, Johannes Kepler University, Linz, Austria. His research areas include comparative welfare state analysis and comparative political economy with a focus on pensions and family policy.

The political economy of pension financialisation: public policy responses to the crisis

Anke Hassel, Marek Naczyk and Tobias Wiß

ABSTRACT
Financialisation has become a key feature of post-industrial economies. This special issue sheds light on pre-funded private pensions as one key component of financialisation, as they turn savings into investment via financial services providers. Public pension systems face financial pressures, resulting from ageing and rising public debt, while financial services are keen to move into the market of private pension provision. Pre-funded private pensions are shaped by regulatory policies that create and correct markets. The financial crisis has triggered policy responses including shifts in investment strategies and also a re-assessment of the role of pre-funded private pensions as a complementary, rather than a superior, source of old-age income. Policymakers' growing awareness of the benefits of collective occupational schemes administered by the social partners may pave the way for a greater role for collective schemes.

Introduction

Pension systems play a crucial role in the evolution of post-industrial economies. Pension policy is not only a social policy that affects retirement income, but also a financial one that impacts savings rates, corporate finance and, indirectly, corporate behaviour.

Funded pensions 'can be designed to create large sums of patient, far-sighted capital, thereby giving rise to a distinctive type of capitalism.' (Estevez-Abe 2001: 190). In Japan, pension funds helped not only to provide funding for public infrastructure projects, but also to supply private manufacturers with patient capital that helped Japanese firms to develop capacities that propelled them to world levels from the 1960s. However the relationship between pension systems and types of capitalism has changed fundamentally in recent decades, as a wave of financialisation has swept the globe (van der

Zwan 2014). The lifting of capital controls, the steep increase in profits from financial activities, the rise of shareholder value – a doctrine that has sometimes been pushed by pension funds – have all characterised the shift from industrial to finance capitalism. At the same time, public pensions have been targeted for partial privatisation, thereby opening up new business opportunities for financial firms, such as insurance companies, mutual funds and banks.

Historically, old-age pensions were understood as a deferred wage, both by trade unions and employers, and were at the core of welfare state expansion. As pension systems make long-term promises for payments in old age, individuals and families rely on them when making life choices. But population ageing, declining growth rates, rising public debt as well as the decreasing participation rates of elderly workers have put pressure on mature pension systems and have made pension reform a salient issue in political discourse. Despite numerous reforms that have lowered pension benefits and increased the retirement age, public pensions still amount to 8.2% of gross domestic product (GDP) and stood at 18% of total government spending in the OECD in 2013 (OECD 2017: 142).

In line with the World Bank's multi-pillar model (Orenstein 2013; World Bank 1994), reforms in recent decades included 'twin processes': the – typically incremental – reduction of public pensions and the expansion of non-state – occupational and personal – pre-funded defined-contribution pensions. This led to a privatisation and marketisation (Ebbinghaus 2015), and ultimately to a financialisation of pensions. Privatisation shifted responsibility for pension provision to private actors, mainly financial services firms, employers and trade unions. Marketisation introduced market mechanisms into both public and private pension plans. Indeed, in both types of plans, clear commitments to guarantee pensions in relation to previous wages at retirement (so-called 'defined benefits') have been increasingly replaced by the 'defined-contribution' principle that consists of offering the insured what they have paid into the system, plus – financial or notional – returns on these contributions, thereby fostering a major reallocation of retirement risks onto individuals.

Pension financialisation lies at the intersection of the privatisation and marketisation of pensions. It refers to the rise of pre-funded defined-contribution plans managed by private financial services providers and to its implications in terms of the growing share of the financial services sector in GDP and employment growth, the growing dependence of pensioners' livelihoods on the performance of financial markets and the growing role of pension funds as providers of capital. Pension financialisation is therefore a subcategory of the broader – and multidimensional – phenomenon of financialisation (cf. van der Zwan 2014; see also Dixon and Sorsa 2009; Ebbinghaus 2011; Engelen 2003; Hacker 2006; Langley 2008).

Despite a general trend towards the financialisation of pensions, three phenomena are striking: First, the extent to which pre-funded private defined-contribution pension plans play a role in mature welfare states still varies considerably. There has been no universal shift of pension systems towards comprehensive private provision. The size of assets held by pension funds – of the defined-contribution and defined-benefit type – in the OECD ranges from close to zero to more than 150% of GDP (Table 1).

Second, there is an important variation in the governance structures and distributional consequences of national systems of pre-funded private pension provision. For example, while some countries (i.e., the United States and the United Kingdom) have 'pure' defined-contribution plans, that fully expose individuals to investment risk, others (e.g., France and Germany) introduced regulations – such as minimum return guarantees – that aim to protect savers from stock market drops (Antolín et al. 2011). Risks do thus not have to be fully attributed to savers.

Third, the financial crisis has had an impact on the provision of pre-funded private – particularly defined-contribution – pensions. Although there has been no general reversal of pension financialisation, regulators, policymakers

Table 1. Pension funds and financialisation in 21 OECD countries.

	Assets of all non-sovereign pension funds as % of GDP		Assets of sovereign pension funds as % of GDP	Market capitalisation of listed domestic companies as % of GDP		Finance and insurance as % of total value added	
	2001–2008	2009–2016	2001–2008	2001–2008	2009–2016	2001–2008	2009–2016
Denmark	124.0	187.6		52.7		5.2	6.1
Canada	110.3	136.5	5.6	111.2	117.7	7.3	7.0
United States	108.3	126.1	14.0	122.1	127.1	7.4	7.0
Netherlands	104.2	145.0		90.3	84.9	6.4	7.9
Switzerland	98.4	119.4		218.0	202.0	11.8	10.2
Australia	83.1	103.6	3.9	115.8	101.1	8.2	8.7
United Kingdom	67.0	91.3		115.7		6.8	7.6
Finland	65.8	63.5		109.9		2.8	2.7
Sweden	41.6	66.6	23.8	84.7		3.9	4.3
Ireland	40.5	45.9	8.1	52.8	44.6	9.1	8.8
Portugal	12.7	10.5	3.7	38.5	31.0	6.9	6.0
New Zealand	12.2	17.9	4.7	34.2	36.1	5.2	5.9
Spain	11.1	13.4	2.5	84.4	74.8	4.9	4.3
Japan	10.8	21.4	26.8	74.9	78.9	5.7	4.7
Norway	6.2	7.7	7.5	53.9	53.3	3.6	4.6
France	5.7	8.8	3.9	79.2	74.3	3.7	4.3
Belgium	4.2	4.5	4.6	66.5	66.0	5.5	6.1
Austria	4.2	5.3		31.9	26.5	5.0	4.5
Germany	4.0	6.0		45.1	43.7	4.8	4.8
Italy	3.1	7.0		41.6	25.6	5.1	6.1
Greece	0.0	0.3		56.4	23.2	4.4	4.8

Source: OECD Global Pension Statistics; World Development Indicators; OECD.Stat.

and pension funds themselves have started to address the negative fall-out of the crisis on pension accounts. One sees a mixed account: in some countries, there was a gradual adjustment towards more conservative investment (UK), but in other cases, asset allocation became even more risky, searching for yields in a low interest rate environment. On the other hand, there was more risk-sharing through collective schemes, while the pressure to join private defined-contribution schemes continued through auto-enrolment. Highly professional financial services industries have been more or less successful in influencing the most recent reforms.

In this collection of articles, we shed light on the evolution of national pensions-finance nexuses – and the variation in pension financialisation – by analysing their emergence, regulation and readjustments. The focus of the analysis is on the response of policymakers to the financial crisis and the fall-out for private pensions. Pension financialisation presents sharp distributional and political dilemmas (Anderson 2019). Individualised financial market risks may increase inequality for pensioners and retirees face 'cohort risk' as falling financial asset prices at the time of retirement hit particular cohorts. Furthermore pension financialisation increases the political influence of financial actors.

Because of the rise of these new risks, we are interested in how different governance arrangements have managed to control them in times of financial crisis, and how policymakers have dealt with different kinds of demands from the insured and from other stakeholders, such as employers and financial services industries. This article first surveys the extent of financialisation of pension policy and its impact on the financialisation of the economy. It then looks more closely at the impact of the financial crisis on private pension provision and policy responses, and presents the articles featured in this special issue. It concludes by zooming in on critical future issues in the governance of multi-pillar pension systems.

Pension financialisation today: no convergence among OECD countries

The financialisation of advanced economies has recently attracted a lot of attention in the context of the public debate on the effects of the financial crisis and growing income inequality. Financialisation is a multidimensional concept that captures a variety of – largely interlinked – developments (van der Zwan 2014: 101–2).

One dimension that has characterised financialisation has been the growing share of the financial services industry in GDP and in employment growth (Boyer 2000). A second facet of financialisation has been the increasing reliance of non-financial firms on earnings generated through financial channels rather than through trade or commodity production and, relatedly, firms' adoption of the doctrine of shareholder value maximisation (Krippner 2005; Lazonick and O'Sullivan 2000). A third very significant development has been the financialisation of households' everyday lives through their increasing use of various financial products, such as private defined-contribution pensions (Martin 2002).

A debate exists about how social policies have been affected by – or might also affect – these developments. The Varieties of Capitalism (VoC) approach has, for a long time, assumed that the deregulation of financial markets and the rise of institutional investors – such as private pension funds – pushing for shareholder value maximisation posed the greatest threat for the resilience of coordinated market economies and their encompassing welfare states (Hall and Soskice 2001). Others have argued that the financialisation of everyday life resulting from the promotion of homeownership – for example because of mortgage holders' attentiveness to interest rate changes or because of the wealth effects of house price appreciation – has eroded public support for redistribution and social insurance arrangements (Ansell 2014; Langley 2008; Schelkle 2012a; Schwartz and Seabrooke 2008). Social policy changes have also been seen as a major driver of financialisation: For example, welfare state retrenchment and its negative impact on the living standards of low and middle-income households is said to have contributed to a boom in consumer credit (Crouch 2009; Krippner 2011).

Old-age pensions have been considered a central constituent of financialisation processes, since they can be pre-funded through an accumulation of assets invested in capital markets (Engelen 2003). The rise of defined-contribution pensions – and the direct link such plans create between the level of benefits and financial market fluctuations – has contributed to turning households into 'everyday' investors (Langley 2008). Pension funds have pushed for a better protection of minority shareholder interests – and, sometimes, for a greater integration of shareholder value maximisation – in investee firms' management practices (Gourevitch and Shinn 2005). Governments have also been increasingly attracted to pension privatisation because, in a context of deindustrialisation and, simultaneously, of the growing internationalisation of finance, they have seen it as a means to increase the competitiveness of their domestic financial industries and, therefore, to boost their countries' economic growth (Naczyk and Palier 2014; see also, World Bank 1994).

While there has been a clear trend towards financialisation in pension policy in recent decades, reforms have not led to convergence among OECD countries. National pension systems have never relied on prefunded private pension provision to the same extent, neither before nor after the era of the retrenchment of public pensions. Moreover, countries' different regulatory approaches have meant that private pension funds are not associated to the same extent with financial sector growth and with a financialisation of non-financial firms. Differences in the regulation of pension funds are responsible for varying degrees of individual financial risks or, in other words, a financialisation of daily life.

It has generally been accepted in the literature that generous public pension schemes are likely to 'crowd out' private pension provisions and that, consequently, the retrenchment of public pensions could help 'crowd in' private plans (Davis 1995; Ebbinghaus 2011). At the same time, it has long been argued that pension systems are a 'locus classicus' of path dependence, for example because of the very long periods of time over which workers accrue their pension rights and of the political resistance to any attempts to change the economic expectations that workers form over time (Myles and Pierson 2001: 306). Even though almost all affluent democracies have cut public pension entitlements over the last three decades (Ebbinghaus 2011), public expenditure on pensions has continued to increase across most OECD countries (see Figure 1). This is the result of financial pressures caused by population ageing, but also of long time lags between the enactment of pension cuts and their implementation (Bonoli and Palier 2007). Similarly, cross-national variation in current spending on private pensions and in the size of pension fund sectors is still, to a large extent, the legacy of regulations introduced several decades ago.

During the post-war period, most countries in Western and Southern Europe introduced generous earnings-related social insurance schemes that provided workers with income maintenance and largely crowded out pre-

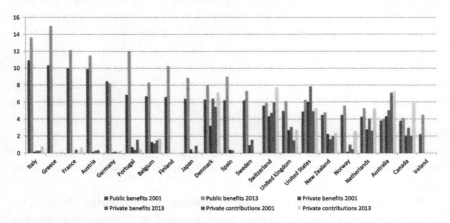

Figure 1. Spending on public/private pensions and contributions to private pension plans as % of GDP, 2001 and 2013. Source: OECD SOCX; OECD Global Pension Statistics. Notes: Data for private benefits in France (2001), Greece (2001) and in Ireland (2001 and 2013) are missing; data for private contributions in France (2001), Ireland (2001 and 2013), Spain (2001 and 2013) and Sweden (2001 and 2013) are missing. For Sweden's private benefits, data were retrieved from OECD.data (2005 benefits for 2001).

funded private pension plans (see top spenders on public benefits in Figure 1). Two notable exceptions in Continental Europe were Switzerland and the Netherlands, where much more basic social insurance pensions (in Switzerland) and universal flat-rate pensions (in the Netherlands) opened enough space for the development of private pension plans. Because of their reliance on basic – often flat-rate – public pensions, the English-speaking countries of Europe, North America and the Antipodes also saw the rise of what some have called 'pension fund capitalism' (Clark 2000). Nordic countries relied on somewhat more complex mixes of public and private arrangements. All of them introduced universal flat-rate pensions for their citizens between the 1930s and 1960s. In the 1960s, Sweden, Finland and Norway – but not Denmark – topped these schemes up with a second public earnings-related pension so as to provide workers with better income maintenance. Occupational pension plans established by employers and unions continued providing an important source of retirement income in Denmark, Norway and Sweden, while in Finland they were all incorporated into the second, public, earnings-related schemes. This explains why Finland has very substantial pension fund assets despite having almost non-existent private pension plans (Table 1 and Figure 1). Japan also relied on a mix of public and private pensions and, like Finland, pre-funded much of its public expenditure through the accumulation of financial assets.

In recent decades, many governments have substantially transformed their public pension systems. For example, Sweden, Finland and Norway have suppressed their highly-redistributive universal pensions and expanded the role of social insurance. Almost all governments have also promoted the expansion of pre-funded private defined-contribution pension plans, not only by cutting public pensions, but also by introducing generous tax incentives for private retirement savings. Yet the general picture that we have drawn of public-private pension mixes in the post-war period is still largely valid today. Continental and Southern European countries (except for the Netherlands and Switzerland) still overwhelmingly rely on public social insurance with public expenditure on public pensions as a percentage of GDP growing acutely in Southern European countries in the wake of the global financial crisis due to economic recession. By contrast, English-speaking countries and Nordic countries (except for Finland) are more mixed.

This does not mean that the private pensions' landscape has remained stable. One of the most significant changes in recent decades has been the gradual replacement of defined-benefit pensions schemes by defined-contribution ones in almost all OECD countries. Another major development is the rise of mandatory or quasi-mandatory private pension provision in countries such as Switzerland, the Netherlands, Denmark, Sweden, Australia and, more recently, New Zealand and the United Kingdom. Even if the size of contributions to private plans and that of total pension fund assets have not grown in a number of Continental and Southern European countries as much as could be expected, given the retrenchment of public pensions (cf. Grødem et al. 2018; Natali et al. 2018), they have grown almost everywhere else (Figure 1 and Table 1).[1]

Pension financialisation and the financialisation of the economy

Has the rise of pre-funded defined-contribution plans managed by private providers of financial services led to a financialisation of the economy? Here, it is vital to distinguish between different dimensions of financialisation. First, there is undoubtedly a positive association between the rise of pre-funded pensions and the growth of the financial sector. The size of assets of non-sovereign pension funds – of the defined-contribution and defined-benefit type – is relatively strongly correlated with the market capitalisation of domestic listed companies (cf. Table 1 – coefficient of correlation of 0.624 for the 2001–2008 period). Economists, financial sector actors and international organisations, such as the World Bank and the OECD, have, for a long time, argued that, by ensuring stable inflows of capital, private pension funds could increase both the depth and the liquidity of capital markets (Naczyk and Palier 2014; see also, Naczyk and Hassel 2019). The correlation between the size of assets of non-sovereign pension funds and the contribution of financial services to total GDP turns out to be weaker compared to the association with companies' market capitalisation (0.493 for 2001–2008 and 0.538 for 2009–2016). The rise of private pension provision can boost the revenues of various providers of financial savings products and typically nurtures the new industries of pension management consultants and intermediaries (Gelepithis 2019). But it is also important to bear in mind that a very large number of private pension schemes are run on a not-for-profit basis and potentially limit the expansion of for-profit insurance companies or mutual funds. This is typically the case of collective occupational schemes, set up as a result of a collective agreement signed between trade unions and employers, especially those of very large industry-level schemes that manage their assets in-house. Such schemes are more prevalent among Nordic countries and the Netherlands. Other important players are (quasi-)public funds (such as Sweden's AP7 Såfa and the UK's NEST) that compete with for-profit providers of personal or occupational pensions.

Although the articles in this special issue do not focus on the financialising impact of pension funds on non-financial firms and entities, previous research has shown that there is also significant variation on that second dimension of financialisation. As already mentioned, pension funds have often been presented as advocates of shareholder value maximisation and, consequently, as drivers of a rise of short-termism among non-financial firms (Lazonick and O'Sullivan 2000). But pension funds are objects of political conflict, and various actors – including managers of non-financial firms and trade unions – have tried to shape regulations so as to turn them into 'patient capitalists' that can improve investee firms' long-term value creation (Estevez-Abe 2001; Naczyk 2016). The patience of pension funds as investors not only applies to their behaviour as shareholders, but also as holders of other financial assets, such as bonds or derivatives (Deeg and Hardie 2016). One area where their investor role is also politicised is that of real estate investment (van Loon and Aalbers 2017). In addition, there have also been major attempts to promote the adoption of environmentally and socially responsible investment practices in the industry (Marens 2004; van der Lugt and Dingwerth 2015). Since actors' preferences and regulations on pension funds' investment practices have varied cross-nationally (McCarthy et al. 2016; Wiß 2015), there is a major need for more comparative research on this issue.

The third salient dimension of financialisation is its relation to households' everyday lives. The received wisdom in the political economy literature is that the rise of pre-funded defined-contribution plans (at the expense of defined-benefit schemes) has directly contributed to expose households to the vagaries of financial markets. Yet, here too, variation is the keyword. Pension funds can pursue more or less risky investment strategies. Previous research had already shown that pension fund managers pursue less risky strategies – that typically rely on investments in fixed-income securities, such as bonds – when trade unions are incorporated in the funds' decision-making structures (Wiß 2015). But the riskiness and volatility of pension fund investment is also often a regulatory issue. While Anglo-Saxon countries usually allow defined-contribution schemes to fully expose plan members to financial market risks, many Continental European countries have introduced regulations that force pension providers to guarantee a minimum rate of return on pension savings. Variations in the allocation of risks are therefore the key theme of this special issue.

Correcting failures in private pension markets after the crisis?

The growing reliance of pension provision on financial markets resulted from more or less deliberate market creation by governments from the 1980s. However, private – particularly defined-contribution – pension plans became increasingly contested and subject to market-correcting measures in the wake of the global financial crisis (see also Schelkle 2012b).

From the 1980s, governments helped to create new markets for private defined-contribution pension plans by cutting public pensions, by making regulations of pre-existing private defined-benefit plans increasingly stringent and by creating tax incentives for the expansion of – personal or occupational – pre-funded defined-contribution plans. The move towards defined-contribution plans was, in general, not driven by deliberate attempts to increase households' exposure to financial market risks, but rather by cautious efforts to reduce governments' long-term pension commitments and to simultaneously increase private responsibility for old-age provision. The financial services industry was keen to step into the breach, as a low inflation-high yield environment became predominant in OECD countries from the 1980s. Governments could also justify the promotion of pension financialisation by pointing out that it had the advantage of creating an inflow of capital in financial markets – and, thus, potentially to promote economic growth – at a time of deindustrialisation. Yet, market-creating pension reforms have expanded the markets for longevity insurance, including their failures. The latter have become increasingly visible after the global financial crisis.

Prefunded private defined-contribution pension plans not only make retirement vulnerable to market volatility; they also put pressure on pension fund managers to achieve high yields, thereby potentially exacerbating market volatility. Governments have thus been under pressure to correct private pension markets in order to ensure stability in pension provision – in other words, in order to achieve the social policy goal of income maintenance in old age. Market-correcting policies include a number of safeguards on investment regulations, such as minimum return guarantees, a set of rules and regulations on investment regarding equities and bonds, a process of de-risking of the investments of private funds, a degree of collective regulation through social partners as well as a partial limitation of financial services industries to dominate the regulation of the market. Defined-contribution pensions can be governed within collective frameworks, which manage market volatility and agency problems quite differently (Anderson 2019; Ebbinghaus and Wiß 2011).

The financial market crisis of 2007/08 and the recent sovereign debt crisis became the stress test for prefunded private pensions. Pension funds lost up to 25% of assets during the 2007/08 financial market crisis, and not all funds have fully recovered. Government regulators and fund managers have faced pressure from their electorates and clients to meet their pension promises. But has the policy mood shifted from market creation to market correction?

This special issue addresses the responses by governments and pension providers to the crisis with regard to governance problems of prefunded private pensions. It particularly aims to contribute to our understanding of the ways governments and private pension providers have sought to reconcile the need for old-age income security and the interests of the industry as well as their own growth models. Although the response of governments and the EU to the 2007/08 financial crisis is already very well documented with regard to public economic and fiscal policy (e.g., Mabbett and Schelkle 2015; Mayntz 2012; Pontusson and Raess 2012) as well as public social policy (e.g., Chung and Thewissen 2011; Hooren et al. 2014; Shahidi 2015; van Kersbergen et al. 2014), in particular labour market reforms, we still lack knowledge about changes in the regulation of pre-funded private pensions in the wake of the crisis – as one key element of financialisation – from a public policy and political economy perspective.

In general, most of the pension reforms before the 2007/08 crisis aimed at market-creation. However, following the financial crisis, one would have expected market-correcting reactions. In fact, several articles in this special issue find that governments, regulators and fund managers have introduced a number of market-correction policies that have aimed at restoring trust in private pensions, minimising risks and resolving governance problems that were previously unresolved, such as the role of fees in private pensions and investment strategies and regulations. Yet, despite the negative fallout from the crisis, market correction policies have not led to a general reversal of pension financialisation. Pre-funded private pensions have become a key component of retirement provision in affluent democracies and have become deeply entrenched, both politically and economically, as part of a new – post-industrial and increasingly financialised – political economy.

Articles in the special issue highlight important trade-offs that policy-makers have faced in reforming private pension plans in the wake of the financial crisis. While the crisis made the volatility of markets highly salient and led to market-correcting responses, governments have been increasingly burdened by public debt and have therefore not had the option of increasing the generosity of public pensions. Moreover, while pension funds have increasingly moved away from volatile equities to more secure bonds, the low-interest environment has made it difficult for them to generate sufficient returns. The trade-off between volatility/risks and returns has been crucially shaped by regulatory decisions made by governments. However, financial market correction does not always result in definancialisation, as markets can be corrected for non-market elements resulting in a reinforcement of financialisation.

The structure of the special issue

The article by Wiß (2019) maps the general development of pension financialisation in the last two decades. He demonstrates that the reliance of pension funds on financial markets has been reinforced in countries as diverse as Germany, the Netherlands and the UK, although the occurrence of two financial market crises (2001/02 and 2007/08) and the still ongoing sovereign debt crisis (since 2011) provided windows of opportunity for policy change. This is echoed by higher individual risks and greater individual responsibility through the extension of coverage of financialised pension (semi-obligatory financialisation) and a shifting away from (final-salary) defined-benefit schemes. Pension fund regulation in all three countries relaxed funding requirements, introduced real market values for the calculation of pension liabilities and/or strengthened financial market expertise in pension fund governance. The article argues that entrenched interests of several actors are an important reason for the reinforcement of pension financialisation despite three financial crises. The financial industry, employers, the state and trade unions have – for different reasons – no interest in the collapse of pension funds.

Ebbinghaus (2019) provides a detailed analysis of the role of organised interests during pension reform processes in the contrasting cases of Germany and the UK. Although the multipillar pension system in the UK has been developed earlier than in Germany, coverage of funded pensions increased in both countries over the last two decades. Pension privatisation and multipillarisation have shifted retirement income provision from non-funded public to private defined-contribution pensions and hence are clearly expression of financialisation. Initially, the position towards financialised pensions was more heterogeneous between employers, the financial sector, trade unions and social advocacy groups. In the context of recent reforms and increasing multipillarisation and financialisation, interest groups adapted their strategies. The organised interest groups of capital and employers supported pension reform initiatives of governments and the declining power of trade unions weakened their defence of the status-quo. Organised labour seems no longer to be as class-oriented and moderate unions welcomed a stronger role for occupational pensions. Despite the financial crisis, they do not see the possibility of a reversal of pension financialisation and embrace multipillarisation, although existing inequalities need to be addressed.

Investment professionals are another group of actors with an interest in pension financialisation, as shown by Gelepithis (2019). So far, most of the literature had explained asset allocation with the preferences of employers (mostly in liberal market economies) or the involvement of trade unions and employee representatives in board decisions (mostly in coordinated market economies). Pension fund governance in the UK has traditionally been seen as employer-led, and pension fund investment behaviour has long been geared towards equities. However, the past two decades have seen UK pension funds 'de-risk' their investment portfolios by shifting their asset allocation away from equities and towards bonds despite no change in pension fund governance. The influence of pension industry professionals, who follow liability-driven investment strategies due to their own risk-return calculations, serves as the main explanation. Faced with dissatisfying performances in the 1980s and 1990s of the 'asset only' investment strategy favouring equities, financial professionals started to disseminate the norm of making investment decisions contingent upon liabilities. Their efforts resulted in statutory minimum funding requirements considering pension funds' asset-liability mismatch. Thanks to highly technical actuarial valuations that are required for liability-driven management, pension fund trustees in the UK, who lacked such expertise, increasingly asked investment consultants for advice or even outsourced investment decisions to asset managers.

Tuytens's (2019) article argues that – in times of financialisation – the state matters for private pension regulation and market correction in liberal countries. The financialisation of pensions creates new conflicts between the pension plan members, who are interested in predictable and high benefits, and pension providers, who aim for returns and profits. Although the existing literature tends to suggest that 'capital' is stronger and will succeed, the article argues that policymakers play an independent role in countering financial interests and improving social outcomes. In the least-likely case of the UK, governments have introduced caps on pension plan charges against the interests of the pension industry. Fiscally constrained governments have considered it to be in their interest to expand good-value-for-money pension plans via cost-reducing regulation (fee caps) in order to avoid pressure and demands for higher public pensions or social assistance because of inadequate private pension provision.

The financialisation of pensions is associated with the introduction of pre-funded pensions that provide benefits based on defined contributions and their financial market returns. However, defined-contribution pensions vary across countries and can take the form of pure defined-contribution plans where individuals are fully exposed to investment risks or more regulated defined-contribution plans where a minimum rate of return prevents major losses. Naczyk and Hassel (2019) analyse the politics behind the introduction of such guarantees within defined-contribution plans. Based on the case study of the introduction of so-called 'Riester' pension plans in Germany in 2001, they emphasise the existence of two – social policy and financial regulation – dimensions in the politics of investment return guarantees. They argue that politicians' choice between predictable benefits (social policy dimension) and equity market development (financial regulation) depends on whether they link the promotion of defined-contribution pensions with reforms of public pensions. The introduction of defined-contribution pensions in combination with cutbacks in public pension benefits represents a high-salient social policy issue resulting in pressure to provide guarantees as compensation. In Germany, this link allowed the insurance industry and parts of trade unions to successfully push for the introduction of such guarantees in the early 2000s.

Beyond nation-states and interest groups, the European Union may drive pension financialisation. Schelkle (2019) provides evidence that the EU does not promote a coherent pension financialisation agenda as one might expect. Instead, the EU's pension strategy is rather accidental and multi-faceted, consisting of a mix of market creation, emulation and correction. Although the EU promotes pre-funded pensions as part of financial market integration, this does not automatically result in the financialisation of pensions. The article illustrates the argument using the reform process of the Pan-European Pension Product (PEPP). The main reasons behind the introduction of PEPP were concerns about pension losses for intra-EU migrants, greater individual responsibility for retirement income, addressing market failures by common standards and transparency, and the closure of pension gaps, rather than promoting the straightforward financialisation of pensions.

In the last contribution to this special issue, Anderson (2019) challenges the financialisation literature that is on average more sceptical about the merits of financialised pensions. Her article provides an overview of the historical development of occupational pension financialisation in Denmark, the Netherlands and Sweden and lays down how the social partners (trade unions and employer associations) managed to organise pre-funded pensions collectively. Cases of employer insolvency and demands by workers and unions for secure and portable pensions resulted in external funding and administration of occupational pensions, allowing the separation of pension reserves from the employer. Furthermore, low or incomplete public pensions crowded in collective occupational pensions for well-paid employers that later had been extended to the entire workforce. Although the levels of pension fund assets are very high and comparable to liberal countries such as the UK and the US, the multipillar pension systems in Denmark, the Netherlands and Sweden are more likely to serve social interests thanks to the equal involvement of employers and trade unions in pension fund governance. Collective pension schemes in these three countries limit the influence of external financial actors and ensure that investments fit with the interests of the plan participants. Although collective pension funds are not risk free, they are capable of combining the advantages of funded pensions with a limited degree of individual risks.

Conclusion: where is pension financialisation heading?

Even though pension funds in almost all OECD countries lost massively during the 2007/08 financial crisis, there is no general reversal of financialisation and no general trend towards greater public provision. Pension financialisation and the broader financialisation of the economy are here to stay. There are two key insights from the articles in this special issue.

The first one is that governments' responses to the risk exposure after financial crises and reactions by financial services providers are far from uniform or even coherent. There is both further financialisation as well as market correction – in the sense of setting limits for the impact of financial markets on old-age incomes – within countries and no convergence towards a common blueprint for multi-pillar pensions, as often proposed by international organisations (e.g., World Bank 1994). As the experience of

Nordic countries and the Netherlands shows, the positive impact of the social partners in the governance of pre-funded private pension plans may improve the legitimacy and attractiveness of collective schemes. But even such schemes – which also invest their assets in financial markets – are not risk free, although they seem to reconcile the drive for pre-funding of pensions with social security in a better fashion than most private pension defined-contribution schemes. In addition, the EU is far from facilitating a systematic policy of pension financialisation by member states but caught in the prerogatives of prioritising labour mobility, individual responsibility and the closure of pension gaps.

The second important insight is that governments have a broader perspective on pensions, beyond the pressures of demographic change and rising dependency ratios. Governments are quite aware that pre-funded pensions play a role for corporate finance, economic growth and financial markets in general. Therefore, if financialisation and pre-funded private pensions are now a fact of post-industrial societies, the challenge is to work towards a governance system that can minimise risk exposure, maximise returns for the insured and ensure proper supervision of the financial services industries. The articles in this special issue point to a number of mechanisms that show that this task is not impossible, despite the various political barriers involved.

Note

1. It should be noted that comparative OECD data presented in this article often do not include pension contributions and assets managed by life insurance companies (e.g. in Germany), thereby underestimating the extent of change.

Acknowledgements

Authors are listed alphabetically and all authors contributed equally to the work. We are grateful to the editors of JEPP for their support of this special issue and to the reviewers of all articles of this collection. We also would like to thank the participants of the July 2016 and May 2017 workshops at the Hertie School of Governance in Berlin (Germany).

Disclosure statement

No potential conflict of interest was reported by the authors.

Funding

This work was supported by the German Federal Ministry of Education and Research (BMBF) under Grant number 01UF1508.

References

Anderson, K. (2019) 'Financialisation meets collectivisation: occupational pensions in Denmark, the Netherlands and Sweden', *Journal of European Public Policy* 26(4). doi:10.1080/13501763.2019.1574309

Ansell, B. (2014) 'The political economy of ownership: housing markets and the welfare state', *American Political Science Review* 108(2): 383–402.

Antolin, P., Schich S. and Yermo, J. (2011) 'The economic impact of protracted low interest rates on pension funds and insurance companies', *OECD Journal: Financial Market Trends* 2011(1): 237–56.

Bonoli, G. and Palier, B. (2007) 'When past reforms open new opportunities: comparing old-age insurance reforms in Bismarckian welfare systems', *Social Policy & Administration*, 41(6): 555–73.

Boyer, R. (2000) 'Is a finance-led growth regime a viable alternative to Fordism? A preliminary analysis', *Economy and Society* 29(1): 111–45.

Chung, H. and Thewissen, S. (2011) 'Falling back on old habits? A comparison of the social and unemployment crisis reactive policy strategies in Germany, the UK and Sweden', *Social Policy & Administration* 45(4): 354–70.

Clark, G. L. (2000) *Pension Fund Capitalism*, Oxford: Oxford University Press.

Crouch, C. (2009) 'Privatised Keynesianism: an unacknowledged policy regime', *British Journal of Politics & International Relations*, 11(3): 382–99.

Davis E. P. (1995) *Pension Funds, Retirement-Income Security and Capital Markets – An International Perspective*, Oxford: Oxford University Press.

Deeg, R. and Hardie, I. (2016) 'What is patient capital and who supplies it?', *Socio-Economic Review* 14(4): 627–45.

Dixon, A. D. and Sorsa, V. P. (2009) 'Institutional change and the financialisation of pensions in Europe', *Competition & Change* 13(4): 347–67.

Ebbinghaus, B. (ed) (2011) *The Varieties of Pension Governance – Pension Privatization in Europe*, Oxford: Oxford University Press.

Ebbinghaus, B. (2015) 'The privatization and marketization of pensions in Europe: a double transformation facing the crisis', *European Policy Analysis* 1(1): 56–73.

Ebbinghaus, B. (2019) 'Multipillarisation remodelled: the role of interest organisations in British and German pension reforms', *Journal of European Public Policy* 26(4). doi:10.1080/13501763.2019.1574875

Ebbinghaus, B. and Wiß, T. (2011) 'Taming pension fund capitalism in Europe: collective and state regulation in times of crisis', *Transfer – European Review of Labour and Research* 17(1): 15–28.

Engelen, E. (2003) 'The logic of funding European pension restructuring and the dangers of financialisation', *Environment and Planning A* 35(8): 1357–72.

Estevez-Abe, M. (2001) 'The forgotten link: the financial regulation of Japanese pension funds in comparative perspective', in B. Ebbinghaus and P. Manow (eds.), *Comparing Welfare Capitalism: Social Policy and Political Economy in Europe, Japan and the USA*, London: Routledge, pp. 191–214.

Gelepithis, M. (2019) 'Re-assessing the role of financial professionals in pension fund investment strategies', *Journal of European Public Policy* 26(4). doi:10.1080/13501763.2019.1574874

Gourevitch, P. A. and Shinn, J. (2005) *Political Power and Corporate Control: The New Global Politics of Corporate Governance*, Princeton: Princeton University Press.

Grødem, A. S., Hagelund, A., Hippe, J. M. and Trampusch, C. (2018) 'Beyond coverage: the politics of occupational pensions and the role of trade unions. introduction to special issue', *Transfer – European Review of Labour and Research* 24(1): 9–23.

Hacker, J. S. (2006) *The Great Risk Shift: The New Economic Insecurity and the Decline of the American Dream*, Oxford, New York: Oxford University Press.

Hall, P. A. and Soskice, D. (eds) (2001) *Varieties of Capitalism: The Institutional Foundations of Comparative Advantage*, Oxford, New York: Oxford University Press.

Hooren, F. van, Kaasch, A. and Starke, P. (2014) 'The shock routine: economic crisis and the nature of social policy responses', *Journal of European Public Policy* 21(4): 605–23.

Krippner, G. (2005) 'The financialization of the American economy', *Socio-Economic Review* 3(2): 173–208.

Krippner, G. (2011) *Capitalizing on Crisis*, Cambridge, MA: Harvard University Press.

Langley, P. (2008) *The Everyday Life of Global Finance: Saving and Borrowing in Anglo-America*, Oxford, New York: Oxford University Press.

Lazonick, W. and O'Sullivan, M. (2000) 'Maximizing shareholder value: a new ideology for corporate governance', *Economy and Society* 29(1): 13–35.

Mabbett, D. and Schelkle, W. (2015) 'What difference does Euro membership make to stabilization? The political economy of international monetary systems revisited', *Review of International Political Economy* 22(3): 508–34.

Marens, R. (2004) 'Waiting for the north to rise: revisiting Barber and Rifkin after a generation of union financial activism in the US', *Journal of Business Ethics* 52(1): 109–23.

Martin, R. (2002) *Financialization of Everyday Life*, Philadelphia, PA: Temple University Press.

Mayntz, R. (ed) (2012) *Crisis and Control – Institutional Change in Financial Market Regulation*, Frankfurt a. M., New York: Campus.

McCarthy, M., Sorsa, V. P. and van der Zwan, N. (2016) 'Investment preferences and patient capital: financing, governance, and regulation in pension fund capitalism', *Socio-Economic Review* 14(4): 751–69.

Myles, J. and Pierson, P. (2001) 'The comparative political economy of pension reform' in P. Pierson (ed.), *The New Politics of the Welfare State*, Oxford: Oxford University Press, pp. 305–33.

Naczyk, M. (2016) 'Creating French-style pension funds: business, labour and the battle over patient capital', *Journal of European Social Policy* 26(3): 205–18.

Naczyk, M. and Hassel, A. (2019) 'Insuring individuals … and politicians: financial services providers, stock market risk and the politics of private pension guarantees in Germany', *Journal of European Public Policy* 26(4). doi:10.1080/13501763.2019.1575455

Naczyk, M. and Palier, B. (2014) 'Feed the beast: finance capitalism and the spread of pension privatization in Europe', Paper presented at the 26th SASE Annual Meeting, Chicago, 10–12 July.

Natali, D., Keune, M., Pavolini, E. and Seeleib-Kaiser, M. (2018) 'Sixty years after Titmuss: new findings on occupational welfare in Europe', *Social Policy & Administration* 52(2): 435-48.

OECD (2017) *Pensions at a Glance 2017: OECD and G20 Indicators*, Paris: OECD.

Orenstein, M. A. (2013) 'Pension privatization: evolution of a paradigm', *Governance* 26(2): 259-81.

Pontusson, J. and Raess, D. (2012) 'How (and why) is this time different? The politics of economic crisis in Western Europe and the United States', *Annual Review of Political Science* 15(1): 13-33.

Schelkle, W. (2012a) 'A crisis of what? Mortgage credit markets and the social policy of promoting homeownership in the United States and in Europe', *Politics & Society* 40(1): 59-80.

Schelkle, W. (2012b) 'In the spotlight of crisis: how social policies create, correct, and compensate financial markets', *Politics & Society* 40(1): 3-8.

Schelkle, W. (2019) 'EU pension policy and financialisation: purpose without powers?', *Journal of European Public Policy* 26(4). doi:10.1080/13501763.2019.1574871

Schwartz, H. and Seabrooke, L. (2008) 'Varieties of residential capitalism in the international political economy: old welfare states and the new politics of housing', *Comparative European Politics* 6(3): 237-61.

Shahidi, F. V. (2015) 'Welfare capitalism in crisis: a qualitative comparative analysis of labour market policy responses to the Great Recession', *Journal of Social Policy* 44(4): 659-86.

Tuytens, P. (2019) 'Countering financial interests for social purposes: what drives state intervention in pension markets in the context of financialisation?', *Journal of European Public Policy* 26(4). doi:10.1080/13501763.2019.1574872

van der Lugt, C. and Dingwerth, K. (2015) 'Governing where focality is low: UNEP and the principles for responsible investment', in K. W. Abboth, P. Genschel, D. Snidal and B. Zangl (eds), *International Organizations as Orchestrators*, Cambridge: Cambridge University Press, pp. 237-61.

van der Zwan, N. (2014) 'Making sense of financialization', *Socio-Economic Review* 12(1): 99-129.

van Kersbergen, K., Vis, B. and Hemerijck, A. (2014) 'The Great recession and welfare state reform: is retrenchment really the only game in town?', *Social Policy & Administration* 48(7): 883-904.

van Loon, J. and Aalbers, M. (2017) 'How real estate became "just another asset class": the financialization of the investment strategies of Dutch institutional investors', *European Planning Studies* 25(2): 221-40.

Wiß, T. (2015) 'Pension fund vulnerability to the financial market crisis: the role of trade unions', *European Journal of Industrial Relations* 21(2): 131-47.

Wiß, T. (2019) 'Reinforcement of pension financialisation as a response to financial crises in Germany, the Netherlands and the United Kingdom', *Journal of European Public Policy* 26(4). doi:10.1080/13501763.2019.1574870

World Bank (1994) *Averting the Old-Age Crisis: Policies to Protect the Old and Promote Growth*, New York: Oxford University Press.

Reinforcement of pension financialisation as a response to financial crises in Germany, the Netherlands and the United Kingdom

Tobias Wiß

ABSTRACT
The financial market crises of 2001/02 and 2007/08 and the sovereign debt crisis that started in 2011 had adverse effects on financialised pensions such as pension funds. In general, moments of crises are major shocks to existing equilibriums and policies and open windows of opportunity for policy change. Did these crises trigger a slowdown or reversal of pension financialisation? This article finds that Germany, the Netherlands and the United Kingdom took similar steps along the pension financialisation path by intensifying the reliance of pension funds on financial markets despite the occurrence of three financial crises. The reinforcement of pension financialisation can be explained by the entrenched interests of several actors in finance, employers, the state, and trade unions, who have no interest in the collapse of pension funds.

Introduction

In light of two major financial market crises in the 2000s that caused stock market downturns and drops in equity returns and the sovereign debt crisis that negatively affected bond investments in highly rated countries, we could expect a decline in the paradigm that markets know best and offer appropriate solutions. Financial crises are major shocks to existing equilibriums and can provide an opportunity for policy change. This article analyses whether Germany, the Netherlands and the United Kingdom (UK) reversed pension financialisation or took further steps along the pension financialisation path.

At its core, financialisation means an increasing reliance of society, the economy and politics on financial market solutions (Epstein 2006). In this article, pension financialisation means the increasing role that financial markets, their actors and their risks play for the provision of pension benefits (Langley 2008; van der Zwan 2014).

A broad research agenda has investigated the effect of financial market crises on public and social policy. Most of the literature focuses on crisis-related public economic and financial policy (Mayntz 2012; Pontusson and Raess 2012) and public social policy, particularly (un)employment policies (Chung and Thewissen 2011; Kiess et al. 2017; Steinebach and Knill 2017; van Hooren et al. 2014). Much less is known about pension fund responses, although most of them suffered during recent crises (Ebbinghaus and Wiß 2011; Pino and Yermo 2010; Wiß 2015b). Bridgen and Meyer (2009) compared the UK and the Netherlands and argue that pension fund developments such as retrenchment are similar despite their contrasting institutional contexts, but they only refer to developments prior to 2009. Although Natali (2018) analyses the extent that occupational pensions contributed to pension financialisation – with the result of country-specific paths – he did not explicitly investigate the response of pension funds to financial crises.

Countries in Central and Eastern Europe and in Latin America provide evidence for a partial or temporary reversal of pension privatisation – not because pension funds suffered in times of market turmoil – but to reduce public debt (Drahokoupil and Domonkos 2012; Naczyk and Domonkos 2016). Recent studies of the political economy of pension financialisation mostly focus on Anglo-American countries (e.g., Berry 2016; Langley 2004). Complementing the literature, this article shows that countries as diverse as Germany, the Netherlands and the UK reacted to financial crises similarly. The Netherlands and the UK have the highest pension fund assets in Europe and therefore are of particular interest. The pension system in Germany relies on financial market solutions to a limited degree and therefore represents a more likely (control) case for a possible reversal.

The following section discusses the theoretical background of path reversal and path reinforcement. After the case selection strategy, the article analyses the development of pension funds during financial crises and reform trajectories. Then, the reasons for the reinforcement of pension financialisation are examined.

Reversal or reinforcement of pension financialisation in times of crisis?

From a historical institutionalist perspective, earlier events and institutions that are in place for a long time impact subsequent developments and reforms (Pierson 2000; Thelen 1999). An established path is very difficult to adapt or switch. External shocks are signs of a critical juncture – representing a rather brief window of opportunity for change (Capoccia 2016) – and are very rare events that allow for major changes to existing policies. The financial market crises of 2001/02 and 2007/08 and the sovereign debt crisis in the years following 2011 represent such shock situations that may trigger a break with past policies. There have been path departures in many OECD countries, from public pay-as-you-go pensions to (partially) privately funded pension schemes, due to demographic changes. Therefore, it is reasonable to assume a taming of the financial-market logic within pension schemes in times of financial crises.

Pension financialisation

Based on recent studies about financialisation (Berry 2016; Langley 2008; van der Zwan 2014, 2017) and own considerations, this article defines five dimensions for assessing pension financialisation:

(1) The introduction or extension of financial-market based pension schemes is an expression of financialisation because it increases the reliance of individuals' future old-age income on financial markets.
(2) More individual choice within financialised pension products requires financial literacy, resulting in a personalisation of financial risks. In the case of lump sums, individuals are responsible for their financial security until death. Furthermore, if individuals can choose a lump sum instead of an annuity, calculative insurance tools are replaced with the financial market interest rate at the time of withdrawal.
(3) The shift from defined benefits (DB) to defined contributions (DC) is associated with financialisation. In the case of DB, individuals receive guaranteed predictable benefits (e.g., 70% of their final salary) and the employer is responsible for compensating shortfalls. In contrast, pension benefits are uncertain in DC schemes because the benefits depend on the performance of contributions invested in financial markets, often combined with individual choice between different investment strategies.

The shift from final-salary to average-salary DB also signals financialisation. In the latter, employees accumulate a defined benefit for each year of employment (for example, two percent (accrual rate) of their salary). However, depending on the scheme rules, entitlements might not be indexed, and adjustments depend on market developments, resulting in a higher attachment to financial markets. In contrast, final-salary DB schemes automatically index benefits (Ghilarducci 1992).
(4) An additional dimension is the method for calculating the pension fund liabilities of DB schemes. Fixed discount rates set by public agencies do not necessarily reflect current market prices and allow for balancing short-term market fluctuations. In contrast, real market values display the current financial market situation in line with finance actors' ideas about the accuracy of markets producing optimum outcomes. Similarly, real financial market values determine

the level of benefits, not fictitious interest rates in DC schemes without a guaranteed return rate.
(5) Finally, pension fund governance is important for financialisation. The composition of pension fund boards determines the influence of external technocratic experts and financial-market actors and their logic on pension fund decisions.

Reversal of pension financialisation

Reversal means a reduction of the financial market logic in funded pension schemes (de-financialisation). Financial crises reveal shortcomings of the status-quo and delegitimise existing practices, resulting in a need for change. In this wake-up moment, political actors may recognise the failures of funded pension systems and introduce changes.

Hall (1993) noted that a complete reversal (of financialisation) would represent a third-order change because the settings of the instruments (e.g., way of financing pensions and calculating benefits), the instruments themselves, and the basic principles behind a policy (e.g., financial markets are the best instrument for the provision of old-age income) are changing. Financial crises could also lead to first- or second-order change, if the overall logic that financial markets know best is not questioned and only corrected. In this case, the shift back to final-salary DB would be a sign of reversal.

According to Blyth (2002), (economic) institutional change requires a change in (economic) ideas. Similar to Hall's third-order change, ideas are very difficult to change. However, based on negative experiences with existing practices and faced with several negative financial market developments, it is reasonable to consider alternative ways of financing and providing pensions. If a policy promotes growth or pension income based on financial market returns but simultaneously has negative consequences such as (individualised) risks of benefit losses in times of financial crises, only one of the competing attributes usually attracts the attention of powerful actors in a predominant way (True et al. 2007). In times of crises, when the negative consequences grow stronger, the centre of attention and the current policy both shift.

During the first great transformation in 1930, the labour movement demanded protection from unregulated markets (embedded liberalism); during the second great transformation in 1970, businesses called for a return to deregulated markets (disembedding markets) (Blyth 2002). Today, we could expect a third transformation when people suffering from negative financial market developments demand public action against individual financial risks by embedding financial markets. However, to gain ground and introduce a transformation, new ideas need support from a coalition of various actors.

Changes in the core beliefs of a dominating (advocacy) coalition often need an external impetus (Sabatier and Weible 2007). Shocks to existing practices reveal failures of the policy itself and of the supporting coalition. This increases doubts about the existing policy and its supporting coalition. The supporting social coalition of a policy reversal can be the same coalition that supported the old policy, if it has changed its ideas, or it can be a new coalition that was previously in a minority position.

Path reinforcement

Regarding path reinforcement, we can distinguish between intensification and non-response. If the status-quo remains intact, the existing path is further used, stabilising and – to a certain degree – reinforcing the path. However, an active response to financial crises is a more realistic scenario, as political actors are expected to react to adverse situations for the collective good. In both cases, the crisis (non-)response is in line with the previous setting. Financial crises reveal failures of the current system and shortcomings are recognised, but political economies do not react in a reversal. Recent studies show that welfare states managed external shocks in line with pre-existing institutions (Chung and Thewissen 2011; Lallement 2011) or path-dependent ideational paradigms (Kiess et al. 2017). Governments are more likely to restore stability in line with well-known pre-crises politics rather than to implement major path-departing reforms. Based on these findings on public social policy responses, we could expect path reinforcement of pension financialisation.

How can we explain the resilience of pension financialisation despite market failures? From a path dependence logic, self-reinforcing processes and entrenched actors' interests reinforce a path (Pierson 2000). If several actors have invested in a path (sunk costs) they will not actively promote a reversal (Ebbinghaus 2005). Before the crises, pension financialisation had become locked-in, making its reversal very unlikely.

As noted above, institutional change requires a change in ideas (Blyth 2002) that is very difficult (Hall 1993; Sabatier and Weible 2007). The idea of financialisation is deeply rooted in the minds of several actors and serves as the dominating blueprint for existing and future pension reforms. However, negative experiences during times of financial crises can trigger learning processes. The result of such a learning process can be that the existing practice is still considered useful and needing improvement, not requiring reversal but necessitating elimination of design failures. Therefore, financialised pensions must omit non-market elements such as benefit guarantees or fictitious interest rates.

Although pension financialisation may lose attraction in times of financial crises, it can be strong enough to serve as a coalition magnet (Béland and Cox 2016) as long as actors with different interests profit from and support it.

Case selection and vulnerability to financial crises

Following a most-different systems design, the article analyses Germany, the Netherlands and the UK. They share a certain degree of pension financialisation, albeit at different levels, that is essential to analyse its reversal or reinforcement. However, they vary in the importance of pension funds for old-age income, their vulnerability to financial crises and pension fund governance.

Occupational pensions are most important for old-age income in the Netherlands, followed by the UK and Germany. Private pension expenses as a share of public pension expenses amounted to only 8% in Germany in 2000, 59% in the Netherlands and 104% in the UK (OECD SOCX). The share of pension fund assets in 2001 as a percentage of the GDP was the highest in the Netherlands (96%), followed by the UK (68%) and Germany (3.5%) (OECD Global Pension Statistics).[1]

Occupational pensions in the Netherlands have been near universal for decades (Anderson 2011). Coverage rates in 2001 were much lower in Germany (52%) (TNS Infratest 2008), and the UK (55%) (ONS 2002). The equity holdings of British pension funds amounted to 71% of their total investments in the year before the financial market crisis of 2001 (UBS 2017), much higher than that in the Netherlands (46%) and Germany (17%) (OECD Global Pension Statistics).[2] This made British pension funds and, to a lower degree, Dutch funds, vulnerable to volatile stock markets. German funds are supposed to suffer most in times of low bond yields due to their high fixed-asset investments. The DB pension plans of British and Dutch pension funds are vulnerable to financial market and sovereign debt crises, as both reduce funding ratios. In the former, low equity prices reduce the value of assets and in the latter, the low interest rates of government bonds reduce the discount rates that are used to calculate the liabilities.

Occupational pensions in the Netherlands are based on industry-level collective agreements. Pension funds are jointly negotiated and administered by the social partners (Anderson 2011). In the UK, occupational pensions were voluntary until 2012. Pension funds are organised at the company level and set up as trusts, and unions and pension fund members lack influence on pension fund governance (Bridgen and Meyer 2011). Occupational pensions in Germany are voluntary. Many industry-level collective agreements cover occupational pensions and the social partners in some industries established collective pension schemes (Wiß 2015a).

The degree of corporatism and trade union involvement in pension fund governance might shape crisis responses. The z-standardised corporatism score from 2000 to 2010 is the highest for the Netherlands (1.47), followed by Germany (0.97) and the UK (−1.63) (own calculation, based on Jahn 2016). From this perspective, trade unions are most likely to tame negative effects of financial crises for employees in the Netherlands and are least likely to in the UK. Furthermore, Germany and the Netherlands represent coordinated market economies that follow an export-led growth model, and the UK is a typical case for a liberal market economy with a demand-led or consumption-led growth model (Hall 2018).

Crises developments

The level of pension fund assets is an indicator of the impact of financial market crises because their development displays the value of pension fund investments. Figure 1 shows the downturn of pension fund assets in the UK and the Netherlands during the financial market crises in 2001/02 and 2007/08 and their subsequent recovery. German pension fund assets were not significantly affected. The volatility of British and Dutch pension fund assets reflect their high equity investments whereas German funds mainly invest in fixed assets.

As the second indicator, the funding ratio measures the degree to which assets cover liabilities (Figure 2) and, as such, is only relevant for DB pensions. Falling equity prices massively reduced the value of assets in the UK during the 2007/08 financial crisis. The shift to more fixed assets in the aftermath of 2008 made them vulnerable to the following sovereign debt crisis with low bond yields. As the result, from 2006 to 2015, 74% of all DB schemes in Britain were in deficit (Pension Protection Fund and The Pensions Regulator 2007–2016).

Funding ratios in the Netherlands generally decreased to 110% in 2002 – even below 100% for many funds – from 150% in 1999 (De Nederlandsche Bank 2005). After a recovery, the average funding ratio decreased again from 147% in 2007 to 98% in 2008 (Figure 2). In Germany, funding requirements are less important as most of the new occupational pension plans since the 2001 reform are DC plans with a nominal guarantee of contributions (Wiß 2018).

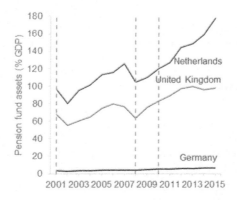

Figure 1. Pension fund assets 2001–2015. Source: OECD Global Pension Statistics. Notes: DE: only *Pensionsfonds* and *Pensionskassen*.

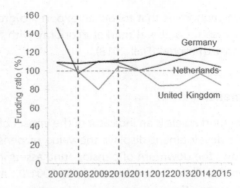

Figure 2. Nominal funding ratios. Source: EIOPA (IORP database). Notes: DE: only *Pensionskassen*. Funding ratios are calculated using national approaches and are comparable to a limited extent.

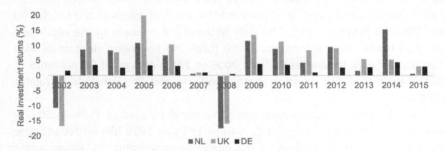

Figure 3. Pension funds' real net investment rate of return. Source: DE and NL 2002–04: OECD (2013); UK 2002–04: UBS (2017); DE, NL, UK 2005–2015: OECD (2016).

The financial market crises of the 2000s had a large negative effect on funds with high equity exposure. Real investment returns decreased massively in 2002 and 2008 in the Netherlands and UK, but not in Germany (Figure 3). The effects of the crises have been more severe and similar for British and Dutch pension funds than for their German counterparts.

Reform trajectories

The Netherlands

As one of the first measures in reaction to the 2001/02 and 2007/08 financial market crises, Dutch pension funds increased contributions to DB schemes to restore sustainable funding ratios. However, contributions could not increase endlessly (amounting to approximately 20% in 2008) and therefore pension fund boards in the Netherlands decided to change the benefit calculation and reduce indexation.

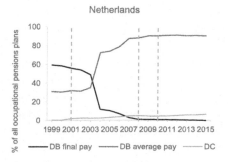 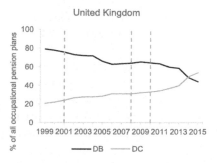

Figure 4. Occupational pension benefit calculation (percent of all pension plans). Source: NL: De Nederlandsche Bank; UK: ONS (2000–2016). Notes: DC plans in the UK include group personal and stakeholder pensions, as they are also work-based schemes.

After the 2001/02 crisis, most pension funds switched from final-salary to average-salary DB plans (Figure 4). Although the social partners agreed on reduced spending for DB schemes by starting to switch to average-salary schemes in 1997 after the government threatened elimination of fiscal incentives, the advent of the financial market crisis in 2001 accelerated the shift (Bridgen and Meyer 2009; Ponds and van Riel 2007).

As part of the 2010 Pension Accord, the social partners and the government agreed to introduce pension contracts that link accrued pension benefits to financial market developments (and life expectancy) (De Deken 2018), paving the way for further financialisation. Accrual rates have been decreasing from approximately 2.25% in 2010 to below 2% since 2013, meaning that employees must work longer to receive the same benefit. As pension funds are still experiencing financial troubles, the Social and Economic Council (SER) – the major advisory board to the government – is currently discussing more individualised pension contracts that combine DC and DB elements (Investment & Pensions Europe 2017c), which would imply a reinforcement of financialisation. Although the initially discussed individualisation of the Dutch second pillar appears to be less likely, future reforms may introduce a less redistributive system with fewer guarantees (De Deken 2018). The new government also plans to introduce the option of a lump sum, giving employees more freedom of choice (Investment & Pensions Europe 2017b).

As a response to the 2001/02 crisis, far-reaching changes in the indexation of pensions took effect in 2007. The government, social partners and the Dutch Central Bank jointly agreed that pension funds must state their indexation policy and management of surpluses and deficits (Anderson 2011). Most pension funds make indexation conditional on the fund's solvency and financial market developments. Full indexation only applies if the funding ratio exceeds 130%. The average indexation decreased from 2.5% in 2008 to approximately 0.5% in 2009 and even further in the following years (2016: 0.05%) (De Nederlandsche Bank), as funding ratios decreased well below 130%.

Another important part of the Dutch crisis response was the regulatory flexibility. Although pension funds in deficit were granted three years to recover in 2007, faced with the 2007/08 crisis, the government extended the recovery period to five years to prevent benefit reductions (De Nederlandsche Bank 2009). In 2015, the recovery period was temporarily extended to 12 years, as many funds did not manage to recover.

The 2007 legislation also changed the calculation of DB liabilities from a fixed 4% interest rate to market values (Ponds and van Riel 2007), and the interest rate for long-term liabilities was reduced in several steps to a 2.4% ultimate forward rate in 2018.[3] This can be interpreted as pension financialisation because DB commitments are now calculated with real market instead of fixed values.

The governance of pension funds also moved further along the path of financialisation. The 2013 Pension Fund Governance Act – aimed at boards with more financial market expertise – introduced five models for pension funds to choose from. They grant more power to external technocratic experts at the expense of employee representatives (De Deken 2017; Kruijf and Vries 2014) in comparison with the old model. However, the overwhelming majority (approximately 90% according to the Dutch Central Bank) has retained the old model with two-tier equal representation.

The UK

Although not all pension measures were explicitly driven by financial crises, they reinforced pension financialisation.

As in the Netherlands, one of the major responses was a change in the benefit calculation. The introduction of minimum funding requirements in 1997, the Financial Reporting Standard 17 in 2002 and the stock market downturns in 2001/02 increased employers' concerns about the unpredictable future costs of DB schemes, which boosted the shift from DB to DC (Bridgen and Meyer 2009; Ponds and van Riel 2007). DB schemes became too costly for British companies, who gradually closed most schemes for new members. Figure 4 shows the steady decline of DB plans from 1999 to 2015, which were substituted with DC plans. The 2008 Pensions Act introduced the stepwise roll-out of automatic enrolment into DC pension plans from 2012 onwards. This represents semi-obligatory or forced financialisation, as employees automatically become members of financial markets (Berry 2016).[4]

Following negative financial market developments, DB indexation was reduced several times to lower employers' financial burden. It was first changed in 2005 to follow the retail price index or 2.5% instead of the previous 5% (Thurley 2017). Since 2011, DB indexation is conditional on the (lower) consumer price index, resulting in lower pension income increases.

Similar to the ongoing discussions in the Netherlands, British employees have had more individual choice over their pension payments since the introduction of pension freedom in 2015 (Natali 2018). Employees are no longer forced to buy an annuity at retirement and can chose a lump sum payment, increasing flexibility (for example, in times of low interest rates) and also individual responsibility and risk (for their financial security until death). Similar to the Netherlands, the 2004 Pensions Act introduced real market values for the calculation of DB liabilities and relaxed minimum funding requirements. Schemes in deficit must prepare a scheme-specific recovery plan with the aim of recovering as quickly as possible, but only if it is affordable for the employer. Previously, all pension funds needed to restore a 100% funding ratio within specified time periods.

In terms of pension fund governance, scandals in the operation of pension funds in the 1990s resulted in changes (Bridgen and Meyer 2011: 283) such as (initially) more member involvement and external control by the newly established Pension Regulator. However, in 2001 a review of pension fund governance (Myners Report) was initiated following a discussion about whether to give more weight to the representative or expert characteristics of fund boards (Clark 2007). Based on this report, the 2004 Pensions Act stressed the importance of expertise and representativeness, but independent and better-trained trustees with at least high-school education (Clark 2007) disadvantage member-nominated trustees. Furthermore, the decline of trust-based pension schemes due to the closure of DB schemes has reduced trade union influence because external asset management and insurance companies are growing in importance with the shift to contract-based DC pensions (Naczyk 2016).

Germany

In line with the reinforcement of pension financialisation, Germany extended the coverage of funded pensions and reduced return guarantees.

A centre-left government reduced public pension benefits and increased the importance of private funded pensions in 2001. Therefore, there was no need for a major regulatory response to the 2001 crisis. Insurance-based pension plans that are organised as direct insurances or pension funds provide a guaranteed rate of return. The market volatility and low bond returns in the 2000s provoked the attention of the Federal Financial Supervisory Authority (BaFin). In 2004, BaFin reduced the guaranteed return rate from 3.25 to 2.75% and between 2007 and 2017 in several steps to only

0.9% due to adverse financial market and bond yield developments. Low or no guaranteed interest rates are in line with pension financialisation because real financial market values and not fixed interest rates determine the level of benefits.

Most German pension funds provide DC-light pension plans that guarantee the nominal value of contributions. Before the sovereign debt crisis, they did not experience problems in providing this very limited guarantee. However, in times of low bond yields (since 2011), low return rates made occupational pensions unattractive for employees. Accumulated negative effects in the aftermath of the sovereign debt crisis resulted in the 2017 occupational pension law that reinforced pension financialisation by introducing pure DC schemes in which employees bear financial market risks and by facilitating auto-enrolment schemes at the industry or firm level (Investment & Pensions Europe 2017a) with the aim of increasing coverage. This promotes the UK-style semi-obligatory financialisation of the 'everyday life' (Langley 2008) of employees. Trade unions only agreed to pure DC plans because the latter must be based on collective agreements, protecting their responsibility and power (Wiß 2018). As a least likely case, Germany took further steps along the path of pension financialisation.

Discussion

What explains the reinforcement of pension financialisation despite three financial crises? The following section is explorative and requires more detailed investigation in further studies. It appears that the idea of financial markets offering appropriate solutions for old-age income is still alive, and state as well as non-state actors promote and shape pension financialisation (Nölke et al. 2013). Financialisation (still) serves as a coalition magnet (Béland and Cox 2016).

Global finance

Many studies place responsibility of financialisation on the increased power of global finance (for an overview, see van der Zwan 2014). The political and economic power of the financial industry play major roles in the process of financialisation, especially regarding changes in a pension scheme's funding calculations. However, despite the massive promotion and support by the global financial industry, financialisation needs to address national political actors for implementation. National political actors are still decisive in policy processes despite the increasing importance of transnational actors (see also Béland 2009). Governments in countries with a social partnership tradition such as the Netherlands and Germany usually consider employers and trade unions for reforms that lie in core areas of social partner regulation (Béland 2009; Schmidt 2002) such as funded occupational pensions.

Government

Governments can have an interest in the continuation of pension financialisation (for Japan and New Zealand, see Estevez-Abe 2001; Trampusch 2017). Politicians who introduced or promoted funded pensions may fear to lose their credibility by reversing them. Furthermore, governments promote pension financialisation to compensate for cuts in public pensions and to strengthen the domestic financial sector, thereby attracting investors, creating new jobs and boosting economic growth (Naczyk and Hassel 2019; Naczyk and Palier 2014).[5] As the Fordist model of wage-led growth is drawing to a close (Baccaro and Pontusson 2016), national political economies need to replace it.[6] Financialisation contributes to financial-led or investment-led growth (Boyer 2000).

According to traditional partisanship theory (e.g., Allan and Scruggs 2004; Huber and Stephens 2001), we could expect that centre-left governments faced with pressure from their electorates over pension promises are more likely to oppose further financialisation than conservative and liberal governments. In contrast, more recent studies show that centre-left parties were drivers of financialisation (Belfrage 2017; Cioffi and Höpner 2006). In our case, the Labour party dominated the years after the 2001/02 and 2007/08 crises in the UK and the Christian-Democrats (CDA) were the largest governing party from 2002 to 2010 in the Netherlands. Despite a different partisan composition of the governments, both countries managed the pension fund crises similarly. In Germany, a centre-left government (1998–2005) established pension funds and, as part of a coalition with conservative parties, intensified pension financialisation by introducing pure DC benefits in 2017. The lack of a partisanship effect is in line with the previous research of Jensen (2012) regarding labour market policy, Vis et al. (2011) regarding immediate social policy expansion after 2008 and Lipsmeyer (2011) regarding welfare spending in times of busts.

Employers

Employers can use financialised pensions as an HR instrument to attract new employees and honour loyalty (Ghilarducci 1992). However, both DB and DC schemes serve this goal and employer preferences shift to DC if DB becomes too costly. In the UK, Bridgen and Meyer (2005) found evidence for the argument that companies have shifted from to DC because many others did so (herd behaviour), and because consultants recommended this cost-cutting strategy. Relaxed funding rules are also in the interest of employers because they reduce the requirement for raising contributions or making repair payments (van der Zwan 2018).

Trade unions

Trade unions, deeply involved in pension fund governance in the Netherlands and recently in Germany, may fear a loss of responsibility, power and credibility if they call for a reversal of financialised pensions. In the form of union (co-)controlled pension funds, unions are part of financial markets, trusting that they can provide secure pension income in the future (Anderson 2019; Keune 2018) (as they did for decades).

Although unions are trying to mitigate negative effects for employees, the call for a reversal by shifting back to DB entails the risk that employers completely close pension schemes due to high DB costs, reducing union power (for a critical view on union influence, see McCarthy 2014). Unions, or a portion of them, have an interest in the partial reversal of pension financialisation (not in the collapse of the whole system), especially in terms of more power in fund boards, but their voice is often not powerful enough. Nevertheless, stronger trade unions in the Netherlands might be the decisive factor determining why there was no radical shift from DB to DC as in the UK, which has rather weak trade unions.

Conclusion

The financial market crises of the 2000s and the 2011 sovereign debt crisis revealed the deficits of funded pensions. Did these crises trigger a reversal of pension financialisation? Despite different institutional contexts, pension systems and varying degrees of pension financialisation prior to the 2000s, Germany, the Netherlands and the UK responded to recent crises in a similar way and reinforced the reliance of pensions on market solutions. They increased individual responsibility and risks by extending coverage (Germany and the UK) and shifting to DC (the UK), pure DC (Germany) or average-career DB with benefits depending on financial market developments (Netherlands). Furthermore, the Netherlands and the UK introduced real market values for the calculation of pension fund liabilities and relaxed funding requirements with the expectation that markets would soon improve by themselves. A stronger focus on financial market expertise in pension fund boards in the Netherlands (depending on the choice of governance model) and the decline of trust-based DB pension schemes in the UK weakened the influence of trade unions on pension fund decisions. The dominating coalition of actors with entrenched interests – global finance, employers and the state –promotes pension financialisation and has no interest in a reversal. The trade unions have no interest in the collapse of the existing system and often they lack powerful voice that would allow for a partial reversal. Most measures in reaction to financial crises did not intend to tame pension fund capitalism or reverse the process of financialisation. Rather, they ensured that pension fund markets function in line with the rationality of financial markets, reinforcing the path of pension financialisation.

Although pension funds in different countries move along a common trajectory, national pension systems vary significantly because they started from different points and levels of pension financialisation. In emphasising the similar crises responses, the existing national variation in pension systems and in regulatory details are not dismissed.

Further research could compare the results with other financialised policies or welfare programmes such as private unemployment and health insurance. Since this article analysed a restricted but diverse set of countries, an application to other countries might be fruitful. The rather tentative explanation of the reinforcement of pension financialisation with entrenched interests also requires further empirical investigation.

The general implication for public policy scholars is that politics does not appear willing to tame pension funds, favouring the financial health of pension funds and markets over social welfare. The question remains whether financialisation leads to de-politicisation when financial markets, not politics, determine social policy.

Notes

1. The OECD data cover only *Pensionsfonds* and *Pensionskassen* for Germany (they account for approximately 25% of all occupational pension plans), explaining the low level of pension fund assets. Insurance-based occupational pension plans and DB book reserve schemes (contributions not necessarily invested in financial markets) are not included in the OECD data.
2. The country differences are qualitatively the same before the 2008 financial market crisis.
3. Since 2012, pension funds can calculate their long-term liabilities with a market-based ultimate forward rate that is less sensitive to short-term fluctuations (Pensions Policy Institute 2014).
4. However, from a social policy perspective, auto-enrolment and nudging may contribute to a more equal distribution of occupational pension plans across employees, reducing inequalities and old-age poverty.
5. In 2014, German pension funds invested 88% of their portfolio in domestic assets and British funds invested 72% (PwC Luxembourg 2015). The share is lower in countries with smaller markets such as the Netherlands (24%). However, domestic pension fund investments as a share of the GDP are very high in the UK (70%), substantial in the Netherlands (30%) and low in Germany (6%), although there was an increase from 2010 to 2015 in all three countries (own calculations based on OECD pension fund data).
6. This article argues that national economies cannot be subsumed under one growth model. Instead, several growth paths coexist within each economy.

Acknowledgements

I would like to thank the three anonymous referees for their very helpful and constructive feedback.

Disclosure statement

No potential conflict of interest was reported by the author.

Funding

This work was supported by the German Federal Ministry of Education and Research (BMBF) under grant number 01UF1508.

References

Allan, J.P. and Scruggs, L. (2004) 'Political partisanship and welfare state reform in advanced industrial societies', *American Journal of Political Science* 48(3): 496–512.

Anderson, K.M. (2011) 'Netherlands: adapting a multipillar pension system to demographic and economic change', in B. Ebbinghaus (ed.), *The Varieties of Pension Governance: Pension Privatization in Europe*, Oxford: Oxford University Press, pp. 292–317.

Anderson, K.M. (2019) 'Financialisation meets collectivisation: occupational pensions in Denmark, the Netherlands and Sweden', *Journal of European Public Policy* 26(4). doi:10.1080/13501763.2019.1574309.

Baccaro, L. and Pontusson, J. (2016) 'Rethinking comparative political economy: the growth model perspective', *Politics & Society* 44(2): 175–207.

Béland, D. (2009) 'Ideas, institutions, and policy change', *Journal of European Public Policy* 16(5): 701–18.

Béland, D. and Cox, R.H. (2016) 'Ideas as coalition magnets: coalition building, policy entrepreneurs, and power relations', *Journal of European Public Policy* 23(3): 428–45.

Belfrage, C. (2017) 'The unintended consequences of financialisation: social democracy hamstrung? The pensions dilemma', *Economic and Industrial Democracy* 38(4): 701–22.

Berry, C. (2016) 'Austerity, ageing and the financialisation of pensions policy in the UK', *British Politics* 11(1): 2–25.

Blyth, M. (2002) *Great Transformations: Economic Ideas and Institutional Change in the Twentieth Century*, New York: Cambridge University Press.

Boyer, R. (2000) 'Is a finance-led growth regime a viable alternative to Fordism? A preliminary analysis', *Economy and Society* 29(1): 111–45.

Bridgen, P. and Meyer, T. (2005) 'When do benevolent capitalists change their mind? Explaining the retrenchment of defined-benefit pensions in Britain', *Social Policy & Administration* 39(7): 764–85.

Bridgen, P. and Meyer, T. (2009) 'The politics of occupational pension reform in Britain and the Netherlands: the power of market discipline in liberal and corporatist regimes', *West European Politics* 32(3): 586–610.

Bridgen, P. and Meyer, T. (2011) 'Britain: exhausted voluntarism – the evolution of a hybrid pension regime', in B. Ebbinghaus (ed.), *Varieties of Pension Governance: Pension Privatization in Europe*, Oxford: Oxford University Press, pp. 265–91.

Capoccia, G. (2016) 'Critical junctures', in: O. Fioretos, T.G. Falleti and A. Sheingate (eds.), *The Oxford Handbook of Historical Institutionalism*, New York: Oxford University Press, pp. 89–106.

Chung, H. and Thewissen, S. (2011) 'Falling back on old habits? A comparison of the social and unemployment crisis reactive policy strategies in Germany, the UK and Sweden', *Social Policy & Administration* 45(4): 354–70.

Cioffi, J.W. and Höpner, M. (2006) 'The political paradox of finance capitalism: interests, preferences, and centre-left party politics in corporate governance reforms', *Politics & Society* 34(4): 463–502.

Clark, G.L. (2007) 'Expertise and representation in financial institutions: UK legislation on pension fund governance and US regulation of the mutual fund industry', *Twenty-First Century Society* 2(1): 1–24.

De Deken, J. (2017) 'The Netherlands: the challenges posed by the unintended universal financialisation of retirement provision', in D. Natali (ed.), *The New Pension Mix in Europe*, Brussels: Peter Lang, pp. 151–82.

De Deken, J. (2018) 'The corrosion of occupational pensions solidarity in the Netherlands', *Transfer: European Review of Labour and Research* 24(1): 43–56.

De Nederlandsche Bank (2005) *Quarterly Bulletin March 2005*, Amsterdam: De Nederlandsche Bank.

De Nederlandsche Bank (2009) *Annual Report 2008*, Amsterdam: De Nederlandsche Bank.

Drahokoupil, J. and Domonkos, S. (2012) 'Averting the funding-gap crisis: East European pension reforms since 2008', *Global Social Policy: An Interdisciplinary Journal of Public Policy and Social Development* 12(3): 283–99.

Ebbinghaus, B. (2005) 'Can path dependence explain institutional change? Two approaches applied to welfare state reform', MPIfG Discussion Paper 05/2, Max Planck Institute for the Study of Societies, Cologne.

Ebbinghaus, B. and Wiß, T. (2011) 'Taming pension fund capitalism in Europe: collective and state regulation in times of crisis', *Transfer: European Review of Labour and Research* 17(1): 15–28.

Epstein, G.A. (2006) 'Introduction: financialization and the world economy', in G.A. Epstein (ed.), *Financialization and the World Economy*, Cheltenham and Northampton, UK: Edward Elgar, pp. 3–16.

Estevez-Abe, M. (2001) 'The forgotten link: the financial regulation of Japanese pension funds in comparative perspective', in B. Ebbinghaus and P. Manow (eds.), *Comparing Welfare Capitalism: Social Policy and Political Economy in Europe, Japan and the USA*, London and New York: Routledge, pp. 190–216.

Ghilarducci, T (1992) *Labor's Capital - The Economics and Politics of Private Pensions*, Cambridge: MIT Press.

Hall, P.A. (1993) 'Policy paradigms, social learning, and the state: the case of economic policymaking in Britain', *Comparative Politics* 25(3): 275–96.

Hall, P.A. (2018) 'Varieties of capitalism in light of the euro crisis', *Journal of European Public Policy* 25(1): 7–30.

Huber, E. and Stephens, J.D. (2001) *Development and Crisis of the Welfare State: Parties and Policies in Global Markets*, Chicago: University of Chicago Press.

Investment & Pensions Europe (2017a) Germany: a disappointing revolution, available at www.ipe.com/pensions/pensions/briefing/germany-a-disappointing-revolution/10017353.fullarticle (accessed January 2018).

Investment & Pensions Europe (2017b) New dutch coalition aims for pensions reform in early 2018, available at www.ipe.com/countries/netherlands/new-dutch-coalition-aims-for-pensions-reform-in-early-2018/10021037.fullarticle (accessed January 2018).

Investment & Pensions Europe (2017c) The Netherlands: still brooding on a new system, available at www.ipe.com/reports/special-reports/top-1000-pension-funds/the-netherlands-still-brooding-on-a-new-system/10020512.fullarticle (accessed January 2018).

Jahn, D. (2016) 'Changing of the guard: trends in corporatist arrangements in 42 highly industrialized societies from 1960 to 2010', *Socio-Economic Review* 14(1): 47–71.

Jensen, C. (2012) 'Labour market- versus life course-related social policies: understanding cross-programme differences', *Journal of European Public Policy* 19(2): 275–91.

Keune, M. (2018) 'Opportunity or threat? How trade union power and preferences shape occupational pensions', *Social Policy & Administration* 52(2): 463–76.

Kiess, J., Norman, L., Temple, L. and Uba, K. (2017) 'Path dependency and convergence of three worlds of welfare policy during the great recession: UK, Germany and Sweden', *Journal of International and Comparative Social Policy* 33(1): 1–17.

Kruijf, J.A.M.D. and Vries, M.S.D. (2014) 'Governance and stakeholder involvement in the Dutch pension industry, lessons for developing countries', *Public Administration and Development* 34(4): 332–44.

Lallement, M. (2011) 'Europe and the economic crisis: forms of labour market adjustment, and varieties of capitalism', *Work, Employment and Society* 25(4): 627–41.

Langley, P. (2004) 'In the eye of the "perfect storm": the final salary pensions crisis and financialisation of Anglo-American capitalism', *New Political Economy* 9(4): 539–58.

Langley, P. (2008) *The Everyday Life of Global Finance: Saving and Borrowing in Anglo-America*, Oxford, NY: Oxford University Press.

Lipsmeyer, C.S. (2011) 'Booms and busts: how parliamentary governments and economic context influence welfare policy', *International Studies Quarterly* 55(4): 959–80.

Mayntz, R. (ed) (2012) *Crisis and Control – Institutional Change in Financial Market Regulation*, Frankfurt a. M. and New York: Campus.

McCarthy, M.A. (2014) 'Turning labor into capital: pension funds and the corporate control of finance', *Politics and Society* 42(4): 455–87.

Naczyk, M. (2016) 'Unemployment and pensions protection in europe: the changing role of social partners. Prowelfare country report: United Kingdom', OSE Paper Series, Research Paper No. 22, European Social Observatory, Brussels.

Naczyk, M. and Domonkos, S. (2016) 'The financial crisis and varieties of pension privatization reversals in Eastern Europe', *Governance* 29(2): 167–84.

Naczyk, M. and Hassel, A. (2019) 'Insuring individuals ... and politicians: financial services providers, stock market risk and the politics of private pension guarantees in Germany', *Journal of European Public Policy* 26(4). doi:10.1080/13501763.2019.1575455.

Naczyk, M. and Palier, B. (2014) 'Feed the beast: finance capitalism and the spread of pension privatization in Europe', Paper presented at the 26th SASE Annual Meeting, Chicago, 10–12 July.

Natali, D. (2018) 'Occupational pensions in Europe: Trojan horse of financialization?', *Social Policy & Administration* 52(2): 449–62.

Nölke, A., Heires, M. and Bieling, H.-J. (2013) 'Editorial: the politics of financialization', *Competition & Change* 17(3): 209–18.
OECD (2013) *Pension Markets in Focus 2013*, Paris: OECD.
OECD (2016) *Pension Markets in Focus 2016*, Paris: OECD.
ONS (2000–2016) *Annual Survey of Hours and* Earnings Pension Tables, Newport: Office for National Statistics.
ONS (2002) *Annual Survey of Hours and Earnings Pension Tables, 2001*, Newport: Office for National Statistics.
Pension Protection Fund and The Pensions Regulator (2007–2016) *The Purple Book - DB Pensions Universe Risk Profile*, Surrey and Brighton: Pension Protection Fund and The Pensions Regulator.
Pensions Policy Institute (2014) *Risk Sharing Pension Plans: The Dutch Experience*, London: Pensions Policy Institute.
Pierson, P. (2000) 'Increasing returns, path dependence, and the study of politics', *American Political Science Review* 94(2): 251–67.
Pino, A. and Yermo, J. (2010) 'The impact of the 2007–2009 crisis on social security and private pension funds: a threat to their financial soundness?', *International Social Security Review* 63(2): 5–30.
Ponds, E.H.M. and van Riel, B. (2007) *The Recent Evolution of Pension Funds in the Netherlands: The Trend to Hybrid DB-DC Plans and Beyond*, Chestnut Hill: Center for Retirement Research at Boston College.
Pontusson, J. and Raess, D. (2012) 'How (and why) is this time different? The politics of economic crisis in Western Europe and the United States', *Annual Review of Political Science* 15(1): 13–33.
PwC Luxembourg (2015) *Beyond Their Borders – Evolution of Foreign Investment by Pension Funds*, Luxembourg: PricewaterhouseCoopers.
Sabatier, P. A. and Weible, C. M. (2007) 'The advocacy coalition framework: innovations and clarifications', in P.A. Sabatier (ed.), *Theories of the Policy Process*, Cambridge: Westview Press, pp. 189–220.
Schmidt, V.A. (2002) 'Does discourse matter in the politics of welfare state adjustment?' *Comparative Political Studies* 35(2): 168–93.
Steinebach, Y. and Knill, C. (2017) 'Social policies during economic crises: an analysis of cross-national variation in coping strategies from 1980 to 2013', *Journal of European Public Policy*: 1–23. doi:10.1080/13501763.2017.1336565.
Thelen, K. (1999) 'Historical institutionalism in comparative politics', *Annual Review of Political Science* 2(1): 369–404.
Thurley, D. (2017) *Occupational Pension Increases*, London: The House of Commons Library.
TNS Infratest (2008) *Situation und Entwicklung der betrieblichen Altersversorgung in Privatwirtschaft und öffentlichem Dienst 2001–2007*, München: TNS Infratest.
Trampusch, C. (2017) 'A state-centred explanation of the finance-pension nexus: New Zealand's pension reforms as a typical case', *Social Policy & Administration*: 1–22. doi:10.1111/spol.12304.
True, J.L., Jones, B.D. and Baumgartner, F.R. (2007) 'Punctuated-equilibrium theory: explaining stability and change in public policymaking', in P.A. Sabatier (ed.), *Theories of the Policy Process*, Cambridge: Westview Press, pp. 155–87.
UBS (2017) *A Long-Term Perspective - Navigating Your Investment Journey: Pension Fund Indicators 2017*, London: UBS Asset Management Ltd.
van der Zwan, N. (2014) 'Making sense of financialization', *Socio-Economic Review* 12(1): 99–129.

van der Zwan, N. (2017) 'Financialisation and the pension system: lessons from the United States and the Netherlands', *Journal of Modern European History* 15(4): 554–84.

van der Zwan, N. (2018) 'The financial politics of occupational pensions: a business interests perspective', in D.O. Nijuis (ed.), *Business Interests and the Development of the Modern Welfare State*, Oxon: Routledge. [forthcoming].

van Hooren, F., Kaasch, A. and Starke, P. (2014) 'The shock routine: economic crisis and the nature of social policy responses', *Journal of European Public Policy* 21(4): 605–23.

Vis, B., van Kersbergen, K. and Hylands, T. (2011) 'To what extent did the financial crisis intensify the pressure to reform the welfare state?' *Social Policy & Administration* 45 (4): 338–53.

Wiß, T. (2015a) 'From welfare states to welfare sectors: explaining sectoral differences in occupational pensions with economic and political power of employees', *Journal of European Social Policy* 25(5): 489–504.

Wiß, T. (2015b) 'Pension fund vulnerability to the financial market crisis: the role of trade unions', *European Journal of Industrial Relations* 21(2): 131–47.

Wiß, T. (2018) 'Divergent occupational pensions in Bismarckian countries: the case of Germany and Austria', *Transfer: European Review of Labour and Research* 24(1): 91–107.

Multipillarisation remodelled: the role of interest organizations in British and German pension reforms

Bernhard Ebbinghaus

ABSTRACT
Recent reforms have responded to demographic ageing and fiscal challenges by shifting toward the multipillarisation of pensions to achieve financial sustainability. Reforms towards privatization and marketization of retirement income provision occurred in Britain and Germany with different pension system legacies. While public opinion supports largely the status quo, the stakeholders, in particular, organized capital and labour, have evolved in their positions towards pension reforms. The analysis seeks to draw out how organized interests have sought to influence mulitipillarisation but also adapted their strategies in the context of increasing financialisation in the two political economies. The position of trade unions, employers' associations, social advocacy groups and the finance sector has increasingly embraced multipillarisation, earlier and more so in Britain than in Germany. A reversal of pension financialisation seems no longer possible but the inequalities and uncertainties need to be addressed in order to make multipillarisation politically sustainable.

Introduction

A large part of today's welfare state is tied to income support for the elderly; this poses a considerable challenge to public finance in the age of austerity. In particular, demographic ageing has become the dominant rationale for governments to scale back public old-age benefits and fostering prefunded pensions. Public policy has aimed to achieve long-term financial sustainability through a paradigmatic shift towards a multipillar architecture. Over the last three decades, pension reforms advanced the twin processes of privatization and marketization of old age income protection across Europe (Ebbinghaus 2015). While privatization led to a shift in responsibility from government to private actors (in particular, employers, unions, and individuals), marketization implied a stronger actuarial link of public pensions to contributions and increased dependency from private savings.

This 'paradigm shift' (Hall 1993) toward multipillarisation has been partially driven by financial interests outside the pension policy community, while burgeoning pension fund capitalism further stimulated the role of finance. Financialisation (van der Zwan 2014), the penetration of financial interests within societies, can be seen as both an engine but also a beneficiary of multipillarisation. The recent financial market crash of 2008, however, has probed the viability of this funded strategy given low investment returns and high risks, leading to renewed criticism of financialisation (Ebbinghaus 2015). It is thus timely to ask: Why has there been a paradigm shift towards multipillarisation and which societal interests does it serve?

Comparing two case studies this article explores the role of organized interests in hampering or advancing marketization and privatization towards multipillarisation in two different pension systems: Britain and Germany. By adopting a most dissimilar country design which looks at the factors leading towards a similar outcome (financialisation), this study analyses Beveridgean basic security versus Bismarckian social insurance (Meyer 2013; Natali 2008; Palier and Bonoli 1995). Based on empirical studies (Ebbinghaus 2011; Leisering 2011) the subsequent analysis summarizes the paradigmatic changes in pension reforms towards marketization and privatization in both countries, connecting these to the interests of stakeholder groups in respect to financialisation.

Following Beveridge's post-war reforms, Britain adopted a basic pension that left ample space for private development. A multipillar architecture has been built early through 'opt-out' of employer-provided occupational pension funds and personal pensions. Despite a rather liberal strategy, the role of the state as a regulator of financialisation and promotor via tax exemptions remains important (Leisering 2011). Poverty problems, uneven access to supplementary pensions, and insecurities of funded pensions have led to major changes that increased public pensions and widened the coverage of funded pensions over the last decade (Meyer and Bridgen 2018; Whiteside 2017). Thus, this Liberal multipillar model became recently rebalanced to address social sustainability issues in respect to access and adequacy in order to maintain it.

In contrast, Germany's Bismarckian pension system has been lagging behind in multipillarism due to compulsory earnings-related public pensions. Only after financial pressure mounted following population ageing, early retirement waves, and unification costs (integrating East German pensions since 1990) did a paradigm shift towards privatization and marketization occur in the 2000s. While public benefits were cut back and retirement age increased, private prefunded pensions have been promoted as a voluntary strategy to fill the income gap left by reduced public pensions. In addition, occupational pensions have been renewed and social partners' role expanded, though these are not necessarily prefunded (Wiß 2018). Germany's conservative welfare state thus embraced multipillarisation belatedly, quite in line with late financialisation (Röper 2018), while still maintaining some corporatist elements.

This uneven convergence towards multipillarism needs further explanation: How have organized interests positioned themselves towards these reforms? My binary comparison focuses on the changing position of interest organizations in pension reforms in Britain and Germany. First, this article discusses the analytical approaches to study pension reforms and the agents of change. This is followed by describing the paradigm shift as the twin processes of marketization and privatization, their reinforcing relationship to financialisation, and the potential effect on risk individualization. The analysis then reviews the differences in interest organizations in overcoming the status quo. Based on a comparative project on popular opinion and the stakeholder interests in Britain and Germany (Ebbinghaus and Naumann 2018a, 2018b; Klitzke 2017, 2018), this article reviews the pension reform dynamics over the last three decades for both countries. In Britain, a rebalancing of the Beveridge multipillar model led to improved public minimum income and an expansion of supplementary pensions, but still fosters an individualization of risks. In Germany, a belated paradigm shift from Bismarckian public pensions aimed at status maintenance to remodel multipillarism occurred, combining voluntarist and collective elements. The conclusion highlights the converging trends toward multipillarisation as engine and result of financialisation. It highlights renewed diversity between the two pension systems but also stakeholder's positioning, discussing also potential implications for the future.

The political economy of multipillarisation

Pension reforms have been analysed from different disciplinary lenses. Economists have focused on demographic ageing as a rationale for an inevitable shift from pay-as-you-go (PAYG) to prefunded pensions in order to achieve long-term financial sustainability (Grech 2013; World Bank 1994). However, the slow actual progress was attributed by political economists and demographers to the status quo oriented ageing electorate (Boeri et al. 2002; Sanderson and Scherbov 2007). Political scientists claimed path dependent feedback (Pierson 1996, 2001) that made radical reforms difficult, not least due to 'blame avoidance' (Weaver 1986) by office-seeking politicians afraid of electoral backlash. Quantitative studies show indeed less severe reforms in pensions than other social policy areas across Europe (Zohlnhöfer et al. 2013). Social policy researchers studied social consequences such as the individualization of risks and raising old age inequalities (Meyer et al. 2007). Moreover, more critical voices pointed at the increasing trend toward financialisation (Berry 2016; Dixon and Ville-Pekka 2009), while increased privatization led to calls for better governance and regulation (Ebbinghaus and Wiß 2011; Leisering 2011).

The paradigm shift toward multipillarisation seems to provide a puzzle given these claims of path dependency. While scholars initially focused on 'veto points' provided by political institutions (Bonoli 2000) to explain cross-national differences in reforms, newer research focused on the electoral competition between political parties (Immergut and Anderson 2007; Immergut and Abou-Chadi 2014). Although the initial path dependence thesis by Pierson (2001) assumed positive returns of past policies, more recently policy analysts pointed at 'negative feedbacks' that induce path departure (Weaver 2010). Actual policy changes show 'anomalies' of the blame avoidance assumption, while the image of 'responsible government capable of taking tough decisions when needed' speaks for 'credit claiming' (Bonoli 2012: 107). Changing public discourse towards a 'need' for a prefunded strategy in ageing societies has been advanced by political actors and economic interests (Leimgruber 2012). Nevertheless, public opinion remains more inclined to prefer the status quo, and is only slowly embracing the reform discourse, such as seeing the state to be less responsible for old age income provision (Ebbinghaus and Naumann 2018b).

In addition to the political factors already mentioned, organized interests have also attempted to influence public policy making as they have a material interest in reform outcomes. Nevertheless, the role of these stakeholders remains more contested between those claiming their importance and those that see them having lost in power (Grady 2013; Pierson 1996). From a power resource perspective (Korpi 1983) we would expect organized interests to advance antagonistic positions based on the capital-labour conflict, though this is dependent on their power and institutional resources. Pension reforms affect the interests of both capital and labour: the marketization shift from PAYG to prefunded pensions, the increase of retirement age, and the retrenchment of benefits have been of major concerns for organized interests. However, there are variations across time and countries in the position and power of unions, employers and other stakeholder interests worth exploring (Grødem et al. 2018; Wiß 2015b).

Organized labour, in particular, unions and also social advocacy groups for pensioners, are expected to defend the status quo of acquired social rights against any retrenchment (Korpi 1983). They should also be more critical about shifts towards private responsibilities without sufficient state regulation or power to negotiate collective solutions (Ebbinghaus and Wiß 2011). If trade unions have enough bargaining power they may pursue occupational pensions as 'second best' strategy (Mares 2003), seeing it as an opportunity to provide services to their waning membership (Keune 2018). For such unions, the 'collectivization of risks' (Johnston et al. 2012) would counter the individualization risk typical of prefunded pensions, for instance, by pooling some risks within a collective scheme.

Today's organized labour, however, seems no longer as class-oriented as implied by power resource theory. Following particularistic strategies, unions might represent only 'insider' interests, while increased dualization, by protecting largely outsiders, reinforces these social inequalities (Naczyk and Seeleib-Kaiser 2015; Seeleib-Kaiser et al. 2012). Some unions representing white-collar or more skilled workers have cooperated with business in order to expand occupational pensions that maintain their status (Naczyk 2013; Wiß 2015a). Post-industrial analyses see unions no longer capable of class solidarity as they face heterogeneous social groups with divergent interests (Armingeon and Bonoli 2006; Häusermann 2010). This thesis would lead us to expect that unions might differ in respect to privatization and marketization of pension provision, some being more inclined to accept inequality and financial risks implied by financialisation than others.

Political economy approaches expect organized capital, both employer associations and the finance sector, to have a material stake in reducing state responsibility and public expenditure as first-order preference (Mares 2003). While employers might prefer their own occupational pensions to attract and retain skilled workers, the finance sector is keen to provide investment management services to occupational pensions or sell individualized saving plans (Naczyk 2013; Natali 2018). Occupational schemes provide an opportunity for outsourcing financial management to banks or investment agencies, while insurances are keen to sell individual or group contracts. Hence it depends on the power balance between organized capital and labour as well as their internal interest differentiation which path emerges. It thus is an empirical question: how do these stakeholders position themselves towards pension reforms?

Decomposing the paradigm shift

In order to assess the paradigm change in both countries, we need to define the main thrust of systemic ('third order') change (Hall 1993). In social policy research, the dependent variable problem is seen as the difficulty to specify welfare state restructuring (Clasen and Siegel 2007). This holds particularly for pension reforms that are rather complex policy changes with long-term impact. Following previous comparative studies (Ebbinghaus 2011; Leisering 2011) we can conclude that pension reforms have led to a paradigm shift toward multipillarisation much earlier in Britain than in Germany. The basic questions to answer here are: how are benefits financed and who is responsible for retirement income? I will argue that these reforms involve the twin processes, the *marketization* of retirement income and the *privatization* of pension responsibility: the 'retreat' of the state through cutting public benefits should be compensated by increased private actor responsibility and prefunding for the future. Both reform thrusts facilitate but also are fostered by *financialisation* in these societies; together they imply also an augmented *individualization* of risks. These four concepts need to be distinguished, though they are partially connected.

Marketization fosters market-based incentives and mechanisms in public policy and beyond (Dixon and Hyde 2002). Increasing the link between pension benefits and paid contributions makes public schemes more commodified even if this may not entail prefunding. The shift from PAYG financing to prefunded pensions entails also marketization, it fosters financialisation through the direct or indirect investment of contributions for future benefits. The introduction of demographic factors or notional defined contributions in public pensions mimics actuarial mechanisms within PAYG systems. We would thus expect the finance sector to have a direct interest in introducing marketization to raise demand for financial services.

Privatization is often an engine in advancing marketization; it entails a shift toward the reallocation of responsibility from the public pillar to non-state actors, including employers and their organizations, unions or works councils as well as individuals (Ebbinghaus and Wiß 2011). Occupational pensions, known as the second pillar, are commonly run by (groups of) employers, while some are collectively negotiated between unions and employers. The third pillar subsumes personal pensions, such as individual savings or insurance contracts for retirement. Although privatization leads to a (partial) 'retreat' of the state from public spending, there might still be regulatory intervention and indirect tax expenditures (Leisering 2011). Moreover, there are important governance issues in respect to resolving the principal-agent conflict between the sponsor and investing agent in addition to the labour-capital conflict between the employer as (co)sponsor and the employee as beneficiary (Ebbinghaus and Wiß 2011). While we expect that employers together with financial services favour privatization, unions may adopt this as their second-best option when expecting opportunities to negotiate occupational pensions (Keune 2018).

Analytically, *financialisation* is a broad political economy concept reaching beyond pensions; it has been defined by van der Zwan's (2014: 101) as 'the web of interrelated processes – economic, political, social, technological, cultural, etc. – through which finance has extended its influence beyond the marketplace and into other realms of social life'. Finance-oriented principles thus encroach into non-market spheres, such as social protection for the elderly, while finance-related agents seek to influence pension policies to promote their products. Historically, it has been shown that the shift toward prefunded pensions makes these more dependent on financial interests (Leimgruber 2012). A study of the finance sector indicates also internal differences between banking, insurance, and investment interests in shaping policy debates on British and German pension reforms (Pieper 2018). Whether and how employers' interests align with finance interests is thus an empirical question.

A social consequence of these reforms is the *individualization* of retirement income risks with societal implications in respect to poverty and inequality. Marketization increases the dependency of retirement income from previous labour market attachments and capability to contribute to public and private pensions, thereby reproducing market inequalities and increasing poverty in old age (Hinrichs and Jessoula 2012). Moreover, privatization limits the possibilities for pooling and compensating social risks (for instance, for years of unemployment or unpaid child caring). Some negotiated occupational schemes between employers and unions might redistribute collectively, while this cannot be the case in personal pensions except through public subsidies (Ebbinghaus and Wiß 2011). Financialisation, particularly when pensions are funded via *defined contribution* (DC) schemes entail an individualization of financial risks (Casey 2012). Given these social implications, unions and social advocacy groups should be most concerned about the likely negative impact of financialisation, marketization and privatization on society, whereas employers and finance interests are more likely to favour financialisation over social concerns.

Overcoming the status quo

Following the path dependency thesis (Pierson 2000), we expect that the institutional settings of the pension systems shape public opinion. In particular, the basic differences between Beveridgean and Bismarckian systems remains strongly institutionalized: two thirds of British respondents (European Social Survey, ESS 2008cit. in Ebbinghaus and Naumann 2018a) are in favour of their public basic flat-rate system by agreeing to the statement that low earners should get the same (or higher) pension than top earners, while two thirds of German respondents endorse the equivalence principle of pension benefits reflecting past income differences enshrined in the social insurance logic (Ebbinghaus and Naumann 2018a, 116). Given that older people (aged 60 and older) tend to vote more frequently in elections than non-elderly voters (1.4 times more in Britain and 1.1 in Germany), the elderly are a pivotal voting bloc in Britain (42%) and Germany (35% of votes actually cast according to ESS 2012; see Ebbinghaus 2017: 214). In light of this 'grey clout' the scope for radical reforms seems rather limited, though pension reforms occurred in both countries despite status quo oriented public opinion. Therefore it is important to investigate whether it is the changing power of organized interests and their evolved strategies in influencing pension policy that matters. Based on interviews (Klitzke 2017, 2018) with agents from the key stakeholders, including unions, social advocacy groups but also employer and finance interests, the following overall patterns of interest constellations can be derived.[1]

Organized labour has faced considerable challenges in both countries, following membership decline and organizational concentration (Ebbinghaus 2017). Around 6 million British employees are today union members or less than a quarter of all employees, but still more than every second public sector worker. British unions are largely organized within the Trades Union Congress (TUC), though membership dropped by half from its peak of 13 million in 1979 when the anti-union Thatcher government came into office. It is a rather fragmented movement in which general and multisector unions coexist with small occupational ones across all sectors. In Germany, the German counterpart (*Deutscher Gewerkschaftsbund*, DGB) has also about 6 million members, having lost more than 3 million since German unification in 1990. Only every fifth employee is organized, though some key industries and the public sector are better organized, while collective bargaining is relatively well institutionalized. The German unions are more neatly organized along sectoral lines, though in the public sector the large united service union (*Vereinte Dienstleistungsgewerkschaft*, ver.di) within DGB competes with the rival civil servant federation (*Deutscher Beamtenbund*, dbb).

As *social advocacy* groups, Britain's National Pensioners' Convention (NPC) or several German welfare organizations with different political or religious background should be noted, though fragmentation among these German social advocacy groups limits finding a common voice for pensioners' interests. In addition, public pension administration such as the National Employment Savings Trust (NEST), set up in 2008 in Britain and the tripartite German social pension insurance (*Deutsche Rentenversicherung*, DRV) in which employees and pensioners vote for representatives in social elections, provide more neutral and informed positions within the pension policy network (Klitzke 2017).

On the side of *organized capital*, the peak employer associations and business clubs in Britain (Confederation of British Industry, CBI, and the Institute of Directors) and German employers (*Bundesverband der deutschen Arbeitgeber*, BDA), industrialists, and handicraft and commerce chambers are important counterparts to unions (Klitzke 2018). In Britain, the employers played already an important role in shaping the reforms of the 1980s given their material interests in occupational pensions, thus they prevented an abolishment of earnings-related state pensions as initially planned by Thatcher (Bonoli 2000). Notably in Germany, the industrialists' club (*Bundesverband Deutscher Industrie*, BDI) has become more critical of public spending since the 1990s, while the employer association (BDA) remained more conciliatory on pension reforms. Britain's Pensions and Lifetime Savings Association (PSLA) and German occupational pension association (*Arbeitsgemeinschaft für betriebliche Altersversorgung*, Aba) organize the interests of employers as sponsors of these schemes, providing expertise but also lobbying within the policy network. For the finance sector, the Association of British Insurers (ABI) and its German counterpart (*Gesamtverband der Deutschen Versicherungswirtschaft*, GDV) are not necessarily always aligned with those of investment firms ('the City') or German general banks and investment interests (*Bundesverband Investment & Asset Management*, BVI), nor do these finance interests always concur with employer and producers' interests (Naczyk 2013; Wiß 2011). Occupational pensions are significant to employers given their human resource strategy of attracting and retaining skilled workers, whereas the finance sector has a commercial interest in promoting prefunded schemes.

One common threat of marketization in response to demographic ageing has been the increase in retirement age in both countries (Hering 2012). The policy positions of organized interests are relatively similar (Klitzke 2018: 37): British and German employers' associations embrace increasing retirement age as their key demand (finance also favours it but sees it as less salient), whereas British and German unions and advocacy groups largely oppose it. There are some differences across unions: British TUC and German DGB take a more stringent policy position than some of its more moderate affiliates (British Unite, German chemical workers union), however, German union representatives identify the issue as more salient than their British counterparts (Klitzke 2018: 38). While in respect to retirement age, the alignment of positions follows our *a priori* expectations, the patterns are more complex in respect to other reform aspects.

The scope and impact of private pensions still differ across both countries. Coverage of occupational pensions among older workers (50 and older) has been around two-thirds in Britain and one third in Germany (Pavolini and Seeleib-Kaiser 2018: 481), and twice as many British retirees rely on private pensions for about double as large a share of their overall pension income compared to Germany (Ebbinghaus 2011: 412/415). Britain has a more advanced pension fund capitalism compared to Germany's reliance on occupational pensions often financed by book reserves (Jackson and Vitols 2001). British organized interests embraced these liberal reforms earlier and more widely than their German counterparts, particularly given the opposition of unions and advocacy groups (Klitzke 2018). As to organized capital, British and German employers both favour advancing occupational pensions. Yet German employers are more eager to limit public pensions given their social contributions taxing labour costs, while British employers are more inclined to protect the basic pension as a minimum floor while limiting their own liabilities (Meyer and Bridgen 2018). As to the finance sector, British pension fund capitalism has provided more opportunities, whereas German banking and insurance interests turned to prefunded pensions only after financial liberalization reforms (Pieper 2018). The analysis of stakeholders thus indicates substantial differences in interests but also cross-national variations in timing and scope that will be explored next.

Rebalancing multipillarism in Britain

The British post-war development of occupational pensions was aided by the opt-out of the second state pension since 1978 and a similar provision for personal funded pensions since 1986. The latter reform occurred when British unions were under considerable attack and lost membership, whereas employers accepted an opt-out for personal DC pensions since their occupational funds were unaffected (Bonoli 2000). After an initial rise in DC contracts, covering every fourth adult, numbers declined after the first decade. Occupational pensions still covered about every second employee (about 40% in private), while assets grew to two-thirds of GDP by the 1990s. Following the Maxwell scandal, pension funds were sterner regulated by the Conservatives in 1995, this was largely accepted by business since it provided an equal playing field. Changes in accounting standards (including European Union regulation in 2005) and equity markets put increased pressure on British firms to limit their pension liabilities. Eventually, this led to a shift from *defined benefits* (DB) toward *defined contribution* (DC) schemes, entailing an individualization of risks (Bridgen and Meyer 2005; Whiteside 2017).

As the private pension pillars have been advanced early in Britain, unions had to adopt their strategies, while employers and finance interests played a dominant role in pension reforms. British unions faced neoliberal reforms not only under Conservatives in the 1980s but also subsequently under New Labour (Grady 2013). Pension fund capitalism became an important feature of pension provision, yet also a risk for current and future retirees. Already after the 2000 downturn, the 2004 Pension Act established a Pension Protection Fund (PPF) and increased regulation but lowered the nominal inflation rate for occupational pensions as compensation. Nevertheless, organized capital (CBI, PLSA, and investment interests) remained critical but they were unable to muster enough power, while the Labour government facing public protest of those affected by bankruptcy set up a compensation fund (Piper 2018: 127). With the financial market crash of 2008, PPF premiums increased rapidly as some DB pension funds defaulted on their liabilities.

Despite its early multipillarisation, only every second British employee was covered by occupational pensions due to declining or low rates in manufacturing and private services by the 2008 financial market crash (Bridgen and Meyer 2011: 274–5). In addition to a decline in occupational pension access, more and more companies shifted from DB to DC pensions by closing old schemes for new entrants due to concerns over increasing liabilities and PPF premiums (Bridgen and Meyer 2005; Whiteside 2017). Public sectors such as administration, health, and education still have high coverage rates

(84% in 2007), remaining the last bastions of DB plans defended by strong unions. For example, most recently (in spring 2018), the British university employees went on strike against the abolition of DB plans by the university supplementary scheme thought to be running considerable liabilities.

As a third pillar, the personal pension introduced with the 1986 'big bang' liberalization of the financial market under Thatcher boosted financialisation. From initially 4 million contracts it became very popular until it reached its peak around 17 million in 1992 (Pieper 2018: 42). After misselling scandals personal pensions stagnated, declining from over 9 million before 2007 by 4 million after the crash within five years (Pieper 2018: A1.1). Together with the problems of coverage among small firms, these developments threatened to leave many British employees with nothing but a meagre basic pension. The Turner commission (led by the former CBI leader) proposed in its reports (2004/5) to increase the basic pension (in lieu of the means-tested supplement), phasing out the second state pension and abolishing contracting out and extending workplace pensions.

Under New Labour, following a 'nudging' strategy advanced by behavioural economics (Thaler and Sunstein 2009), the Pension Act 2008 introduced auto-enrolment for contributions (minimum 8%) by rolling it out from larger to smaller firms by 2016. Thus employees not covered by occupational pensions would be automatically enrolled into a DC plan at their workplace (every three years unless individuals decide otherwise). Auto-enrolment indeed reversed the trend: coverage increased by 5 million largely due to new members in the private sector. By 2016, the majority of 15 million working people have DC occupational plans (51%), a minority still profits from DB pensions (16%) and around a third are auto-enrolled in DC workplace plans (Pensions Regulator 2016). However, the abolition of a life annuity requirement upon retirement by the Conservative-Liberal coalition in 2015 intensified the individualization of financial market hazards and longevity risks for the sake of 'freedom and choice' in line with financialisation (Natali 2018: 458).

At the same time, New Labour also enacted a striking proposal to improve the basic state pension, which both the subsequent Coalition and Conservative governments maintained (Meyer and Bridgen 2018; Whiteside 2017). Unions and social advocacy groups were largely supportive of more state intervention in line with their members and public attitudes at large. The more striking fact was that British employers and finance organizations were in favour of an improved state basic pension quite in contrast to a priori expectations. Apparently, British employers and pension providers saw the flat-rate public pension as insufficient; indeed a higher minimum would help supplementary pensions topping up to more adequate retirement income.

Fostering belated multipillarism in Germany

The paradigm shift occurred much later in Germany, given the legacy of Bismarckian social insurance aiming at maintaining living standards. Piecemeal changes to contributions and benefits maintained the public PAYG pensions until a consensual reform gradually phased out early retirement was passed in late 1989. After unification, the Bismarckian pension system became extended to the East thanks again to PAYG financing, but the financing via social contributions added to the labour cost problems. The finance sector and economic experts called for a paradigm shift towards private prefunded pensions, breaking away from past interparty and bipartite consensus. However, some occupational pensions had already existed in many medium- to large-sized firms as a fringe benefit, particularly in manufacturing and finance (Jackson and Vitols 2001). Additionally, a negotiated occupational scheme for public employees (Wiß 2011) mirrored partly the generous final salary granted to tenured civil servants (*Beamte*).

German unions have traditionally defended the public PAYG pensions against any retrenchment, while employers have embraced reforms towards sustainability given demographic ageing and unification costs. A paradigm change occurred also in respect to reversing once popular early retirement policies, though unions, by and large representing more older and retired workers than younger ones, have been particularly opposed to increases in retirement age. During the 1990s, the pension debate shifted toward the sustainability of public pensions and the need for prefunded pensions. However, first steps by the Conservative-Liberal Kohl government were abolished by the incoming red-green Schröder government in 1998 but eventually led to even more advanced reforms as it promoted financialisation soon afterwards.

While German public pension reforms had tinkered with gradual adjustments to the fiscal and demographic pressures before, the paradigm shift towards multipillarisation was advanced by the red-green government in early 2000s. The so-called Riester pension, named after former deputy metal workers' union leader and then Social Democratic labour minister, introduced a voluntary funded personal pension to compensate for the gap caused by cutbacks in public benefits. This multipillar turn was more in line with employers and finance interests but also the moderate chemical sector union, while all other unions and social advocacy groups contested the non-compulsory DC pension (Klitzke 2017: 141).

The final law passed in May 2001, using state subsidies to promote voluntary contributions (up to 4% of salary) of low-income earners and parents with children. Initially, the insurers (represented by GDV) expected two-thirds of all employees to sign up voluntarily (Willert 2013: 301), but take up was slow and, only after further improvements, 12 million contracts had been signed by 2008. A decade later 17 million plans or every second employee had signed up, though some stopped paying contributions for lack of resources but also due to low returns since the 2008 crash. The imposed capital guarantee favoured the interests of insurances, which sold two-thirds of all contracts (Pieper 2018: 46), partly compensating for having lost favourable tax-status of life insurances. Indeed, finance was heavily involved in the reform, and the red-green government used the pension reform to advance its broader policy-shift towards financialisation (Röper 2018).

In addition, employers and unions had lobbied for changes fostering occupational pensions traditionally provided by larger German companies and the negotiated scheme for public employees. Voluntary deduction from salary (*Entgeltumwandlung*) for occupational pensions was made possible under collective agreements. In the chemical, construction and metal manufacturing sectors, the unions negotiated pension schemes with employers (Wiß 2011). The negotiated non-tenured public employee scheme was changed toward DC, while over one million civil servants (*Beamte*) still profit from a favourable (non-funded) final-salary retirement pay. Today 17 million people live in households with access to occupational pensions (about 20 million members). Nevertheless a coverage gap still exists for those with low education (1.6 times higher coverage among tertiary educated), for migrants (1.3 more natives) and gender (1.4 more men than women), whereas there is an overrepresentation (1.8 times) in the public sector (Pavolini and Seeleib-Kaiser 2018: 484–6).

The paradigm shift entailed also parallel reforms which reduced future public pension benefits due to demographic adjustments and retirement age extension. The unions had lost much of their influence in parliament by then (Trampusch 2005). They were divided between the metal and public service unions that defended the status quo of public pensions and the moderate chemical workers unions that favoured negotiating occupational pensions (Wiß 2011). Even a decade later, these differences still matter in the positioning of German unions towards funded occupational and personal pensions (Klitzke 2016: 154–6). Although the social associations are the most critical reform opponents, DGB launched a campaign before the 2017 elections to push for a reinforcement of the public pension. The second Grand Coalition (2013–2018) under Merkel found a compromise to improve former mothers' pension credits ('Mütterrente') favoured by the Conservatives and exemptions from retirement age increases for workers with long contribution records ('Rente mit 63') demanded by Social Democrats (and DGB unions). The subsequent Grand Coalition (2018–) has been more cautious in giving in to union demands and postponed decisions until the report of a new pension commission.

Discussion

Financialisation has increased with the shift towards further privatization and marketization in Britain and Germany, shifting the balance of interests towards employers and financial services. The binary comparison of rather dissimilar pension systems showed that both have been exposed to similar demographic sustainability concerns and financialisation tendency, though with distinct timing and to varying degrees. Public opinion support for status maintenance in German social insurance contrasts to anti-poverty orientation of the British basic pension tradition. Despite the popularity of the status quo, path departure was possible when organized interests, particular employers, finance interests and moderate unions embraced such reforms. Multipillarisation happened earlier in Britain than in Germany.

Governments of all colours had been engaged in advancing pension reforms towards financialisation in both countries, though this would not have been possible without the keen support of organized capital and the weakness of labour in defending the status quo. The two systems, however, saw contradictory changes towards a multipillar architecture. Most recently, Britain improved the minimum income function of the basic pension (abolishing the earnings-related supplement), bringing it more in line with Beveridge's initial intention, public opinion, and union demands. Interestingly, this was only achieved once British business and finance eventually supported this 'rebalancing' over the last decade. Quite in contrast, German employers called for public pension cutbacks due to ageing since the 1990s. Indeed, the demographic challenge, early retirement and unification costs have led to a paradigm shift away from intergenerational solidarity to a multipillar architecture. This happened against public opinion and the status defence of unions, as the red-green government engaged in a double strategy of cutting public pensions while extending private voluntary options to fill the retirement income gap. Paradoxically, it was Germany that advanced the marketization of pensions for demographic sustainability reasons since 2000s, while Britain has recently been more concerned about minimum income protection underneath the supplementary pensions that also were extended.

In terms of financialisation, Britain had built up a multipillar architecture earlier, assisted by opt-outs for pre-exiting occupational pension funds and for personal DC pensions. While occupational pensions had been traditionally DB schemes, employers were under marketization pressure to minimize their liabilities and move toward DC plans, entailing individualized risks similar to personal pensions. The financial market crash provided further urgency as DB schemes were underfunded and any bankruptcy raised premiums. British unions were able to moderate the erosion of DB rights in the better organized public sectors but failed to do so in the remaining economy for lack of bargaining power. Consequentially, the main problem is the low coverage of private supplementary pensions, particularly for those in low grades and smaller firms. It was less the unions but the coalition of employers and finance services that aligned with reforms pursued by governments of both partisan colours: improving public pension, abolish earnings-related state pension, and promoting private supplementary pensions through auto-enrolment. In Britain, the dual transformation was an upgrading of the public minimum and a widening of privately funded pensions, though unions were unable to stem the erosion of DB rights, particularly outside the public sector.

Quite in contrast, Germany's pension policy long ignored the co-existing occupational pension pillar that was largely unfunded fringe benefit and the generous DB arrangements in the public sector. The dual transformation of the 2000s, however, brought not only cutbacks in public pensions but also expanded occupational pensions and introduced partly subsidized voluntary DC pensions. These reforms were pushed through by a left-green government against considerable reservations by unions, while employers and finance interests had propagated such a paradigm shift since the 1990s. Subsequently, German unions have gained a more active role in negotiating occupational pensions, though DGB and its members still lobby for a roll back of pension cuts and are against retirement age increases. During the last two Grand Coalitions of Chancellor Merkel some partial concessions to unions and advocacy groups occurred, though the multipillar architecture remains reaffirmed. The debate about improving minimum income in old age to prevent poverty has gained momentum recently, while closing the gaps in coverage of supplementary pension remains also a challenge. Germany could learn from Britain to tackle both problems by fostering minimum pension provision and using automatic enrolment to boost supplementary pension coverage.

Outlook

The financial market crash of 2008 has had a considerable impact on current funded schemes as well as on the ongoing pension reform discourse. The financial market crash and subsequent European debt crisis has led to a major drop in pension fund assets and lowered the long-term prospects of funded pensions. In Britain, the Brexit referendum and subsequent decision to leave the European Union on 29 March 2019 has led to additional uncertainties about the British financial market and its long-term regulatory regime. Whether unions will be able to defend remaining DB schemes under more difficult circumstances remains to be seen; the pension fund protection has become ever more expensive and this might get worse if bankruptcies increase due to a post-Brexit downturn.

In the case of occupational DC plans or personal pensions (such as Riester), the lower returns and uncertain prospects have led to dissatisfaction with such savings, particularly for those close to retirement. Thus the future of funded pensions is not as secure as it seemed when financialisation had its heydays before 2008. The British move towards providing better minimum income protection in old age seems also to be necessary in Germany in order to prevent a growth in old age poverty. Even if in both countries the coverage gap of supplementary pensions can be closed, the very nature of funded pensions will lead to reproduction of income inequality in old age. To what degree this is acceptable to both societies or whether public opinion subsequently turns against financialisation remains a question to be addressed in the future.

Note

1. In addition to the secondary analyses, the description of position is based on semi-open interviews which were conducted with representatives from interest organizations in Britain (12 in 2011) and Germany (15 in 2012), see Klitzke (2017) for details.

Acknowledgements

The author is grateful to Julia Klitzke for conducting the interviews with stakeholders as part of the project A6 'Welfare State Reforms from Below' (PI: Ebbinghaus), funded by the German Research Foundation as part of the Collaborative Research Centre 884, Political Economy of Reform, University of Mannheim, Germany. The author thanks the editors of the special issue and the anonymous referees for their constructive feedback.

Disclosure statement

No potential conflict of interest was reported by the author.

Funding

This work was supported by Deutsche Forschungsgemeinschaft [grant number SFB 884/A6].

ORCID

Bernhard Ebbinghaus http://orcid.org/0000-0001-9838-8813

References

Armingeon, K. and Bonoli, G. (2006) *The Politics of Postindustrial Welfare States: Adapting Postwar Social Policies to New Social Risks*, London: Routledge.

Berry, C. (2016) 'Austerity, ageing and the financialisation of pensions policy in the UK', *British Politics* 11(1): 2–25.

Boeri, T., Boersch-Supan, A. and Tabellini, G. (2002) 'Pension reforms and the opinions of European citizens', *American Economic Review* 92(2): 396–401.

Bonoli, G. (2000) *The Politics of Pension Reform: Institutions and Policy Change in Western Europe*, Cambridge: Cambridge University Press.

Bonoli, G. (2012) 'Blame avoidance and credit claiming revisited', in G. Bonoli and D. Natali (eds.), *The Politics of the New Welfare State in Europe*, Oxford: Oxford University Press, pp. 93–110.

Bridgen, P. and Meyer, T. (2005) 'When do benevolent capitalists change their mind? Explaining the retrenchment of defined-benefit pensions in Britain', *Social Policy & Administration* 39(7): 764–85.

Bridgen, P. and Meyer, T. (2011) 'Britain: exhausted voluntarism – The evolution of a hybrid pension regime', in B. Ebbinghaus (ed.), *The Varieties of Pension Governance*, Oxford: Oxford University Press, pp. 265–91.

Casey, B.H. (2012) 'The implications of the economic crisis for pensions and pension policy in Europe', *Global Social Policy* 12(3): 246–65.

Clasen, J. and Siegel, N.A. (2007) *Investigating Welfare State Change: The 'Dependent Variable Problem' in Comparative Analysis*, Chelthenham: Elgar.

Dixon, J. and Hyde, M. (2002) 'Marketization of social security: a cross-national perspective', *Review of Policy Research* 19(3): 5–13.

Dixon, A. and Ville-Pekka, S. (2009) 'Institutional change and the financialisation of pensions in Europe', *Competition and Change* 13(4): 347–67.

Ebbinghaus, B. (2011) *The Varieties of Pension Governance: Pension Privatization in Europe*, Oxford: Oxford University Press.

Ebbinghaus, B. (2015) 'The privatization and marketization of pensions in Europe: a double transformation facing the crisis', *European Policy Analysis* 1(1): 56–73.

Ebbinghaus, B. (2017) 'The role of trade unions in pension policymaking and private pension governance in Europe', in D. Natali (ed.), *The New Pension Mix in Europe*, Brussels: Peter Lang, pp. 207–37.

Ebbinghaus, B. and Naumann, E. (2018a) 'Class, union, or party allegiance? Comparing pension reform preferences in Britain and Germany", in B. Ebbinghaus and E. Naumann (eds.), *Welfare State Reforms Seen from Below*, London: Palgrave, pp. 107–28.

Ebbinghaus, B. and Naumann, E. (2018b) 'The popularity of pension and unemployment policies revisited', in B. Ebbinghaus and E. Naumann (eds.), *Welfare State Reforms Seen from Below*, London: Palgrave, pp. 155–86.

Ebbinghaus, B. and Wiß, T. (2011) 'Taming pension fund capitalism in Europe: collective and state regulation in times of crisis', *Transfer* 17(1): 15–28.

Grady, J. (2013) 'Trade unions and the pension crisis: defending member interests in a neoliberal world', *Employee Relations* 35(3): 294–308.

Grech, A.G. (2013) 'Assessing the sustainability of pension reforms in Europe', *Journal of International and Comparative Social Policy* 29(2): 143–62.

Grødem, A.S., Hagelund, A., Hippe, J.M. and Trampusch, C. (2018) 'Beyond coverage: the politics of occupational pensions and the role of trade unions', *Transfer* 24(1): 9–23.

Hall, P.A. (1993) 'Policy paradigms, social learning, and the state. The case of economic policymaking in Britain', *Comparative Politics* 25: 275–97.

Häusermann, S. (2010) 'Solidarity with whom? Why organised labour is losing ground in continental pension politics', *European Journal of Political Research* 49: 223–56.

Hering, M. (2012) 'Live longer, work longer? Intergenerational fairness in retirement age reforms in Germany and the United Kingdom', in P. Vanhuysse and A. Goerres (eds.), *Ageing Populations in Post-Industrial Democracies*, London: Routledge, 79–105.

Hinrichs, K. and Jessoula, M. (2012) *Labour Market Flexibility and Pension Reform. Flexible Today, Secure Tomorrow?* Basingstoke: Palgrave.

Immergut, E. and Anderson, K. (2007) 'The dynamics of pension politics', in E. Immergut, K. Anderson and I. Schulze (eds.), *The Handbook of West European Pension Politics*, Oxford: Oxford University Press, pp. 1–45.

Immergut, E.M. and Abou-Chadi, T. (2014) 'How electoral vulnerability affects pension politics: introducing a concept, measure and empirical application', *European Journal of Political Research* 53(2): 269–87.

Jackson, G. and Vitols, S. (2001) 'Between financial commitment, market liquidity and corporate governance: occupational pensions in Britain, Germany, Japan and the USA', in B. Ebbinghaus and P. Manow (eds.), *Comparing Welfare Capitalism*, London: Routledge, pp. 171–89.

Johnston, A., Kornelakis, A. and Rodriguez d'Acri, C. (2012) 'Swords of justice in an age of retrenchment? The role of trade unions in welfare provision', *Transfer* 18(2): 213–24.

Keune, M. (2018) 'Opportunity or threat? How trade union power and preferences shape occupational pensions', *Social Policy & Administration* 52(2): 463–76.

Klitzke, J. (2017) 'Beveridge and Bismarck remodelled: The positions of British and German organised interests on pension reform', Mannheim: dissertation, University of Mannheim, available at https://ub-madoc.bib.uni-mannheim.de/42079/.

Klitzke, J. (2018) 'Membership or influence logic? The response of organized interests to retirement age reforms in Britain and Germany', in B. Ebbinghaus and E. Naumann (eds.), *Welfare State Reforms Seen From Below*, London: Palgrave, pp. 27–54.

Korpi, W. (1983) *The Democratic Class Struggle*, London: Routledge.

Leimgruber, M. (2012) 'The historical roots of a diffusion process: the threepillar doctrine and European pension debates (1972–1994)', *Global Social Policy* 12(1): 24–44.

Leisering, L. (2011) *The New Regulatory State: Regulating Pensions in Germany and the UK*, London: Palgrave.

Mares, I. (2003) *The Politics of Social Risk. Business and Welfare State Development*, New York: Cambridge University Press.

Meyer, T. (2013) *Beveridge Statt Bismarck! Europäische Lehren für die Alterssicherung von Frauen und Männern in Deutschland*, Bonn: Friedrich Ebert Stiftung.

Meyer, T. and Bridgen, P. (2018) 'Individualisation reversed: the cross-class politics of social regulation in the UK's public/private pension mix', *Transfer* 24(1): 25–41.

Meyer, T., Bridgen, P. and Riedmüller, B. (2007) *Private Pensions Versus Social Inclusion? Non-State Provision for Citizens at Risk in Europe*, Cheltenham: Elgar.

Naczyk, M. (2013) 'Agents of privatization? Business groups and the rise of pension funds in Continental Europe', *Socio-Economic Review* 11(3): 441–69.

Naczyk, M. and Seeleib-Kaiser, M. (2015) 'Solidarity against all odds: trade unions and the privatization of pensions in the age of dualization', *Politics and Society* 43(3): 361–84.

Natali, D. (2008) *Pensions in Europe, European Pensions*, Brussels: PIE Lang.

Natali, D. (2018) 'Occupational pensions in Europe: Trojan horse of financialization?' *Social Policy & Administration* 52(2): 449–62.

Palier, B. and Bonoli, G. (1995) 'Entre Bismarck et Beveridge: "Crises" de la Sécurité Sociale et Politique(s)', *Revue française de science politique* 4(45): 668–99.

Pavolini, E. and Seeleib-Kaiser, M. (2018) 'Comparing occupational welfare in Europe: the case of occupational pensions', *Social Policy & Administration* 52(2): 477–90.
Pieper, J. (2018) *New Private Sector Providers in the Welfare State*, London: Palgrave.
Pierson, P. (1996) 'The new politics of the welfare state', *World Politics* 48(2): 143–79.
Pierson, P. (2000) 'Increasing returns, path dependence, and the study of politics', *American Political Science Review* 94(2): 251–67.
Pierson, P. (2001) *The New Politics of the Welfare State*, New York: Oxford University Press.
Röper, N. (2018) 'German finance capitalism: the paradigm shift underlying financial diversification', *New Political Economy* 23 (3), 366–390.
Sanderson, W.C. and Scherbov, S. (2007) 'A near electoral majority of pensioners: prospects and policies', *Population and Development Review* 33(3): 543–54.
Seeleib-Kaiser, M., Saunders, A. and Naczyk, M. (2012) 'Shifting the public-private mix: a new dualization of welfare', in P. Emmenegger, S. Häusermann, B. Palier and M. Seeleib-Kaiser (eds.), *The Age of Dualization: The Changing Face of Inequality in Deindustrializing Societies*, New York: Oxford University Press, pp. 151–75.
Thaler, R.H. and Sunstein, C.R. (2009) *Nudge: Improving Decisions About Health, Wealth, and Happiness*, London: Penguin.
Trampusch, C. (2005) 'From interest groups to parties: the change in the career patterns of the legislative elite in German social policy', *German Politics* 14(1): 14–32.
van der Zwan, N. (2014) 'Making sense of financialization', *Socio-Economic Review* 12(1): 99–129.
Weaver, K. (2010) 'Paths and forks or chutes and ladders? Negative feedbacks and policy regime change', *Journal of Public Policy* 30(2): 137–62.
Weaver, K.R. (1986) 'The politics of blame avoidance', *Journal of Public Policy* 6(4): 371–98.
Whiteside, N. (2017) 'Britain's pension reforms: A new departure?', in D. Natali (ed.), *The New Pension Mix in Europe*, Brussels: PIE Lang, pp. 177–200.
Willert, M. (2013) *Regulierte Wohlfahrtsmärkte: private Altersvorsorge in Deutschland und Großbritannien*, Frankfurt: Campus.
Wiß, T. (2011) *Der Wandel der Alterssicherung in Deutschland. Die Rolle der Sozialpartner*, Wiesbaden: VS Verlag.
Wiß, T. (2015a) 'From welfare states to welfare sectors: explaining sectoral differences in occupational pensions with economic and political power of employees', *Journal of European Social Policy* 25(5): 489–504.
Wiß, T. (2015b) 'Pension fund vulnerability to the financial market crisis: the role of trade unions', *European Journal of Industrial Relations* 21(2): 131–47.
Wiß, T. (2018) 'Divergent occupational pensions in Bismarckian countries: the case of Germany and Austria', *Transfer* 24(1): 91–107.
World Bank (1994) *Averting the Old Age Crisis: Policies to Protect the Old and Promote Growth*, Oxford: Oxford University Press.
Zohlnhöfer, R., Wolf, F. and Wenzelburger, G. (2013) 'Political parties and pension generosity in times of permanent austerity', *World Political Science Review* 9(1): 291–318.

Re-assessing the role of financial professionals in pension fund investment strategies

Margarita Gelepithis

ABSTRACT
Funded pensions are now established components of most mature retirement income systems. The value of global pension fund assets is higher than ever before, and the way these assets are invested affects both the welfare of future retirees, and the performance of national economies. Recent research has identified systematic cross-national variation in the investment behaviour of pension funds, explaining it through the preferences and influence of employer-sponsors and plan members. Yet the ongoing 'de-risking' of UK pension funds remains puzzling. Informed by the UK case, this article develops the argument that variation in pension fund asset allocation reflects the independent influence of networks of investment professionals who construct and institutionalise norms of liability driven investment.

Introduction

Funded pensions, where retirement income is paid out of accumulated financial assets rather than current income, are now firmly established components of most mature retirement income systems (OECD 2016). The public policy importance of funded pensions has been cemented by strained Pay-As-You-Go (PAYG) arrangements, contributing to a 'financialisation of the everyday' (van der Zwan 2014) in which a range of social risks are increasingly insured on financial markets.

Despite being hard hit by two financial crises in the 2000s, the value of global pension fund assets is higher than ever (OECD 2018). The way these sizable assets are invested is of consequence not only for the welfare of future retirees (Wiß 2015; Yermo and Pino 2010: 18), but also for the structure and performance of national economies (Clark 2000, 2017; Dixon 2008; Shiller 2000).

Recent comparative research has identified systematic cross-national variation in the investment behaviour of pension funds (OECD 2016: 19; Yermo and Pino 2010). To explain this variation, emphasis has been placed on understanding the investment preferences of employer-sponsors and plan members (Ebbinghaus 2012; McCarthy et al. 2016; Wiß 2015), as well as on understanding how pension fund governance structures the investment influence of these actors (Ebbinghaus and Wiß 2011: 355–371).

Patterns of United Kingdom (UK) pension fund investment are puzzling by such accounts however. A Liberal Market Economy (LME) where pension fund governance is 'employer led' (Ebbinghaus and Wiß 2011: 355–358), the UK is a context in which pension fund investment should be strongly geared towards equities. Yet, despite stability in the investment preferences and influence of employer-sponsors and plan members, the past fifteen years have seen UK pension funds 'de-risk' their investment portfolios and shift their asset allocation away from equities towards bonds.

In this article I examine the UK case and develop the argument that pension fund asset allocation is not a straightforward reflection of the investment preferences and influence of employer-sponsors and plan members. Rather, it is in large part shaped by the independent influence of their agents – networks of investment professionals who have constructed and institutionalised norms of liability driven investment.

In the next section, I review existing explanations of variation in pension fund asset allocation. Section III presents the puzzle of the UK case, and section IV develops the expectations that inform my analysis. In section V, I present a narrative of the UK case, drawing on interview and documentary evidence to trace the process of change in pension fund investment decision-making since the 1990s. The final section is a discussion of this case in relation to the expectations that inform it. I set out the theoretical implications of my argument, with reference to recent developments in the strikingly different German context.

Employer-sponsors and plan members in pension fund investment strategies

Among institutional investors, pension funds stand out for the long-term nature of their liabilities. As a result, a first wave of political economy scholarship saw pension funds as a homogenous class of investor, expected to bolster equity markets by investing long-term in risky assets such as corporate stocks (Goyer 2006: 400; Jackson and Vitols 2001: 6). By linking the investment strategies of pension funds to the nature of their liabilities, this strand of scholarship saw pension fund capitalism as a key feature of LMEs, as well as a potentially transformative force in Coordinated Market Economies (CMEs) (Dixon and Sorsa 2009; Hall and Sockice 2001).

More recently, a second wave of scholarship has drawn attention to heterogeneity in the investment behaviour of pension funds. It has identified cross-national differences in pension fund asset allocation, challenging the idea that pension fund capitalism is a force for convergence to the Liberal model. Far from adopting homogenous investment behaviour, pension funds in LMEs tend to adopt 'risky' investment strategies based on relatively equity-heavy portfolios, while pension funds in Coordinated and Mixed Market Economies (MMEs) tend to adopt 'conservative' investment strategies based on investment portfolios that are relatively bond-heavy, (Wiß 2015: 139).

Underlying this stylised pattern of cross-national differences in asset allocation are corresponding differences in pension fund governance. In CMEs and MMEs, the governing boards of pension funds are composed of members typically chosen by both sponsoring employers and employees (Stewart and Yermo 2008: 6). The resulting strong plan member representation on pension fund governing boards is expected to ensure close alignment of the fund's investment strategy with the preferences of the fund's beneficiaries (Stewart and Yermo 2008). In particular, member representatives are expected to skew the portfolio towards investments that are typically considered to be more conservative, such as government and corporate bonds (Ebbinghaus and Wiß 2011: 367–371; Stewart and Yermo 2008; Useem and Mitchell 2000).

By contrast in LMEs, pension funds tend to take the legal form of a trust, in which trustees must administer the plan's assets in the sole interests of the plan participants (Stewart and Yermo 2008). There are few or no legal requirements for member representation and occupational pensions tend to be 'employer led', with plan members exerting more limited investment influence (Ebbinghaus and Wiß 2011: 355–358; Stewart and Yermo 2008). Since employers are expected to prioritise lower contributions over stable and sustainable future benefits, such governance arrangements are seen to favour investment in equities (Ebbinghaus and Wiß 2011; Harper 2008; Stewart and Yermo 2008; Useem and Mitchell 2000).

Qualifying this stylised picture, McCarthy et al. show that plan members do not always prefer lower yield, lower risk investments, and employer sponsors do not always prefer to invest in riskier assets (McCarthy et al. 2016). Rather, the investment preferences of business and labour are dynamic, influenced by pension fund financing needs, governance arrangements and regulatory context. In this way, McCarthy et al. explain changes in investment patterns that have occurred in the absence of change in the relative investment influence of business and labour (McCarthy et al. 2016: 760–762).

In sum, as political economists have increasingly sought to explain variation in pension fund investment behaviour, they have shifted their attention away from the long-term nature of pension fund liabilities (Goyer 2006; Hall and Sockice 2001; Jackson and Vitols 2001), towards the investment preferences and influence of employer-sponsors and plan members (Ebbinghaus 2012; McCarthy et al. 2016; Wiß 2015). Overwhelmingly, the underlying premise of second wave accounts of pension fund investment is that whether as 'principals' who delegate and monitor the investment decisions of appointed 'agents', or through direct representation on the pension fund boards, it is employers and employees who are ultimately responsible for making decisions about broad asset allocation.

A puzzling case of 'de-risking'

The UK case stands out as puzzle when viewed in light of such explanations. While known for being heavily invested in equities in line with its 'employer led' pension fund governance arrangements (Ebbinghaus 2011; OECD 2013; Wiß 2015; Yermo and Pino 2010), the UK has seen a substantial and long-term shift away from equity exposure and towards bonds since 1994 (Myners 2001: 54). Equity exposure more than halved after 2003, while bond exposure has increased by over 50 per cent in the same time period (see Figure 1). As Figure 2 shows, this shift is particularly notable in comparative context.

The trend is all the more striking because it precedes the immediate post-crash years when OECD countries retreated from equities (Antolin and Stewart 2009; Ebbinghaus 2012; Wiß 2015; Yermo and Pino 2010), and has carried on strong throughout an OECD-wide 'search for yield' in the protracted low interest rate environment (OECD 2015). Although there has also been a simultaneous trend towards increased investment in 'other' assets, the overall trend has been towards assets typically seen as 'conservative' – even if 'other' investments are all classed as risky.

It is difficult to understand this shift in broad asset allocation with reference to the investment preferences and influence of employers and employees. The shift takes place without a corresponding increase in employee influence in pension fund governance. Moreover, two broad trends in

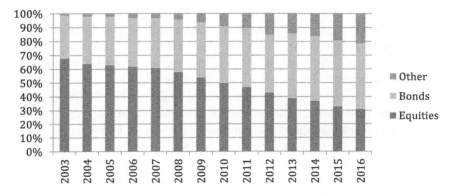

Figure 1. Broad asset allocation in UK pension funds. Source: Mercer (2016).

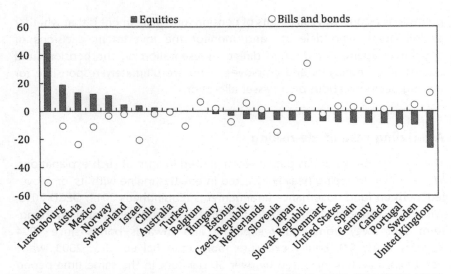

Figure 2. Variation of investments in equities, bills and bonds, 2004–2014 (OECD 2015).

workplace pension provision are likely to have shifted the investment preferences of employers further towards 'risky' asset allocation. The first is the well-documented trend from Defined Benefit (DB) to Defined Contribution (DC) arrangements (Munnell 2006). The second is a less commonly analysed trend within DC arrangements from trust-based to contract-based provision (Ashcroft 2009; UK Parliament 2013).

In DB arrangements, which are almost always trust-based in the UK (UK Parliament 2013), trustees acting as agents of the employer-sponsor have the duty to meet a pre-defined level of benefits. Since they face a considerable downside to failing to meet this target but derive limited benefit from exceeding it, they are usually incentivised to invest in a risk averse way (Bank of England 2014: 20). In DC schemes, the employee/employer pay an agreed amount into the pension fund, but the income received by the employee in retirement is dependent on investment returns, scheme charges, and annuity rates at retirement. In trust-based DC schemes, plan trustees have no duty to meet a defined level of benefits but they do have a duty to act in the interests of scheme members (Ashcroft 2009: 5).

In contract-based DC schemes, which make up over half of UK DC schemes and are the main growth area in the UK pensions market (Ashcroft 2009), pension funds are managed by a third party, such as an insurance provider, and operate on the basis of a contract between the scheme member and the provider. Since the provider responsible for making decisions on asset allocation is not bound by a duty of trust to plan members (UK Parliament 2013), contract-based schemes have an incentive to maximise returns, and are expected to be less conservative in their asset allocation than trust-based schemes (Ashcroft 2009; Bank of England 2014: 20).

In sum, the strong trend away from DB and towards contract-based DC pension provision should have shifted the investment preferences of UK employers further towards 'risky' asset allocation. In the absence of a simultaneous increase in employee influence in UK pension fund governance, it is therefore difficult to understand the ongoing aggregate de-risking of UK pension funds with reference to the investment preferences and influence of employers and employees.

Bringing financial professionals back in

In explaining the puzzle of the UK case, I embrace the institutionalism of existing accounts of variation in asset allocation. My analysis is guided by the assumption that asset allocation decisions are made by political actors whose influence and preferences are shaped by – and also shape – the institutional context. In existing accounts of pension fund investment behaviour, employer-sponsors and plan members are the key political actors, and corporate governance arrangements constitute the relevant institutional context. But in the analysis of the UK case that follows, I draw on recent research which points to the importance of financial professionals, and the broader institutional context of financial regulation.

According to this research, financial professionals involved in pension fund capitalism such as asset managers, actuaries, and pension consultants exert an independent influence over pension fund investment strategies. Pension fund trustees increasingly take asset allocation decisions on the basis of advice from investment consultants (Jenkinson et al. 2016; Tonks 2005), and there has been an increase in 'outsourced' asset management in which pension fund trustees or governing boards delegate not only the implementation of asset management, but also key aspects of investment strategy including high-level asset allocation decisions (Clark and Unwin 2017; Tonks 2005). Labour trustees in particular are increasingly likely to delegate investment decisions to financial professionals (Verma and Weststar 2011).

Financial professionals have their own distinct investment preferences. In particular, the literature paints a picture of international networks of financial professionals who construct and disseminate the investment norms guiding pension fund asset allocation. These norms are informed by investment beliefs – lenses through which financial markets are analyzed (Franzen 2013; Koedijk and Slager 2010). They constitute a 'paradigm of pension investment' (Ambachtsheer 2005) or 'standard of investment knowledge' formulated and adopted on a global scale (Franzen 2013: 15). Of particular importance here is a shared educational background among investment professionals schooled in modern investment theory by universities, business schools, and international accreditation bodies like the Chartered Financial Analyst Institute (Franzen 2013).

Accounts of financial professionals enacting a global paradigm of pension investment tend to homogenise the investment behaviour of pension funds, and cannot in isolation explain observable variation in asset allocation. One way to account for such variation may be to combine these insights with those of research about how regulation constrains and shapes pension fund investment behaviour. In particular, recent work has pointed to the role of quantitative investment limits (Ebbinghaus and Wiß 2011) and accounting standards (Amir et al. 2010; Dixon and Monk 2009) in pension fund decision-making, highlighting the tendency of such regulation to foster more conservative investment behaviour.

In the analysis that follows, I proceed inductively to develop an explanation for the de-risking of UK pension funds. I draw on documentary and interview evidence (see appendix for interview list) to trace the process of change in investment decision-making across the UK occupational pensions landscape. Looking beyond the investment preferences and influence of plan members and employer-sponsors, and informed by the research outlined above, I pay particular attention to the investment preferences and influence of financial professionals and the regulatory context in which they operate.

The UK 'de-risks'

I start the analysis at the publication of the Myners Review of Institutional Investment (Myners 2001). This review was commissioned in 2000 by the first Blair government, to examine possible investment distortions within UK financial institutions. As the first authoritative exposition of financial industry influence in UK pension fund investment, the report forms the starting point for the case. I then step back two decades, to trace the process of 'de-risking' back to the changing investment norms of financial professionals since the late 1980s.

Financial industry influence in DC and DB investment before 2000: the Myners Review

The influence of investment professionals over asset allocation is clearest in contract-based schemes. In its discussion of DC pensions, the Myners Review concluded that while in theory members of contract-based DC schemes could shape investment behaviour by voting with their feet, in practice this occurred 'only in a minority of cases' (Myners 2001: 54). A group of twenty-five life insurers were defining asset allocation,[1] within a small market of passive consumers that offered few incentives for financial innovation (Myners 2001; Interview 4). Investment practices were overwhelmingly characterised by 'lifestyling' – asset allocation would mechanically shift from equities to bonds as plan members neared retirement (Ashcroft 2009; Myners 2001).

Although the influence of investment professionals was most obvious in contract-based schemes, it was not confined to them. In trust-based schemes, whether DB or DC, it was the responsibility of the trustees to make investment decisions on behalf of the plan members. Yet, according to the Myners Review, trustees were 'heavily dependent on advisers' for investment decision-making – including for strategic asset allocation decisions (Myners 2001: 8). The advisers in question were investment consultants, operating primarily within branches of actuarial firms (Myners 2001: 64).

Investment consulting for pension funds had emerged as a business in the UK in the early 1980s, and grew fast in the 1990s. Trustees were not required to have expertise in investment – only to 'obtain proper advice' about it (Pensions Act 1995). They therefore usually lacked professional qualifications in finance and were increasingly seen to possess neither the resources nor the expertise to make investment decisions (Myners 2001: 4). Overall, the review concluded: 'although in law trustees are making the strategic asset allocation, in practice, there must be considerable doubt over the extent to which they are exercising genuine decision-making power' (Myners 2001: 9).

In seeking investment advice, trustees had little choice between distinct investment allocation options. The investment consulting industry was 'small and highly concentrated' (Myners 2001: 9), with 70 percent of the market split among four firms: Watson Wyatt, William Mercer, Bacon and Woodrow, and Hymans Robertson (Myners 2001: 64). The reliance of both DC and DB schemes on investment advice that was so concentrated reinforced the development of dominant industry-wide investment norms, and the adoption of similar investment strategies across pension funds. Concentration had led to 'a commonality of investment policy among pension funds' and trustees were aware the advice offered by investment consultants did not vary greatly from practice to practice (Myners 2001: 70).

Changing investment norms

While homogenous, investment norms have not remained static over time. In the 1980s 'asset only' investment approaches were dominant (Aon Hewitt 2014; Chambers et al. 2005). Assets were invested in an 'off the shelf' (Aon Hewitt 2014: 4) or 'one size fits all' (Myners 2001) way, and asset allocation was not tailored to specific schemes. In particular, trustees ignored the liability profiles of their schemes, and 'mature and young schemes were invested side by side' (Aon Hewitt 2014: 4). Assets were chosen for their growth potential, and pension funds were seen as long-term investors ideally placed to benefit from asset classes that were subject to higher volatility in the short term, but higher returns in the long run (Blake 2003: 6).

Pension funds were encouraged to maintain a static and 'balanced' split across asset classes, typically consisting of 70 percent equities and 30 percent bonds and other assets. Since balanced funds targeted a performance benchmark consisting of the average return on a peer group of funds with a similar strategy (Chambers et al. 2005: 3), there were powerful herding incentives for asset allocation (Myners 2001: 56). Over time, this meant that even greater weight was given to equities as a result of their high historical returns (Chambers et al. 2005: 3). Under 'asset only' investing, UK pension schemes led the 'cult of equity' (Sutcliffe 2005), and equities peaked at 79 percent of the aggregate DB portfolio in 1994 (Bank of England 2014; Pension Protection Fund 2016).

Already by the late 1980s and early 1990s however, actuaries and investment consultants had begun to construct an alternative investment paradigm, in which liabilities rather than assets were central. In response to growing dissatisfaction with the investment performance of leading balanced fund managers, analysis by investment consultants cast doubt on the ability of fund managers to consistently add value by tinkering with investments within prescribed asset allocation boundaries (Myners 2001: 54). Instead, drawing on academic studies (e.g., Ambachtsheer 1987; Leibowitz 1986; Winklewoss 1982), pensions consultants began to stress the importance of making investment decisions with liabilities in mind.

Consultants trained in actuarial science began to recommend the use of Asset Liability Management (ALM) to assist trustees in setting their asset allocation strategy (Myners 2001: 54). This involved the use of quantitative techniques to structure the asset portfolios of pension schemes by paying 'due regard to the structure of their liabilities' (Blake 2003). The practice began to take hold among large pension schemes, and by 1990 an estimated 30 percent of UK DB pension funds were applying ALM (Blake 2003).

Liability-driven investment becomes institutionalised

The increased attention that trustees were advised to pay to liabilities was encouraged by the Minimum Funding Requirement (MFR), introduced in 1997. A response to public concerns about the security of occupational pensions following the Maxwell scandal, the MFR introduced for the first time the requirement that pension schemes hold a minimum level of assets to meet their liabilities (Thurley 2008). As a result, it highlighted the need for trustees to consider their fund's potential asset-liability mismatch (Thurley 2008). Crucially, the MFR was designed and drafted by the Faculty and Institute of Actuaries. Actuarial and consulting firms, who benefited from the corresponding requirement that pension trustees obtain professional actuarial valuations for their funds (Thurley and McInnes 2017), were key in introducing this regulatory development that encouraged liability sensitive investing (Blair 1995; Blake 2001).

As pensions consultants promoted liability sensitive investment within the new regulatory framework, the use of peer benchmarked balanced funds declined steadily (Aon Hewitt 2014; Chambers et al. 2005; Franzen 2013). By the end of the 1990s, it was barely half as prevalent as it had been at the beginning of the decade (Myners 2001: 54). ALM became increasingly common practice, and sophisticated asset-liability models were developed by North American and British researchers in close co-operation with practitioners (e.g., Mulvey and Towers-Perrin 1996). Initially confined to the biggest pension funds, ALM was 'implemented in cascades starting at the largest market player' and gradually became the industry standard (Franzen 2013: 120).

As the use of ALM spread, it further reinforced the influence of investment consultants in strategic asset allocation decisions. The investment alternatives produced by ALM depended heavily on the underlying assumptions of the asset-liability model. Yet trustees lacked the technical expertise to challenge complex models or their underlying qualitative judgments. Among schemes using an asset-liability model at the time of the Myners Review, trustees were involved in the setting of underlying assumptions in only 30 per cent of cases. Myners concluded that consultants were 'the sole source of serious qualitative input' to asset-liability models (Myners 2001: 59).

Gradually, the UK started to shift away from the 'cult of equity' towards asset allocation that was more closely shaped by the liability structure of UK DB pension schemes. In particular, asset allocation began to reflect the demographic differences between funds, as well as a number of what investment professionals call 'technicals' such as inflation and interest rates (Interview 1). As an increasing number of corporate DB pension funds began to close to new entrants, DB scheme membership came to consist of a greater, and increasing, proportion of retirees and a smaller, and decreasing, proportion of members in the accumulation phase. From 1994, this maturing of pension plan liabilities within the new context of liability-sensitive investment drove a decrease in aggregate DB allocation to equities and an increase in allocation to index-linked bonds (Mercer 2014; Pension Protection Fund 2016).

This trend was further strengthened by the publication of the Myners Review. Drawing heavily on consultation responses from the financial community, the Review sought to institutionalise a scheme-specific funding standard reflecting the maturity structure of the liabilities of each pension scheme. This recommendation, which was immediately accepted by the government (HM Treasury and the Department for Work and Pensions 2001), further incentivized the selection of asset classes on the basis of their volatility match with scheme liabilities. In addition, the review had the effect of further strengthening the investment advisor relative to both the actuary and the fund manager (Blake 2003), encouraging pension funds to 'spend more on asset allocation' to improve investment decision making and investment returns (Myners 2001: 60).

The Myners Review was closely followed by the implementation of FRS17 in 2003. This accounting standard faced criticism from both unions and employer sponsors, but was accepted by the investment industry. It became policy in a depoliticised way, on the basis of the professional judgment of the Accounting Standards Board (Bridgen and Meyer 2009; Veron 2007). FRS17 replaced the MFR, but continued to reinforce the shift of pension fund assets into bonds (Blake 2003).

Crises reinforce the trend towards liability-driven investment

The final chapter of the UK's de-risking story begins with the 'perfect pension storm' of falling equity markets and simultaneously falling interest rates between 2000 and 2003. This toxic combination eroded assets while sending liabilities soaring. It signalled the end of the traditional balanced mandate of a fixed portfolio mix of equities and bonds, as it became apparent that this approach exposed pension schemes to considerable funding gaps (Franzen 2013). Moreover, the regulatory response, which took the form of the Pensions Act of 2004 and the creation of the Pensions Regulator (tPR), strengthened the imperative for trustees to avoid funding gaps (Franzen 2010; Interview 4).

The global financial crisis of 2007–2008 inspired no further regulation relevant to strategic asset allocation. However, interview evidence suggests a perception among trustees of a hardening of the stance of tPR towards funding gaps (Interview 4, Interview 5). This perception has further discouraged trustees from questioning investment advice (Interview 4).

As a result, almost two decades since the Myners Review first identified the heavy dependence of trustees on investment consultants, the influence of the consulting industry is at an all time high (CMA/IFF Research 2018; Competition and Markets Authority 2018; OMB Research 2016) and the overwhelming majority of clients purchase advice on strategic asset allocation (Bank of England 2014: 19, 36). Trustees continue to have little choice in asset allocation since the provision of investment advice remains highly concentrated – now in the hands of the 'big three' investment consultancies, Mercer, Aon Hewitt, and Willis Towers Watson.[2] ALM is standard in the market, with nearly 90 percent of schemes basing their investment decisions at least in part on an asset-liability study (Bank of England 2014: 19, 36; Franzen 2013: 244). Moreover, within the practice of ALM, the link between assets and liabilities has been successively tightened (Franzen 2013: 243).

Changing patterns of asset allocation in DB and DC investment

The industry's emphasis on liability driven investment has resulted in similar asset allocation for a given set of liabilities across firms (Bank of England 2014: 20; Bank for International Settlements 2007). Differences in scheme maturity correspond closely with differences in the relative proportion of the fund's portfolio invested in equities and bonds (Pension Protection Fund 2016), and go a long way towards explaining the much greater degree of 'de-risking' by corporate pension funds as compared to the local authority pension funds (Bank of England 2014: 39). Over time, maturing liabilities have driven the continued aggregate decrease in DB allocation to equities. By 2016, equity allocation had fallen to just 30 per cent of the aggregate DB portfolio (Mercer 2014; Pension Protection Fund 2016), while total bond allocation had risen to 51 per cent (Bank of England 2014; Pension Protection Fund 2016).

The de-risking of UK pensions has overwhelmingly been driven by the asset allocation patterns among DB schemes (Mercer 2014; Pension Protection Fund 2016). While there has been some de-risking among DC schemes, most continue to rely primarily on equities (Schroders 2016). In 2016, the average default DC fund of a FTSE 350 firm invested just under 67 per cent of its total assets in developed equities, only 16 per cent in bonds, and 13 per cent in alternatives (Schroders 2016).

Yet, this risk-heavy profile does not reflect a starkly different underlying investment strategy on the part of the investors of DC pension scheme assets relative to those of DB schemes (Interview 4; Interview 5; Interview 1). While DC schemes do not have liabilities strictly speaking, the dominant investment practice of 'lifestyling' – recently super-ceded by conceptually similar individual 'glidepaths' – ensures that asset allocation in DB and DC schemes is shaped by scheme demographics to a similar extent (Interview 4; Interview 5; Interview 1). Thus the high equity exposure of DC schemes primarily reflects the fact that they are still – on aggregate and relative to DB schemes – young and in the accumulation phase (Interview 1, Interview 3, Interview 5).

Moreover, asset allocation in DC schemes is increasingly structured 'as if' to match liabilities, taking into account the expected effect of changes in 'technicals' like interest and inflation rates on individual benefits (Interview 5; Interview 3). Two of the 'big three' investment consulting firms pioneered Liability Driven Investment (LDI) for DC schemes (Payne 2006), and asset allocation started to become less equity-heavy, despite the youth of the sector (Ashcroft 2009).

Discussion and Conclusion

The starting point for the preceding narrative was that it is difficult to understand the ongoing de-risking of UK pension funds with reference only to the investment preferences and influence of plan members and employer-sponsors. Although employers continue to have more of a role in pension fund governance than employees, and the spread of DC arrangements means that employers bear less of the risk of pension fund investment decisions, the share of equities in pension fund portfolios has declined steadily over the past 25 years.

In analysing the UK case, I have been guided by recent research highlighting the independent influence of financial professionals in shaping pension fund investment behaviour, and the regulatory context in which they operate. My findings lend support to these insights, but also allow us to go beyond them.

The UK case shows how pension fund asset allocation was shaped by the independent influence of networks of investment professionals – most notably, a concentrated industry of actuaries and investment consultants – who constructed and institutionalised norms of investment that increasingly took into account the specific structure of pension fund liabilities.

In the context of liability driven investment practices, the de-risking of UK pension funds has been fuelled mainly by the sharply maturing liability profiles of DB schemes. Pension scheme demographics, as well as other 'technicals' such as inflation and interest rates, emerge from the UK case as important economic values that shape asset allocation in the context of liability sensitive investing.

The implication of this is that the homogenous class of institutional investors, identified by first wave accounts of financialisation, should not necessarily constitute pressures for institutional convergence. Rather, the liability-focused investment norms constructed by these investors bring about variation in asset allocation, according to the economic and demographic circumstances that structure pension fund liabilities. In this way, homogenous investment norms may be important in explaining variation in pension fund investment patterns, both across countries and over time.

As expected, regulation also had an important role to play in shaping asset allocation. The Minimum Funding Requirement, FRS17, and the Pensions Act of 2004 all contributed to the de-risking trend, by incentivizing pension funds to closely match their assets to their scheme's liabilities. Yet, the analysis presented here gives causal primacy to the agency of investment professionals rather than to the regulatory context. The case study shows how the beginnings of the shift towards liability-sensitive investment preceded all relevant regulatory activity. Pensions consultants and actuaries initiated the underlying change in investment norms, and were also the key players in the introduction of the MFR.

My account of UK de-risking does not depart from the institutionalism of existing accounts of variation in asset allocation. Asset allocation decisions are still made by political actors, whose preferences and influence shape and are shaped by the institutional context. Within the bounds of institutionalism however, my theoretical contribution is twofold.

First, I show that patterns of pension fund asset allocation are only partially shaped by employer sponsors, by plan members, and by the institutions of corporate governance. At least in some cases, they are defined by the independent influence and preferences of investment professionals, and the regulatory context which they help shape and in which they operate.

Second, ideas play a more central role in my argument than they do in existing explanations. While existing explanations depart from the premise that some assets are more risky than others, the explanation developed here shows how the concept of risk is itself socially constructed, with implications for investment preferences. Under asset-only norms of investment, demographic differences among pension schemes did not lead to differences in asset allocation. But where the risk of holding an asset is understood relative to the liabilities it must fund, pension fund demographics, as well as prices like interest rates and inflation rates, become central to strategic asset allocation decisions.

If the argument developed in this paper is correct, we should observe pension schemes with similar demographics, facing similar market prices, and operating within similar regulatory environments to display similar patterns of asset allocation – regardless of the system of corporate governance. Although beyond the scope of this article to offer a quantitative or in-depth qualitative test of whether this is the case, recent developments in Germany seem to offer preliminary support for the argument. A CME with diametrically different pension fund governance arrangements to the UK, and lacking an established and powerful pensions industry, Germany constitutes a tough test for the argument developed in this paper.

In the early 2000s, two new occupational pension vehicles – Pensionsfonds and Contractual Trust Arrangements (CTAs) – were introduced to the German pension system. These vehicles were subject to very few investment restrictions. They were to operate in a regulatory context similar to that of UK pension funds, and much more liberal than that of existing retirement savings vehicles (Ottawa 2008; Rössler 2000).

This investment freedom attracted financial professionals to a country where pensions consultants and asset managers had previously had little investment influence (Wagner 2006). The industry brought with it a 'more holistic asset-liability approach' to making strategic investment decisions than the asset-driven approach that dominated investment decision-making in existing vehicles (Cresswell 2017). The new pension funds adopted asset allocation practices similar to those of equivalent UK DB schemes (Interview 2), resulting, as Figure 3 shows,[3] in a higher aggregate equity exposure than

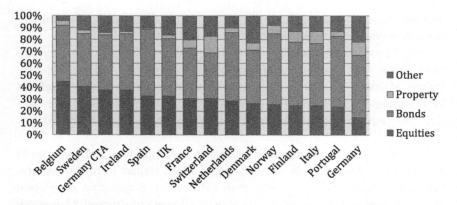

Figure 3. Broad strategic asset allocation by country. Source: (Mercer 2015).

(more mature) DB funds in the UK, and a much higher exposure than the regulated pension vehicles (Mercer 2011, 2012, 2013, 2014, 2015, 2016).

Particularly striking is that this equity-heavy asset allocation occurred in the context of CTA and Pensionsfonds governance arrangements that have tended to reflect existing patterns of German corporate governance in terms of employee representation (Rössler 2000). Indeed, unregulated vehicles have quickly become popular with unions, who expressed little concern about investment consequences of regulatory freedom, and have embraced the outsourcing of investment management to investment professionals (Ziegler 2008).

The arrival of these newcomers to the German pension landscape may also produce pressure for change in investment practices in Pensionskasse, Direktversicherungen, and Unterstützungskasse, the traditional, regulated German occupational pension vehicles. Restricted by quantitative limits on investment in each asset class (ABA 1999) and by BaFin's strict stress-test parameters (Franzen 2010; Ottawa 2014), these vehicles continue to have among the lowest equity exposures of all the European pension industries, investing only 13 per cent of their portfolios in equities on average between 2011 and 2016 (Mercer 2011, 2012, 2013, 2014, 2015, 2016).

Yet, industry commentators have noted a 'quiet revolution' among regulated vehicles in terms of an increased influence of consultants and fund managers (Ottawa 2013; Röhrbein 2012a, 2012b), and most regulated pension funds now express a desire for higher exposure to equity depending on individual fund demographics (Franzen 2010; Ottawa 2014).

A CME without a long-established pensions industry, Germany constitutes an unlikely case for this paper's argument. Yet even here, there are signs that asset allocation is being similarly shaped by the liability-driven investment norms of financial professionals, within the confines of a bipartite regulatory framework.

Notes

1. See Myners (2001: 128) for full list of insurers and their respective market shares.
2. The big three account for over 50% of the market, while the top six firms account for an estimated 70% of DB schemes (NAPF 2014).
3. The graph focuses on CTAs for reasons of data availability. These make up over 80% of the assets of unregulated vehicles (Franzen 2010; Schmid and Menne 2014).

Acknowledgements

This paper has benefited from the expertise of seven generous interviewees, three excellent reviewers, and each one of the STARS workshop participants. I am particularly grateful to Waltraud Schelkle, Anke Hassel, Tobias Wiß and Pieter Tuytens.

Disclosure statement

No potential conflict of interest was reported by the author.

References

ABA (1999) 'Germany: More than just a savings issue', *Investment and Pensions Europe*, October Magazine, available at https://http://www.ipe.com/germany-more-than-just-a-savings-issue/12582.fullarticle.
Ambachtsheer, K. P. (1987) 'Pension fund asset allocation: In defence of a 60/40 equity/debt asset mix', *CFA Institute Financial Analysts Journal* 43(5): 14–24.
Ambachtsheer, K.P. (2005) 'Why pension fund management needs a paradigm shift', in G. Clark and O.S. Mitchell (eds), *Reinventing the Retirement Paradigm*, Oxford: OUP, pp. 188–205.
Amir, E., Guan, Y. and Oswald, D. (2010) 'The effect of pension accounting on corporate pension asset allocation', *Review of Accounting Studies* 15(2): 345–66.
Antolin, P. and Stewart, F. (2009) 'Private pensions and policy responses to the financial and economic Crisis', *Financial Market Trends*, Paris: OECD, pp. 127–41.
Aon Hewitt. (2014) *The Evolution of Pension Scheme Investing: Looking Beyong DGFs to Fiduciary Management*, London: Hewitt Risk Management.
Ashcroft, J. (2009) 'Defined contribution arrangements in Anglo-Saxon countries', *OECD Working Papers on Insurance and Private Pensions*, Paris: OECD.
Bank for International Settlements (2007) 'Institutional investors, global savings and asset allocation', *CGFS Papers* (vol. 27).
Bank of England (2014) 'Procyclicality and structural trends in investment allocation by insurance companies and pension funds', *Discussion Paper by the Bank of England and the Procyclicality Working Group*, London: Bank of England.
Blair, C. (1995) 'Pension fund regulation', *Research Paper 95/10*, London: House of Commons Library.

Blake, D. (2001) 'UK pension fund management: how is asset allocation influenced by the valuation of liabilities?' *The Pension Institute Discussion Paper 0104*:1–4.

Blake, D. (2003) 'UK pension fund management after Myners: The hunt for correlation begins', *Journal of Asset Management* 4(1): 32–72.

Bridgen, P. and Meyer, T. (2009) 'The politics of occupational pension reform in Britain and the Netherlands: the power of market discipline in liberal and corporatist regimes', *West European Politics* 32(3): 586–610.

Chambers, A.J. et al. (2005) 'Liability driven benchmarks for UK defined benefit schemes', Paper presented at the The Institute of Actuaries Finance and Investment Board conference, London.

Clark, G. (2000) *Pension Fund Capitalism*, Oxford: OUP.

Clark, G. (2017) 'The financial legacy of pension fund capitalism', in R. Martin and J. Pollard (eds), *Handbook on the Geographies of Money and Finance*, Cheltenham: Edward Elgar, pp. 66–91.

Clark, G. and Unwin, R. (2017) 'The outsourced chief investment officer model of management and the principal-agent problem', *The Journal of Retirement* 4(3): 28–41.

CMA/IFF Research (2018) *The Market for Investment Consultancy Services and Fiduciary Management Services: Experiences and Views of Pension Scheme Trustees*, London: CMA.

Competition and Markets Authority (2018) *The Market for Investment Consultancy Services and Fiduciary Management Services: Experiences and Views of Pension Scheme Trustees*, London: IFF Research.

Cresswell, N. (2017) 'Asset allocation: investors embrace change', *IPE*, April Magazine, available at https://http://www.ipe.com/pensions/pensions-in/germany/asset-allocation-investors-embrace-change/10018260.article.

Dixon, A.D. (2008) 'The rise of pension fund capitalism in Europe: an unseen revolution?', *New Political Economy* 13(3): 249–70.

Dixon, A.D. and Monk, A.H.B. (2009) 'The power of finance: accounting harmonization's effect on pension provision', *Journal of Economic Geography* 9(1): 619–39.

Dixon, A.D. and Sorsa, V. (2009) 'Institutional change and the financialisation of pensions in Europe', *Competition and Change* 13(4): 347–67.

Ebbinghaus, B. (2011) *Varieties of Pension Governance: Pension Privatization in Europe*, Oxford: OUP.

Ebbinghaus, B. (2012) *Varieties of Pension Governance Under Pressure: Funded Pensions in Western Europe*, Munich: Dice.

Ebbinghaus, B. and Wiß, T. (2011) 'Taming pension fund capitalism in Europe: collective and state regulation in times of crisis', *Transfer: European Review of Labour and Research* 17(1): 15–28.

Franzen, D. (2010) 'Managing investment risk in defined benefit pension funds', *OECD Working Papers on Insurance and Private Pensions*, Paris: OECD.

Franzen, D. (2013) 'The impact of regulation on the asset investment of defined benefits pension funds', DPhil dissertation, Department of Economic Geography, University of Oxford.

Goyer, M. (2006) 'Varieties of institutional investors and national models of capitalism: the transformation of corporate governance in France and Germany', *Politics and Society* 34(3): 399–430.

Hall, P.A. and Sockice, D. (2001) 'An introduction to varieties of capitalism', in P.A. Hall and D. Soskice (eds), *Varieties of Capitalism: The Institutional Foundations of Comparative Advantage*, Oxford: Oxford University Press, pp. 1–68.

Harper, J.T. (2008) *Board of Trustee Composition and Investment Performance of US Public Pension Plans*, Toronto: Rotman International Centre for Pension Management.

HM Treasury and the Department for Work and Pensions (2001) *Myners Review of Institutional Investment in the UK: The Government's Response*, Westminster: HM Treasury.

Jackson, G. and Vitols, S. (2001) 'Between financial commitment, market liquidity, and corporate governance', in B. Ebbinghaus and P. Manow (eds), *Comparing Welfare Capitalism*, London: Routledge, pp. 171–89.

Jenkinson, T., Jones, H. and Martinez, J.V. (2016) 'Picking winners? Investment consultants' recommendations of fund managers', *The Journal of Finance* 71(5): 2333–70.

Koedijk, K. and Slager, A. (2010) *Investment Beliefs: A Positive Approach to Institutional Investing*, Basingstoke: Palgrave Macmillan.

Leibowitz, M. L. (1986) 'Total portfolio duration: A new perspective on asset allocation', *CFA Institute Financial Analysts Journal* 42(5): 18–29.

McCarthy, M., Sorsa, V. and van der Zwan, N. (2016) 'Investment preferences and patient capital: financing, governance, and regulation in pension fund capitalism', *Socio-Economic Review* 14(4): 751–69.

Mercer (2011) *European Asset Allocation Survey*, London: Mercer.
Mercer (2012) *European Asset Allocation Survey*, London: Mercer.
Mercer (2013) *European Asset Allocation Survey*, London: Mercer.
Mercer (2014) *European Asset Allocation Survey*, London: Mercer.
Mercer (2015) *European Asset Allocation Survey*, London: Mercer.
Mercer (2016) *European Asset Allocation Survey*, London: Mercer.

Mulvey, J. (1996) 'Generating scenarios for the towers perrin investment system', *IMFORMS Journal on Applied Analytics* 26(2): 1–122.

Munnell, A.H. (2006) 'Employer-sponsored plans: The shift from defined benefit to defined contribution', in G.L. Clark, A.H. Munnell and M.J. Orszag (eds), *The Oxford Handbook of Pensions and Retirement Income*, Oxford: OUP, pp. 359–381.

Myners (2001) *Myners Review of Institutional Investment: Final Report*, London: HM Treasury.

OECD (2013) *Annual Survey of Large Pension Funds and Pension Reserve Funds: Report on Pension Fund's Long Term Investments*, Paris: OECD.

OECD (2015) *Pension Markets in Focus*, Paris: OECD.

OECD (2016) *Pension Markets in Focus*, Paris: OECD.

OECD (2018). *Pension funds' assets (indicator)*, available at https://data.oecd.org/pension/pension-funds-assets.htm.

OMB Research (2016) *Trustee Landscape Qualitative Research: Further Investigations Into Board Dynamics and Trustee Training*, London: The Pensions Regulator.

Ottawa, B. (2008) 'Taking the CTA to the Mittelstand', *Investment and Pensions Europe*. May Magazine, available at https://http://www.ipe.com/taking-the-cta-to-the-mittelstand/27917.fullarticle.

Ottawa, B. (2013) 'German investors shift towards active management', *IPE*, 9 July, available at https://http://www.ipe.com/german-investors-shift-towards-active-management-survey/54167.article.

Ottawa, B. (2014) 'Stress tests thwarting German schemes' equity investments, experts warn', *Investment and Pensions Europe*. May Magazine, available at https://http://www.ipe.com/stress-tests-thwarting-german-schemes-equity-investments-experts-warn/10001375.fullarticle.

Payne, B. (2006) 'British DC plans use liability-driven investing', *Pensions & Investments*, 12 June, available at http://www.pionline.com/article/20060612/PRINT/606120735/british-dc-plans-use-liability-driven-investing.

Pension Protection Fund (2016) *The Purple Book*, London: PPF.

Röhrbein, N. (2012a) 'German asset management: a quiet revolution', *IPE*, October Magazine, available at https://http://www.ipe.com/german-asset-management-a-quiet-revolution/47671.fullarticle.

Röhrbein, N. (2012b) 'German asset management: in the market for advice', *IPE*, September Magazine, available at https://http://www.ipe.com/german-asset-management-in-the-market-for-advice/47668.article.

Rössler, N. (2000) 'Germany's CTA does pensions the UK way', *Investment and Pensions Europe*, December Magazine, available at https://http://www.ipe.com/germanys-cta-does-pensions-the-uk-way/13783.fullarticle.

NAPF (2014) Schemes' satisfaction with investment consultants remains steady, in-house expertise grows and consultants' tenure shortens, finds NAPF survey [Press release]. Retrieved from http://www.plsa.co.uk/PressCentre/Press_releases/0389-Schemes-satisfactionwith-investment-consultants-remains-steady.aspx.

Schmid, C. and Menne, V. (2014) 'Germany: long-term horizons and pensions', *Investment and Pensions Europe*, April Magazine,, available at https://http://www.ipe.com/pensions/pensions-in/germany-long-term-horizons-and-pensions/10001421.article.

Schroders (2016) *FTSE Default DC Schemes Report*, London: Schroders.

Shiller, R.J. (2000) *Irrational Exuberance*, Princeton, NJ: Princeton University Press.

Stewart, F. and Yermo, J. (2008) 'Pension fund governance: challenges and potential solutions', *OECD Working Papers on Insurance and Private Pensions*, Paris: OECD.

Sutcliffe, C. (2005) 'The cult of equity for pension funds: should it get the boot?', *Journal of Pension Economics and Finance* 4(1): 57–85.

Thurley, D. (2008) *Standard Note SN/BT/1215: Minimum Funding Requirement*, London: House of Commons Library.

Thurley, D. and McInnes, R. (2017) *Briefing Paper: Defined Benefit Pension Scheme Funding*, London: House of Commons Library.

Tonks, I. (2005) 'Pension fund management and investment performance', in G.L. Clark, A.H. Munnel and M.J. Orszag (eds), *The Oxford Handbook of Pensions and Retirement Income*, Oxford: OUP, pp. 456–80.

UK Parliament (2013) 'Improving governance and best practice in workplace pensions: scheme governance', available at http://www.publications.parliament.uk/pa/cm201213/cmselect/cmworpen/768/76805.htm on 08/01/17.

Useem, M. and Mitchell, O.S. (2000) 'Holders of the purse strings: governance and performance of public retirement systems', *Social Science Quarterly* 81(2): 489–506.

van der Zwan, N. (2014) 'Making sense of financialization', *Socio-Economic Review* 12(1): 99–129.

Verma, A. and Weststar, J. (2011) 'Token presence or substantive participation? A study of labor trustees on pension boards', *Journal of Labor Research* 32(1): 39–60.

Veron, N. (2007) *The Global Accounting Experiment*, Brussels: Bruegel.

Wagner, J. (2006) 'Rules trigger CTA boom', *IPE*, February Magazine, available at https://http://www.ipe.com/rules-trigger-cta-boom/18566.article.

Winklevoss, H. E. (1982) 'Plasm: Pension liability and asset simulation model', *CFA Institute Financial Analysts Journal* 38(2): 585–594.

Wiß, T. (2015) 'Pension fund vulnerability to the financial market crisis: the role of trade unions', *European Journal of Industrial Relations* 21(2): 131–47.

Yermo, J. and Pino, A. (2010) 'The impact of the 2007-2009 crisis on social security and private pension funds', *International Social Security Review* 63(2): 5–30.

Ziegler, J.N. (2008) 'At the nexus of social policy and capital markets: pension reform and enterprise governance in Germany', *IRLE Working Paper No. 174-08*.

Appendix: Interview List

I include evidence from seven semi-structured elite interviews conducted between May and July 2018:

Interview 1, Asset manager: Senior Retirement Strategist, Vanguard Asset Management Ltd.

Interview 2, Actuary: Head of Strategic Development at Pensions Insurance Corporation.

Interview 3, Consultant: Head of UK DC Solutions, Aon.

Interview 4, PLSA Policy Lead: Defined Benefit and Investment Policy Lead, Pensions and Lifetime Saving Association (PLSA).

Interview 5, In-house asset manager: Head of Strategy Coordination, Universities Superannuation Scheme (USS).

Interview 6, Union-appointed trustee: UCU-appointed Director of the USS Board of Trustees.

Interview 7, Employer-appointed trustee: UUK-appointed Director of the USS Board of Trustees.

Countering financial interests for social purposes: what drives state intervention in pension markets in the context of financialisation?

Pieter Tuytens

ABSTRACT
Welfare financialisation creates conflicts between the social objectives of households and the commercial interests of financial welfare providers. This paper investigates under what conditions regulations' that counter financial interests are more or less likely. It argues that our analytical focus should shift away from gauging the relative strength of organised interests or voter mobilisation, towards a better understanding of how policymakers play an independent role in shaping regulatory decisions in line with their own long-term objective: promoting private pension provision as an alternative to more extensive public provision. To support this argument, this paper examines a least-likely case study – namely the puzzling shift in the UK over the past two decades towards stricter regulation of the pension industry. Overall, the paper suggests that variation in regulatory decisions reflects the efforts by policymakers to balance the commercial viability and social-political stability of private pension provision.

Introduction

Welfare privatisation generally increases the dependence of households on investment in financial welfare products to protect themselves against the uncertainties of life (Martin 2002; van der Zwan 2014). Private providers of these products have played an important role in promoting financialisation of welfare provision, with pension policy as a prominent example (Hacker 2002; Naczyk 2013). However, welfare financialisation creates new conflicts between the social objectives of households and the commercial interests of the financial sector. Returns on financial investments need to be shared between households and commercial providers: higher profit margins for the latter mean fewer resources dedicated to social objectives such as old age income security. While some scholars are optimistic about the ability of financialisation to 'emancipate' individuals that were previously excluded from participating in financial markets (see discussion in Erturk et al. 2007), others anticipate a less benign outcome where private providers manage to reap much of the return on investment at the expense of beneficiaries (e.g., Blake et al. 2014).

Shaping and correcting financial welfare markets can play an important role in tipping these distributional struggles in favour of households (Schelkle 2012). Especially in the past few years, there has been a tendency towards stricter regulatory interventions in private pension markets (Sier 2016). Yet governments do not seem to come down clearly on either side of the fence: while policymakers do not give free reign to financial actors, efforts to constrain financial firms in order to promote social objectives are often hesitant and limited in scope. Such interventions to improve social outcomes in the private welfare sphere are indeed not self-evident when they are resisted by well-organised private pension providers, often without clear electoral reward due to the complexity of these measures (Hacker 2002). Hence in order to develop a better understanding of the dynamics that shape the outcome of welfare financialisation, we need to ask what drives these regulatory interventions that go against the interests of the financial sector.

This paper argues that we have to pay more attention to the state as an autonomous actor, playing an independent role in shaping financialisation on basis of its own interests. In doing so, it proposes to shift our analytical attention away from more traditional approaches that understand policy interventions as a response to electoral pressure or the waning influence of financial actors. Rather than analysing states as 'transmission belts' that translate pressure into decision, this paper argues that fiscally constrained governments have their own stake in the outcome of welfare financialisation: namely the long-term viability of private pension provision as an alternative to more expansive public provision. This means that decisions to intervene in pension markets are not so much steered by demands of voters or organised interests, but rather by policymakers' assessment of whether intervention promotes their own objective or not. More specifically, this paper argues that interventions actively aim at balancing both the social and commercial viability of private pension provision. Existing efforts to explore the welfare-finance nexus tend to focus predominantly on the financial consequences of social policies (Ebbinghaus and Manow 2001; Estévez-Abe 2001; more recently revived by Naczyk 2013); whereas this paper explores more explicitly the interaction between social and financial considerations. By providing a more nuanced understanding of how governments shape financialisation, this paper addresses the broader concern that 'the role of the state remains underdeveloped in this body of scholarly work' (van der Zwan 2014: 113).

In order to support the argument that interventions that counter interests of financial welfare providers are driven by the independent objectives of policymakers, rather than pressure from voters or organised interests, this paper investigates a least-likely case of such interventions: namely the puzzling shift in the UK over the past two decades towards stricter regulation of private pension providers. The Pensions Act 2014 introduced a far-reaching legislative framework that imposes new constraints on pension providers, including stricter reporting requirements and an unprecedented charge cap limiting the annual management charges on a large number of private schemes. This is a significant achievement given the well-organised financial sector in the UK; certainly when compared to the failure of similar efforts to bring down charges only one decade earlier. The introduction of a charge cap on regulated products in the early 2000s was eventually watered down following intense industry lobbying. Even more remarkable is the fact that it was a Labour-led government that backed down to industry pressure in 2004, whereas the recent regulatory push is preceded by a coalition of Conservatives and Liberal Democrats. This paper argues that this regulatory shift cannot be accounted for by an increase in political salience or reduced influence of the financial sector in the wake of the financial crisis. Instead it shows how the shift reflects a different assessment by policymakers in both governments as to whether stricter intervention promotes their shared objective of expanding private pension savings. The analysis is based on qualitative text analysis of the relevant parliamentary debates (identified using Hansard[1]), as well as secondary sources such as press articles (identified using Nexus[2]), surveys and other publically available sources. Additional interviews have been conducted with stakeholders who were directly involved in the negotiation process and representative of both the pensions industry and transparency advocates (see overview[3]).

This state-centric approach to studying intervention in private pension markets has several implications for how we understand the dynamics of shaping welfare financialisation. First, this approach suggests that we should pay more attention to how policymakers try to steer the actions of private actors in order to promote their own objectives. Secondly, it shows that the financial crisis did not create problems but merely intensified existing challenges. Finally, it suggests that the politics of regulating private welfare provision are characterised by a continuous negotiation between legislators and industry. Overall, this paper expects that all regulatory outcomes will eventually reflect a negotiated balance between commercial viability on the one hand, and social-political viability on the other.

The rest of this paper is structured as follows. The first two sections focus on reviewing the relevant literature and presenting the proposed argument to explain state interventions in the context of welfare financialisation. The subsequent section explains the puzzling shift in the UK towards stricter regulation on basis of the proposed state-centric argument. The fourth section evaluates alternative explanations based on shifts in political salience and organised interest mobilisation, showing that these alternatives do not withstand closer scrutiny. In the conclusions, I discuss how this state-centric approach to studying intervention in private pension markets applies to countries other than the UK, as well as the wider implications for how we understand the dynamics of shaping welfare financialisation.

Established explanations for state intervention in financial welfare markets

Market failures feature prominently in explanations for state intervention in financial markets (for an overview see Moloney 2010). Markets for financial welfare services are indeed characterised by several important market-failures, in particular information asymmetries (Barr 2012: 209). Most people don't understand the basic financial concepts that are required to make good decisions (Mitchell and Lusardi 2011). Complexity in financial products means that 'some people end up with high-cost options because they lack the necessary information or capacity to make good choices.' (Barr 2012: 210). Furthermore, most people don't shop around to find the best deal, which hinders competition on which markets depend to drive prices down (Pitt-Watson and Mann 2012). Nonetheless, keeping in mind that the main problems of private pension costs were well understood since the 1990s (see for example Orszag and Stiglitz 2001; Whitehouse 2001), market failure as such cannot account for variation in the timing and scope of interventions.

A widespread political-economy explanation for variation in state intervention refers to the ability of industry to shape regulations to serve its special interests. The theoretical argument that policymakers will prioritise narrow, specific interests over those of the public at large has been made under several monikers, including the 'logic of collective action' (Olson 1965), the 'privileged position of business' (Lindblom 1977), and 'regulatory capture' (Peltzman 1976; Stigler 1971). The basic argument is that it is easier and less costly for a smaller group with high stakes in the outcome to mobilise and influence regulatory decisions, than it is for larger groups with smaller stakes. Business groups in particular are well-positioned to ensure that their preferences are reflected in regulatory decisions. Not only does business possess structural and instrumental power over elected politicians (Culpepper 2015; Hacker and Pierson 2002; Lindblom 1977); special interests can also 'capture' regulators and administrators on basis of their industrial expertise or by offering the prospect of attractive career opportunities (for recent reviews, see Bó 2006; Etzioni 2009).

Nevertheless, the ability of welfare providers to influence policy-decisions is restricted by the responsiveness of policymakers to electoral pressure (Gingrich 2011; Gingrich and Häusermann 2015). Culpepper has argued that capture by special interest groups is more likely when the 'political salience' of the issue at stake is lower – meaning that decisions are not likely to affect voters' behaviour (Culpepper 2010). When voters do care about decisions, decision-makers also take public opinion into account; reducing the scope for business to exert their influence on basis of their expertise or strategic communication of structural importance.

In conclusion, to explain state interventions in financial welfare markets, past scholarship suggests that we have to look at the relative strength of organised interest groups, as well as the level of political salience. Accordingly, the puzzling shift in the UK should be explained by higher willingness of voters to punish and reward the government on basis of introducing stricter intervention; or by changes in the relative influence of organised interests (such as declining influence of the financial sector). However, as I will show in the empirical section, these hypotheses do not seem to be supported by observation.

Towards a better explanation: bringing the state back in

This paper argues that established frameworks have important limitations when trying to account for what drives governments to intervene in financial welfare markets. As discussed, most prevalent accounts share a focus on how policymakers respond to 'external pressure' – be it electoral pressure or that of organised interest groups. By reducing the role of policy-makers to that of a transmission belt – translating pressure into decisions – prevailing approaches fail to detect the importance of the state as an independent actor. In contrast, this paper claims that governments play a key role in shaping the distributional conflict between households and financial providers. This goes back to the broader research agenda aimed at 'bringing the state back in' (Evans et al. 1985; Skocpol 2008); namely by recognising that states are 'autonomous actors' who 'formulate and pursue goals that are not simply reflexive of the demands or interests of social groups, classes, or society' (Skocpol 1985: 9).

Accordingly, this paper argues that governments play an autonomous role in shaping welfare financialisation in order to promote their independent interests. Rather than making far-reaching ex ante assumptions as to what drives policymakers, I argue that specifying those interests is ultimately an empirical matter. In the context of welfare financialisation, this paper suggests that governments are interested in promoting the success of private welfare provision as a viable alternative to public provision (see also Ebbinghaus and Whiteside 2012; Leisering 2011; Mabbett 2012; Trampusch 2018). Failure to deliver a politically stable distribution of pension benefits creates the threat that public provision will have to step back in at some point. This concern is clearly formulated by Adair Turner:

The increasing inequality of pension provision will create major social stress; and those who lose out are likely to lobby and vote for *ad hoc* rather than intelligently planned changes to the state system, and will be a powerful political force given the increasing proportion of elderly people in the population. (Pensions Commission 2004: 170)

Hence governments have a clear stake in the long-term success and stability of private welfare provision.

Arguing that policymakers' decisions are guided by their own objective to promote the long-term viability of private welfare provision does not mean that policymakers act in isolation from electoral feedback or industry pressure. While policymakers take re-election prospects and cooperation by financial actors into account, this still leaves them with considerable discretion in terms of whether and how to intervene. Interventions in financial welfare markets depends on the *assessment* of policymakers as to whether such intervention promotes or hinders the achievement of long-term stability of private provision; rather than on their responsiveness to electoral feedback or pressure by mobilised interest groups. In the UK case, both governments shared the same objective to expand private savings, yet the policy strategy to achieve this had changed. It was this different policy approach that prompted a different assessment as to whether stricter intervention is necessary; not an increase in willingness to go against industry interests or to promote private savings. In conclusion, this paper argues that governments play a key role in shaping welfare financialisation and accompanying distributional struggles.

A state-centric approach to explaining the puzzling shift towards stricter regulations of pension costs in the uK

While the provision of financial vehicles and related services is never without costs, it is crucial for beneficiaries to keep those costs as low as necessary (Blake et al. 2014: 48). Regulatory intervention could significantly reduce the cost of private welfare provision, yet tend to be strongly resisted by financial actors. At the same time, such interventions do not necessarily translate into clear electoral rewards because proposals are technical, boring and difficult to explain. Earlier efforts by Labour to bring down charges for asset management – for example by introducing a 1% charge cap for Stakeholder Pensions in the early 2000s – were eventually watered down following intense industry lobbying; resulting in a much more generous cap of 1.5%. Yet one decade later, the Conservative-led coalition government managed to introduce a new legislative framework that includes, among other measures, a charge cap of 0.75% for the new regulated schemes – limiting fees even more than the cap that was initially defeated by the industry. How can we explain the puzzling shift in the UK towards stricter regulatory intervention that actively goes against industry interests in order to improve social outcomes, given the unsuccessful attempts less than a decade earlier?

Why did Labour relaxed regulations in 2004?

Labour introduced an earnings-related public pension scheme in the 1970s (the 'State Earnings-Related Pensions Scheme' or SERPS), which would have resulted in more generous, encompassing public pension provision. Yet this outcome was never achieved as the subsequent Conservative government curbed the expansion of SERPS, for example by re-indexing benefits to prices and promoting contracting-out to private schemes (Bridgen and Meyer 2011: 272–73). Since the early 1980s, subsequent governments in the UK did much effort to keep public pension provision at a minimum; leaving the task to achieve adequate pensions to voluntary initiative within markets (Esping-Andersen 1990; Moran and Schulze 2007). However, persistently low levels of private savings were increasingly perceived to be problematic. After returning to power in 1997, Labour assessed that low and even middle-income earners who don't have access to occupational pensions will not have pension benefits above the minimum income level, leaving up to a third of future pensioners facing poverty (Secretary of State for Social Security 1998: 1). At the same time, Labour refused to increase public provision as doing so was considered to be unaffordable (Secretary of State for Social Security 1998: 30). This established the background for new reform initiatives aimed at promoting private pension savings. The solution was to introduce a regulated low-cost product that is sufficiently appealing to buy on voluntary basis: the Stakeholder Pension. A key characteristic of this product was the 1% charge cap to keep costs low. However, this initiative failed to achieve its objective to expand coverage of lower income households (Pensions Commission 2005: 48). The government decided to revise the product, which opened up a window of opportunity for the pension industry to get rid of the charge cap on regulated products. The industry had been strongly critical of these constraints, judging them too stringent to make selling the product worthwhile (ABI 2002; House of Commons 2001: 15). At that point, the industry was not in a comfortable position to convince the government. Both the expert review that informed the revision (HM Treasury 2002: 23) and the Treasury itself strongly insisted on maintaining the price cap, the latter stating that 'the Government has a high threshold for persuasion for moving from a flat 1% charge' (HM Treasury and DWP 2003: 19). Nevertheless, following two years of intense lobbying, the Treasury dropped its insistence on the charge cap and decided to relax the cap to 1.5% (Financial Times 2004).

Why did the Treasury eventually give in to pressure from the life insurance industry? All evidence strongly indicates that the government caved in because it feared that sticking to the cap would result in certain failure of its strategy to expand private savings; this for the simple reason that the pension industry would not sell the regulated products. The Association of British Insurers made clear that doing so would be 'unprofitable' (Work and Pensions Committee 2003: 57), while big insurers were already reported to have gone on a 'seller's strike' (The Guardian 2002). Confronted with this threat to boycott the new product, the Treasury financial secretary admitted that 'the government had to strike a balance between the interests of consumers and the economics of the market.' (statement by Ruth Kelly in The Guardian 2004). When pressed about this in the Commons, she explained why the government conceded to the financial sector:

> What we want them to do is open their doors to low to moderate income consumers—that is the ultimate goal of this—and to encourage people to save who have previously not saved. If that is the ultimate result, then I think this policy will have been successful. (Select Committee on Treasury 2004, Q2134)

In conclusion, the government relaxed the price cap in 2004 because it was convinced that doing so was necessary to achieve its core objective – namely expanding private saving levels. The government was inclined to stick to a strict price cap; but assessed that doing so was likely to result in failure of the stakeholder strategy. On the other hand, abandoning such strict regulations would give the stakeholder regime at least a shot at success.

Why did the coalition government introduce stricter regulations in 2014?

Disappointed with the earlier efforts to promote private savings on a purely voluntary basis, both Labour and the Conservatives became convinced that some level of compulsion was necessary (Bridgen and Meyer 2011; House of Commons 2008). This resulted in a cross-party agreement in 2008 to introduce a new strategy to expand private savings that was based on the idea of 'auto-enrolment'. This requires employers to subscribe their workers to a private scheme and to contribute to it, unless the employee decides to opt out. For those employers who do not actively select a scheme for their workers, the government designed NEST (the National Employment Savings Trust); a semi-private default scheme, executed by private associations but heavily regulated by the state to control investment risks and achieve low costs. However, the existing commercial pension schemes that operate alongside NEST remained largely unregulated and shielded from competition by NEST (by capping the contributions to NEST).

From early onwards these unregulated private schemes have been accused of sustaining high and hidden charges. Both experts and media tried to raise public awareness of this problem (see for example the reports by the RSA 2009, 2010; as well as a series of articles – published by the Daily Mail between 2009 and 2010 – declaring a 'war on hidden charges'). To deal with such criticism and to encourage savings, pension industry associations took several initiatives aimed at 'dispelling fears of hidden costs' (quote by Saunders, chief executive of the Investment Management Association; Financial Times 2012). By taking the lead in 'clearing out its own house' through self-regulation, the pension industry explicitly aimed at pre-empting concrete regulatory interventions (Work and Pensions Committee 2012, ev34). The pre-emptive strategy of the industry seemed to work very well. The government explicitly welcomed industry efforts to 'sort its own house out' as being far better 'than the Government trying to be over-prescriptive' (Steve Webb, then Pensions Minister; House of Commons 2011, Column 126WH). By the end of 2011, both government and industry seemed to settle on self-regulation as the preferred approach to deal with the issue of high charges. Steve Webb declined requests for intervention as late as early 2013 (Work and Pensions Committee 2013: 91). So why did the coalition government eventually decide to employ 'hard regulations' to intervene in the pensions sector? This is not self-evident, given its reluctance and keeping in mind that, only a few years earlier, even a left-of-centre government that was predisposed to stick to its regulatory guns eventually backed down to industry demands.

To explain this regulatory shift, I argue that government officials were driven by the concern that taking no action against high charges would undermine its renewed strategy to promote private savings. The lack of public trust in private pensions has long been considered a key element of the problem of low savings as it is 'holding back a wider retirement savings culture' (Brandon Lewis (Conservatives); House of Commons 2011, Column 108WH). While auto-enrolment is designed as a way around this problem, legislators from all sides of the political spectrum feared that the possibility of people being steered into bad schemes would further deteriorate trust in private pensions and result in wide-scale opt-outs. Gregg McClymont (Labour) argued that: 'If we permit confidence to be damaged, because auto-enrolment does not succeed, many people could opt out, which would jeopardise auto-enrolment.' (House of Commons 2011: Column 122WH). Or in the words of Lord Freud (Conservatives): 'we must restore public faith in the concept of pension saving and, behind this, pension charges are key' (House of Lords 2012: Column 1641). Even if people remain in bad-value schemes, both Labour and Conservative legislators feared this could lay the basis for a future mis-selling scandal: 'No members of the Committee, and especially the Minister, would want a situation in which pensions are mis-sold. Often, however, mis-selling takes many years to come to light. Bearing in mind the resistance that business has to further regulation, will the Minister assure the Committee that there will be sufficient regulation to ensure that inappropriate pensions are not sold in the first place, rather than regulations being introduced after the event?' (Teresa Pearce (Labour); House of Lords 2011, Column 254) or David Mowat (Conservatives): 'I fear that unless those measures are adopted, auto-enrolment will compound a failure that could easily become our next mis-selling scandal.' (House of Commons 2012: Column 847). In conclusion, legislators from both sides of the aisle were concerned about the prospect of auto-enrolment being derailed by the possibility that people are pushed in bad-value schemes.

Despite initial reluctance, the Department for Work and Pensions (DWP) came to acknowledge over the course of 2013 that these are not abstract concerns. In the spring of 2013, the DWP was finalising its proposals on how to deal with the surge of 'small pension pots'. Every time workers move between jobs, they leave behind a relatively small amount of savings with their old employer – an unintended but very expensive consequence of auto-enrolment. The government sought to solve this problem by automatically transferring peoples' older funds into their most recent scheme (unless the worker decides differently). Yet the widespread occurrence of bad-value schemes meant that in many occasions the government would be actively moving peoples' lifetime savings from a good scheme into a bad value scheme. So when the Office for Fair Trading published a damning report in the summer of 2013, arguing that 'competition alone cannot be relied upon to drive value for money for all savers in the DC workplace pension market' (OFT 2013: 14), Steve Webb eventually conceded and proposed a series of strict regulations aimed at preventing the worst outcomes for savers – including the charge cap on default schemes (i.e., higher charges are allowed as long as the saver makes an active decision to join a more expensive scheme). This rationale can be illustrated by this extended quote by Steve Webb while defending his policy decision in the House of Commons:

> There is an issue of what happens if money is automatically transferred from a "good" scheme to a "bad" scheme, and I accept that point. That is why we are regulating for scheme quality. It should not just be a worry that someone's small pension pot gets auto-transferred to a bad scheme; it should be a worry that an entire work force have been auto-enrolled into a bad scheme. We should not have bad schemes and must deal with that. That is why we are tackling pension scheme quality, which includes a range of issues such as governance, investment, costs and charges. (Steve Webb (Liberal-Democrats); House of Commons 2013: Column 772)

In other words, the main driver behind regulatory intervention was the concern that bad-value schemes would be detrimental for establishing trust in auto-enrolment and thereby undermine the long-term success of their strategy to expand private savings.

Alternative explanations and why they don't hold up

In the previous section I argued that the regulatory shift in the UK resulted from a different assessment by policymakers on how to best promote their own interests. But why accept this argument, rather than more readily available explanations? The most obvious alternative is that the financial crisis triggered public outcry and electoral pressure on politicians to act more forcefully against the financial sector. This pressure on legislators eventually convinced the DWP to intervene, with the pension industry in a weakened position to object to these new rules. This section investigates whether the regulatory shift can be explained respectively by shifts in political salience, or by shifts in organised interest mobilisation. I conclude that none of these shifts was sufficiently significant to explain the difference in regulatory outcome.

The role of electoral considerations

The first alternative explanation for the shift in regulatory decisions is an increase in political salience. Voters who did not care about hidden and excessive pension charges in the past might care nowadays, this in response to the financial crisis or given the higher prominence of private pensions following auto-enrolment. This implies at the very least that voters are aware of the issue of high pension cost (let alone that they are mobilised). However, all evidence strongly suggests that political salience was low and remains so today. Several surveys show that most people are simply not aware of pension costs or their size; this applies to individual scheme members (OFT 2013; YouGov and B&CE 2015) as well as the employers who have to select schemes for their workers (DWP 2014; Wood et al. 2012). In fact, a widely shared analysis of the problem is precisely that high charges persist because there is a serious lack of public awareness of these charges (FSCP 2014; Harrison, Blake and Dowd 2012; OFT 2013; Pitt-Watson and Mann 2012).

One could object that even if people are not aware of this specific issue, there certainly is a less articulated anger against the financial sector. Regulatory interventions in this area could be a political initiative to show voters that the government is taking tough action against the financial sector, this with the intention to reap electoral benefits. If that is the case, we should at the very least find indications that parties showcase their efforts during the subsequent general election. Nonetheless, this expectation is not supported by empirical analysis of party manifestos and press coverage in the run-up to the general election in May 2015 (see endnotes for methodological notes).[4] The issue of regulating private pensions was barely mentioned in written press during the six months preceding the election. During the main televised debates, nobody came close to claiming credit for standing up against the pension industry (or even to touching on this topic). Conservatives did not even bother to mention it in their party manifesto (while the other parties only included a vague reference to the importance of good value pensions). So in conclusion, there is no evidence that either Labour or the governing parties sought to politicise this issue for reasons of electoral gain.

The role of organised interest groups

Another possible reason why regulatory intervention succeeded in 2014, is that the pension industry was no longer able to resist mounting pressure by those advocating for more transparency. We could indeed expect that the financial crisis has harmed the legitimacy of the financial service sector, reducing its ability to block regulations. However, this explanation cannot account for the timing of the reform shift towards 'hard' regulatory intervention. If the financial crisis deteriorated the legitimacy of the financial sector, this reduced influence must have been apparent well before 2013. Yet as indicated in the previous section, the regulatory preferences of the DWP and the pensions industry were well-aligned until early 2013. Until that point, the government made clear that it fully supports the softer approach based on 'self-regulation' that was actively promoted by the industry (see for example the joint effort by the Investment Management Association, the Association of British Insurers, the Society of Pension Consultants and the National Association of Pension Funds that resulted in a 'Joint Industry Code of Conduct'; NAPF 2012). Daniel Godfrey – who was leading the Investment Management Association (IMA) at that point – confirmed that the approach by the government at that time was well-aligned with the IMA strategy (Interview with Daniel Godfrey). At the same time, transparency advocates recall that their demands were more or less ignored for several years (Interviews with Andy Agathangelou and David Pitt-Watson). Given that there are no indications for a sudden demise in the organisational strength of the pension industry in the first half of 2013, we need to look beyond industry influence to account for the regulatory shift.

Increasing pressure by pro-regulation groups could be a better explanation for the shift towards 'hard' regulations in 2013. However, if it is correct that state interventions were designed as a concession to mounting pressure by pro-transparency interest groups, then we should expect that the content of reforms reflects the content of their demands. The problem for this hypothesis is that this expectation does not apply to the central and most contentious part of the reform package, namely the price cap. Given that the price cap is the element that was most forcefully opposed, it is the intervention where we would *least* expect the government to introduce it without strong external pressure. Yet in that period there was no consensus regarding the appropriateness of the price cap among experts and consumer associations, let alone a concerted push to force the government to adopt this measure against strong resistance by the pensions industry. For example, only one of the consumer advocates invited to the Work and Pensions Committee evidence session in January 2013 univocally defended the introduction of the charge cap; all others were reluctant to recommend this measure to the Committee members (personal communication with Dominic Lindley; confirmed in official minutes – see Work and Pensions Committee 2013: 64). Also the influential report by the Office for Fair Trading did not recommend the introduction of a price cap (OFT 2013). Much of their reluctance can be explained by the worry that the imposition of a cap could encourage some providers to raise their charges towards that figure, resulting in higher charges overall. In order to understand why the DWP still introduced the price cap, despite the lack of strong pressure, it is worth including a longer quote by Daniel Godfrey, who headed the Investment Management Association at that time. He recalls a personal meeting with Steve Webb, justifying his decision:

> [Steve Webb] said: 'I understand in a theoretical world, that obviously that [i.e., the industry-led governance code] would be preferable. But I'm responsible for 40.000 schemes and no matter how good your governance code is, that doesn't give me comfort that all 40.000 schemes will become well-governed. And so the easiest way I can make sure that they at least don't do too much harm is to bring in the charge cap.' So I think that was the reason; the killer argument for the government, was I suppose the difficulty of policing the governance which in theory would have been a better solution. (Interview with Daniel Godfrey).

The key point here is that the reform package was not simply a concession to external pressure. Organised interest groups certainly facilitated reforms by providing evidence regarding the prominence and impact of bad value schemes. Yet the timing and content of reform proposals strongly suggest that such influence got traction because it aligned with the governments' broader concerns regarding the viability of auto-enrolment.

Conclusions

This paper focused on conflicts between the commercial interests of private pension providers and the social interests of households who increasingly depend on such financial products for old age income security. How can we explain the prevalence of regulatory interventions that go against concentrated, financial interests in order to promote broader, social objectives? Whereas traditional accounts explain such interventions as a response to electoral pressure or mobilisation by organised interest groups, this paper argues that governments play an autonomous role in shaping private pension markets. Policymakers have their own stake in promoting the long-term viability of private welfare; hence reducing pressure on public provision. So in order to explain variation in state intervention in financial welfare markets, we have to focus more on policymakers and how they assess such interventions in the light of their own objectives. Studying the recent shift towards stricter regulations in the UK as a least-likely case of regulatory interventions that go against financial interests to promote social objectives provided empirical support to this argument.

While the shift towards stricter regulation in the UK was selected as a hard case, it reflects a much wider trend of government initiatives aimed at reducing the cost of private pension provision (for an overview, see Sier 2016). In line with the expectation of this paper, this broader shift does not seem to be driven by angry voters, but by the growing concern that private pensions will end up in trouble in the longer run if unadjusted. Interestingly, this also applies to countries where social partners and non-profit pension funds dominate private pension provision. The Netherlands provides a telling example. Responding to pressure by the Dutch financial markets regulator (Autoriteit Financiële Markten), legislators threatened social partners in 2011 with legal intervention if their collective pension funds failed to take action to reduce costs and improve transparency regarding their members (AFM 2011; De Telegraaf 2010; Het Financieele Dagblad 2011). Despite initial resistance, funds managed to reduce costs significantly through restructuring and renegotiating contracts with commercial providers (AFM 2015; Sier 2016).

The proposed state-centric approach has at least three wider implications for analysing the dynamics of government intervention in financial welfare markets. First of all, it suggests that policymakers currently fear dispirited voters more than angry voters. While angry voters care about improving private pensions, most households who do not trust financial welfare simply do not participate in private schemes. Non-participation in private pensions when public provision is curtailed creates a huge problem for policymakers; failure to prevent sharp drops in living standards is most likely to result in uncontrolled demands on the public system in the long run (Pensions Commission 2004: 170). To avoid ever greater compulsion (which carries its own political risk, Mabbett 2012), policymakers have to build up public trust in the value of private pensions (Taylor-Gooby 2005; Vickerstaff et al. 2012). Secondly, the argument requires us to think more nuanced about the role of the crisis in explaining the recent surge in state intervention in private pension markets. Rather than triggering a public outcry that elicits response from policymakers, the financial crisis and subsequent low-interest environment push policymakers into action because lower returns intensifies the already existing challenge to make private pensions viable. Finally, the proposed analytical approach suggests that more attention should go to the on-going negotiations between legislators and the pension industry. While there is the need to improve the social viability of private welfare provision, this certainly does not mean that legislators will consistently go against industry interests. Because governments rely on the cooperation of financial welfare providers, there are clear limits to its ability to enforce regulations on these firms. Private providers, on the other hand, also tend to depend on the state for their commercial success; mainly because they generally benefit handsomely from state measures aimed at encouraging participation in private schemes (e.g., fiscal incentives). Therefore this paper expects that all regulatory outcomes will eventually reflect a negotiated balance between commercial viability on the one hand, and social-political viability on the other.

Notes

1. Hansard search query: 'pension' AND 'charges'; complemented with targeted reading of the relevant Special Reports by the Treasury Committee as well as the Work and Pensions Committee (analysed all results since 2010; targeted analysis for earlier years).
2. Nexus search query: 'pensions' AND 'charges' – In headline & lead paragraphs – UK National Newspapers (analysed all results since 1999).
3. Selection of relevant stakeholders is based on the names that featured most prominently in parliamentary debates and oral evidence sessions by the Work and Pensions Committee:

    - *Representing transparency-advocates*: Andy Agathangelou (Director Transparency Task Force; 15-08-2018); David Pitt-Watson (Tomorrow's Investor project leader; 21-08-2018); Christopher Sier (Financial Services Consumer Panel; 24-08-2018); Dominic Lindley (Which?; email correspondence).
    - *Representing pensions industry associations*: Daniel Godfrey (Investment Management Association; 30-08-2018).
    - *Exploratory interviews*: Chris Curry (Direction Pensions Policy Institute; 23-03-2017); Gregg McClymont MP (Shadow Pensions Minister; 04-07-2017).

4. The review of written press coverage is based on the 1910 results rendered by NEXIS search within UK publications (query: Private AND Pensions AND Charges; period between 1 Nov 2014 and 7 May 2015). The review of televised debates is based on transcripts of the British Party Leaders' Election Debate (ITV, 2 April 2015), the Opposition Parties Election Debate (BBC1, 16 April 2015) and press reporting of debates.

Acknowledgements

This paper has benefited tremendously from the insightful comments by Karen Andersen, Nick Barr, Margarita Gelepithis, Bob Hancké, Anke Hassel, Deborah Mabbett, Marek Naczyk, Waltraud Schelkle, Tobias Wiß, Noel Whiteside and the three anonymous reviewers.

Disclosure statement

No potential conflict of interest was reported by the author.

References

ABI (2002) *Stakeholder Pensions – Closing the Savings Gap*, London: Association of British Insurers.
AFM (2011) *Kosten Pensioenfondsen Verdienen Meer Aandacht*, Amsterdam: Autoriteit Financiële Markten.
AFM (2015) *Vermogensbeheer- En Transactiekosten Pensioenfondsen in Beeld*, Amsterdam: Autoriteit Financiële Markten.
Barr, N. (2012) *The Economics of the Welfare State*, Oxford: Oxford University Press.
Blake, D., Harrison D. and Dowd K. (2014) *Value for Money - Assessing Value for Money in Defined Contribution Default Funds*, London: The Pensions Institute.
Bó, E. (2006). 'Regulatory capture: A review' *Oxford Review of Economic Policy* 22(2): 203–25.
Bridgen, P. and Meyer, T. (2011) 'Britain: Exhausted Voluntarism', in B. Ebbinghaus (ed.), *The Varieties of Pension Governance*, Oxford: Oxford University Press, pp. 255–91.
Culpepper, P. (2010) *Quiet Politics and Business Power*, Cambridge: Cambridge University Press.
Culpepper, P. (2015) 'Structural power and political science in the post-crisis era', *Business & Politics* 17(3): 391–409.
De Telegraaf (2010) 'AFM: Pensioenfonds Moet Opener Worden over Kosten; Hoogervorst Wil Financiële Bijsluiter', *De Telegraaf*, 27 November.
DWP (2014) *Landscape and Charges Survey 2013: Charges and Quality in Defined Contribution Pension Schemes*, London: Department for Work and Pensions.
Ebbinghaus, B. and Manow, P. (2001) *Comparing Welfare Capitalism : Social Policy and Political Economy in Europe, Japan and the USA*, London/New York: Routledge.
Ebbinghaus, B. and Whiteside, N. (2012) 'Shifting responsibilities in Western European pension systems: what future for social models?', *Global Social Policy* 12(3): 266–82.
Erturk, I., Froud, J., Johal, S., Leaver, A. and Williams, K. (2007) 'The Democratization of finance? Promises, outcomes and conditions', *Review of International Political Economy* 14(4): 553–75.
Esping-Andersen, G. (1990) *The Three Worlds of Welfare Capitalism*, Cambridge: Polity.
Estévez-Abe, M. (2001) 'The forgotten link: The financial regulation of Japanese pension funds in comparative perspective', in B. Ebbinghaus and P. Manow (eds.), *Comparing Welfare Capitalism : Social Policy and Political Economy in Europe, Japan and the USA*, London/New York: Routledge, pp. 190–214.
Etzioni, A. (2009) 'The capture theory of regulations—revisited', *Society* 46(4): 319–23.
Evans, P., Rueschemeyer, D. and Skocpol, T. (1985) *Bringing the State Back In*, Cambridge: Cambridge University Press.
Financial Times (2004) 'Treasury rethinks cap on savings fees', *Financial Times*, 18 June.
Financial Times (2012) 'We need to dispel fears of "hidden costs"', *Financial Times*, 6 May.
FSCP (2014) *Investment Costs - More Than Meets the Eye*, London: Financial Services Consumer Panel.
Gingrich, J. (2011) *Making Markets in the Welfare State: The Politics of Varying Market Reforms*, Cambridge: Cambridge University Press.

Gingrich, J. and Häusermann, S. (2015) 'The decline of the working-class vote, the reconfiguration of the welfare support coalition and consequences for the welfare state', *Journal of European Social Policy* 25(1): 50–75.
The Guardian (2002) 'Stakeholder pensions flop', *The Guardian*, 23 November.
The Guardian (2004) 'Anger at lifting of 1% fee cap on savings', *The Guardian*, 18 June.
Hacker, J. (2002) *The Divided Welfare State: The Battle Over Public and Private Social Benefits in the United States*, Cambridge: Cambridge University Press.
Hacker, J and Pierson, P. (2002) 'Business power and social policy: employers and the formation of the American welfare state', *Politics & Society* 30 (2): 277–325.
Harrison, D, Blake, D. and Dowd, K. (2012) *Caveat Venditor*, London: Pensions Institute.
Het Financieele Dagblad (2011) 'Inzichtelijk Pensioen; Als Fondsen Falen, Moet Overheid Ingrijpen', *Het Financieele Dagblad*, 13 April.
HM Treasury (2002) *Medium and Long Term Retail Savings in the UK: A Review* (Sandler Review), London: HM Treasury.
HM Treasury and DWP (2003) *Proposed Product Specifications for Sandler 'Stakeholder' Products - Consultation Document*, London: HM Treasury.
House of Commons (2001) *Stakeholder Pensions - Research Paper 01/69*, London: House of Commons.
House of Commons (2008) *Public Bill Committee - Pensions Bill*, London: House of Commons.
House of Commons (2011) *Westminster Hall Debate on 'Pension Plan Charges'*, London: House of Commons.
House of Commons (2012) *House of Commons Debate on 'Pension Industry'*, London: House of Commons.
House of Commons (2013) *House of Commons Debate on 'Pensions Bill'*, London: House of Commons.
House of Lords (2011) *House of Lords Debate on 'Pensions Bill'*, London: House of Lords.
House of Lords (2012) *House of Lords Debate on 'Pensions: Occupational Pensions*, London: House of Lords.
Leisering, L. (2011) *The New Regulatory State: Regulating Pensions in Germany and the UK*, Basingstoke: Palgrave Macmillan.
Lindblom, C. (1977) *Politics and Markets: The World's Political and Economic Systems*, New York: Basic Books.
Mabbett, D. (2012) 'The Ghost in the machine pension risks and regulatory responses in the United States and the United Kingdom', *Politics & Society* 40(1): 107–29.
Martin, R. (2002) *Financialization of Daily Life*, Philadelphia: Temple University Press.
Mitchell, Olivia S., and Lusardi, A. 2011. *Financial Literacy: Implications for Retirement Security and the Financial Marketplace*. Oxford: Oxford University Press.
Moloney, N. (2010) 'Financial services and Markets', in R. Baldwin, M. Cave and M. Lodge (eds.), *The Oxford Handbook of Regulation*, Oxford: Oxford University Press, 437–56.
Moran, M. and Schulze, I. (2007) 'United Kingdom: pension politics in an Adversarial System', in E. Immergut, K. Anderson and I. Schulze (Eds.), *The Handbook of West European Pension Politics*, Oxford: Oxford University Press, 49–96.
Naczyk, M. (2013) 'Agents of privatization? business groups and the rise of pension funds in continental Europe', *Socio-Economic Review* 11(3): 441–69.
NAPF (2012) *Pension Charges Made Clear: Joint Industry Code of Conduct Telling Employers About DC Pension Charges*, London: National Association of Pension Funds.
OFT (2013) *Defined Contribution Workplace Pension Market Study*, London: Office for Fair Trading.

Olson, M. (1965) *The Logic of Collective Action*, Cambridge: Harvard University Press.

Orszag, P. and Stiglitz, J. (2001) 'Rethinking pension reform: 10 myths about social security systems', in R. Holzman (ed.), *New Ideas About Old Age Security: Toward Sustainable Pension Systems in the 21st Century*, Washington, DC: World Bank, pp. 63–70.

Peltzman, S. (1976) 'Toward a more general theory of Regulation', *Journal of Law and Economics* 19: 211–40.

Pensions Commission (2004) *Pensions: Challenges and Choices - The First Report of the Pensions Commission*, London: Pensions Commission.

Pensions Commission (2005) *A New Pension Settlement for the Twenty-First Century - The Second Report of the Pensions Commission*, London: Pensions Commission.

Pitt-Watson, D. and Mann, H. (2012) *Seeing Through British Pensions - How to Increase Cost Transparency in UK Pension Schemes*, London: RSA.

RSA (2009) *Pensions for the People: Addressing the Savings and Investment Crisis in Britain*, London: RSA.

RSA (2010) *Tomorrow's Investor: Building the Consensus for a People's Pension in Britain*, London: RSA.

Schelkle, W. (2012) 'In the spotlight of crisis: how social policies create, correct, and compensate financial markets', *Politics & Society* 40(1): 3–8.

Secretary of State for Social Security (1998) *A New Contract for Welfare: Partnership in Pensions*, London: The Stationery Office Limited.

Select Committee on Treasury (2004) *Examination of Witnesses (Questions 2190-2139)*, London: House of Commons.

Sier, C. (2016) *The Drive Towards Cost Transparency in UK Pension Funds*, London: Financial Services Consumer Panel.

Skocpol, T. (1985) 'Bringing the state back in: strategies of analysis in current research', in P. Evans, D. Rueschemeyer and T. Skocpol (Eds.), *Bringing the State Back In*, Cambridge: Cambridge University Press, pp. 3–38.

Skocpol, T. (2008) 'Bringing the state back in: retrospect and prospect the 2007 Johan Skytte prize lecture', *Scandinavian Political Studies* 31(2): 109–24.

Stigler, G. (1971) 'The theory of economic regulation', *The Bell Journal of Economics and Management Science* 2(1): 3–21.

Taylor-Gooby, P. (2005) 'Uncertainty, trust and pensions: the case of the current UK reforms', *Social Policy & Administration* 39(3): 217–32.

Trampusch, C. (2018) 'A state-centred explanation of the finance-pension nexus: New Zealand's pension reforms as a typical case', *Social Policy & Administration* 52(1): 343–64.

Van der Zwan, N. (2014) 'Making sense of financialization', *Socio-Economic Review* 12(1): 99–129.

Vickerstaff, S., Macvarish, J., Taylor-Gooby, P., Loretto, W. and Harrison, T. (2012) *Trust and Confidence in Pensions: A Literature Review*, London: Department for Work and Pensions.

Whitehouse, E. (2001) *Administrative Charges for Funded Pensions: An International Comparison and Assessment*, Paris: OECD.

Wood, A., Wintersgill, D. and Baker, N. (2012) *Pension Landscape and Charging: Quantitative and Qualitative Research with Employers and Pension Providers*, London: Policy Research Institute.

Work and Pensions Committee (2003) *Third Report of the Work and Pensions Committee - The Future of UK Pensions*, London: House of Commons.

Work and Pensions Committee (2012) *Automatic Enrolment in Workplace Pensions and the National Employment Savings Trust - Eighth Report of Session 2010–12 - Volume I:*

Report, Together with Formal Minutes, Oral and Written Evidence, London: House of Commons.

Work and Pensions Committee (2013) *Improving Governance and Best Practice in Workplace Pensions - Sixth Report of Session 2012–13 - Volume II - Oral and Written Evidence*, London: House of Commons.

YouGov and B&CE (2015) *Pensions Survey*, London: YouGov.

Insuring individuals ... and politicians: financial services providers, stock market risk and the politics of private pension guarantees in Germany

Marek Naczyk and Anke Hassel

ABSTRACT
Studies of the rise of private defined-contribution pensions traditionally focus on social policy concerns about the allocation of risks and costs for beneficiaries and employers. There is, however, another – low-salience, financial – dimension of pension privatisation. Regulations introducing minimum return guarantees in private pensions impact financial markets because they incentivise fund managers to invest plan portfolios in fixed-income securities rather than in equities. While different segments of the financial industry have divergent preferences over such guarantees, policy-makers are caught in a dilemma: Should they prioritise predictable benefit levels or equity market development? Using the case of the introduction of Germany's 'Riester-Rente', we argue that, as politicians linked the introduction of private defined-contribution plans with cuts in statutory pensions, the re-emergence of a high-salience, social policy image of pensions helped insurance firms' and some trade unionists' case for minimum guarantees to prevail, thereby hindering equity market development in Germany.

Introduction

In recent decades, European governments have promoted the rise of private defined-contribution plans that, instead of guaranteeing workers a set level of their wages at retirement, offer them what they have paid into the system, plus returns on investments (Ebbinghaus 2015; Orenstein 2013). Since such plans tie benefit levels more closely to workers' contribution records and to the performance – and volatility – of financial markets, social scientists associate their rise with a 'great risk shift' (Hacker 2006; Mabbett 2012) and a financialisation of pensions (Engelen 2003; Langley 2008; van der Zwan 2014). Yet the distributional consequences of the expansion of private defined-contribution plans have varied across countries due to regulatory differences

(EIOPA 2011). While 'pure' defined-contribution plans that fully expose individuals to investment risk predominate in countries such as the United States and the United Kingdom, many other countries have introduced regulations that protect savers from stock market drops (Antolín et al. 2011). For example, Austria, Germany and Slovenia force most providers of occupational and personal pensions to guarantee a minimum rate of return on participants' pension assets. What drives the introduction of such guarantees in defined-contribution pensions?

To build a theory on the regulatory choices policy-makers face when privatising pensions, we have analysed distinct episodes of an almost decade-long political process that culminated in the introduction of 'Riester' pension plans in Germany in 2001. Riester plans are voluntary personal pension plans in which individuals select the level of their own contributions and the financial services provider that manages the plan's assets. A key characteristic of Riester plans is that plan managers are legally obliged to guarantee that, at retirement, plan members receive at least the nominal value of all their contributions. This provision makes Germany one of the countries whose personal pensions deviate the most from a 'pure' defined-contribution design that fully exposes individuals to investment risk. Germany is also an important case because, although it has epitomised Bismarckian welfare states with generous, publicly-provided social insurance (Esping-Andersen 1990) and coordinated market economies with non-market coordination of firms' activities (Hall and Soskice 2001), it has seen market mechanisms greatly rise in importance in its social protection and economic systems (Streeck 2009).

Based on this case study and on the emerging literature on the 'welfare-finance nexus' (Estévez-Abe 2001), we argue that the politics of investment return guarantees can only be understood by simultaneously looking at two – social policy and financial regulation – sides of pensions. Minimum return guarantees are both a social policy instrument that reallocates risks in pension provision and a financial regulation tool that impacts the allocation of savings in capital markets and, more broadly, the financing of the economy. Pure defined-contribution plans allow fund managers to allocate a very large part of pension assets in – typically quite volatile – equities. By contrast, minimum return guarantees force pension plan managers to invest a larger chunk of plan portfolios in fixed-income securities, such as bonds and derivatives, because these – traditionally less volatile – instruments allow managers to meet minimum return targets with greater certainty (Antolín et al. 2011: 25).

The two dimensions of pensions directly structure the constellations of actors involved in the politics of investment return guarantees. Debates on pension guarantees involve traditional social policy actors, such as party politicians, bureaucrats, trade unions and employers. But they also give a central role to the main providers of private pension products, i.e., financial services providers. Insurance companies, banks and mutual funds have divergent preferences over whether the state should require pension providers to guarantee investment returns because, due to their different business models, they do not have the same capacity to offer such guarantees (Wehlau 2009). As recipients of pension fund investments, stock exchanges also have strong interests in this regulatory area.

As they have to decide on the regulations governing private plans, politicians are caught between contradictory pressures. In coordinated market economies – such as the German one – where, in an era of financial liberalisation, firms have relied ever less on banks and increasingly on equity markets to fund their activities, the expansion of equity-oriented – and, therefore, preferably guarantee-free – pension plans has been considered a very powerful vehicle for creating a stable source of funds in equity markets. Yet, such lightly regulated and equity-oriented plans create the risk that plan participants lose savings in case of a market downturn.

We argue that politicians' choice over whether they prioritise relatively predictable benefit levels or equity market development is crucially influenced by how they link the introduction of private defined-contribution pension plans with other pension reforms. When they decide to link it with cuts in existing public pensions, mobilisation against retrenchment maintains or reasserts an image of pensions as a high-salient, social policy, issue and puts policy-makers under immense pressure to introduce guarantees. By contrast, when they do not do so, the creation of defined-contribution plans presents the image of a relatively low-salient, financial regulation, issue and politicians have a lot of latitude to introduce lighter regulations.

The rest of the article is organised as follows: The first section provides an overview of the existing literature on the politics of pension privatisation and further specifies the theoretical framework. The second section presents the German case study. The conclusion discusses how the 2001 Riester reform has linked with other reforms in the German political economy and suggests avenues for future research.

The two sides of pension privatisation

Research on the political dynamics behind public pension cuts and the expansion of defined-contribution plans has initially focused on a conservative backlash against the welfare state (Hacker 2004; Pierson 1994), but has growingly highlighted how centre-left governments have pushed through reforms in a context of 'permanent austerity' and population ageing (Pierson 2001; see also Häusermann 2010; Huber and Stephens 2001). Employers have been another protagonist of these changes because of their influence in the political arena (Häusermann 2010), and also because of the cuts made by many firms in occupational pension plans that were traditionally used for building peaceful labour relations and retaining skilled workers (Bridgen and Meyer 2005; Hacker 2004). Organised labour has also been a major player, due to its capacity to mobilise against reforms through demonstrations or elections (Anderson and Meyer 2003; Ebbinghaus 2011). However, many trade unions have consented to promote more collective occupational schemes through collective bargaining, so as to make cutbacks in public pensions more palatable to employees and to prevent an excessive marketisation of pension provision (Naczyk and Seeleib-Kaiser 2015; Trampusch 2006a, 2006b; Wiß 2012).

Most literature assumes that actors' stance in the politics of privatisation is driven by their concerns over the generosity and costs of pensions *qua* social policy. This is despite the fact that pension arrangements are a crucial element of many countries' financial systems. The financial significance of pension schemes has been most evident in Anglo-Saxon liberal market economies (LMEs), where large firms rely heavily on equity markets to secure finance (Hall and Soskice 2001). By 1990, pension funds held as much as one third[1] of equities quoted in American and British stock markets (Davis 1995: 181). In the German, Japanese and Nordic coordinated market economies (CMEs), where firms have traditionally been more reliant on retained earnings to fund their activities, pension schemes based on 'book reserves' – schemes that are financed through tax-deductible provisions set up on the liability side of companies' balance sheets – have been a key vehicle for helping managers to retain corporate earnings within their firms (Estévez-Abe 2001). Private pension arrangements have also impacted finance on an international scale: As Anglo-Saxon pension funds started investing their portfolios in the shares of firms based in CMEs, many of these firms have integrated the Anglo-Saxon principle of 'shareholder value' in their management practices, thereby raising concerns over a financialisation of CMEs and their convergence on the liberal variant of capitalism (Clark 2003; Engelen 2003; Lazonick and O'Sullivan, 2000; van der Zwan 2014).

Given these links between pensions and finance, a growing body of literature has shown two main ways in which the 'welfare-finance nexus' shapes pension politics (Estévez-Abe 2001). Firstly, the financial dimension of pensions strongly influences actors' preferences over pensions' institutional design. For example, as increasingly stringent international accounting standards have forced publicly-listed firms to report their occupational schemes' assets and liabilities on their balance sheets, using a 'fair' valuation based on current market conditions, such companies have preferred to transform their – liability-heavy – defined-benefit plans into – liability-free – defined-contribution plans (Clark 2003; Dixon and Monk 2009). Employers and trade unions also try to shape pension plan regulations, so as to be able to influence the type of assets in which pension funds invest and the time horizon of these investments (McCarthy et al. 2016; Naczyk 2016; Wiß 2015).

Secondly, when the welfare-finance nexus is taken into account, it becomes evident that financial services providers are important actors in this area. Some have highlighted the role of life insurance companies in the development of supplementary pensions since the late nineteenth century (Leimgruber 2008; Meyer and Bridgen 2012; Naczyk 2013). However, mutual funds and asset management companies controlled by banks have also become active in pension provision in recent decades (Oelschläger 2009). These different segments of the financial services industry offer very different types of pension products and have therefore diverging – and intense – preferences over pension plan regulation (Wehlau 2009). Insurance companies' business model typically relies on offering relatively predictable benefits paid out in the form of an annuity and is underpinned by industry-specific prudential rules and supervisory practices (Quaglia 2011). By contrast, mutual funds and asset management companies do not usually offer annuities and typically market pure defined-contribution products by promising high long-term returns from portfolios heavily invested in equities. Since different types of financial firms will attempt to frame the political debate so that politicians adopt regulations that advantage their own products, examining their political activities is a precondition for understanding the politics of private pension guarantees. With their strong interests in directing investments towards equity markets, stock exchanges' political role in the area of pension fund regulation can also not be neglected.

How do politicians decide on the regulations governing private pension plans? While most literature assumes that politicians' choices are purely determined by social policy concerns about the allocation of risks and costs, an approach that takes into account the welfare-finance nexus implies that politicians also weigh up the impact of pension plan regulations on the financial system. This is not only because financial services providers who defend specific regulations may deploy arguments revolving around this financial dimension, but also because financial markets have often been high on politicians' agenda (Trampusch 2018). In the post-1970s context of deindustrialisation and globalisation, many governments have sought to stimulate the development of domestic capital – especially equity – markets in order to allow more firms to tap into them to expand their activities. In fact, financial reform has been pursued across much of the political spectrum, as the centre-left has attempted to surpass the right as a champion of economic modernisation (Cioffi and Höpner 2006). Given the importance of financial development, proponents of pure defined-contribution plans – such as mutual funds, asset management companies and stock exchange professionals – have tried to strike a responsive chord with reformist politicians by emphasising how the expansion of such plans would increase and stabilise the supply of funds in domestic equity markets.

This context ties in neatly with Culpepper's (2011) framework on the role of business in policy-making. Building on standard public policy theory (Baumgartner and Jones 1993), Culpepper points out that the power of business varies between policy areas. The business community is particularly powerful on policy issues that receive low media attention and are decided in informal settings. The higher the salience of an issue and the more formal the institutional arena governing it, the greater the likelihood will be that business will be defeated and that it will have to build alliances with other actors. While the business community might be tempted to shift the arena from high to low salience venues and from formal to informal venues, other – civil society or party – actors will do the opposite. For them, the framing of an issue as a high-salience issue governed by formal policy processes is preferable for winning the battle over policies. The political battleground is therefore dependent on the framing of an issue and the defining of the venue for battle.

Traditionally, pension policy has been dominated by those caring for old age interests and represented by a powerful and high-salience policy image of protecting pensioners against poverty. This traditional framing has been challenged by the rise of new financial services providers who have been able to frame defined-contribution pensions as a low-salience financial regulation issue intimately connected with equity market development. Yet the success of this challenge could be thwarted if some actors managed to shift the policy image of defined-contribution plans back to a high-salience social policy one.

We argue that, paradoxically, it is not the direct mobilisation of opponents of 'pure' defined-contribution plans against their introduction, but rather politicians' decision to link the introduction of such plans with cuts in existing public pensions that allows these opponents – mainly the insurance industry and some segments of organised labour – to thwart their introduction. As long as policy-makers disconnect the introduction of pure defined-contribution plans from cuts in public pensions, it remains a technical issue and creates an environment of 'quiet politics' that prevents opponents of such plans from gaining enough momentum. By contrast, if defined-contribution plans are introduced in combination with retrenchment, the whole pension reform package becomes much more politicised and allows arguments about the threats posed by the volatile pension plan portfolios of pure defined-contribution plans for the level of pensions to be heard in the public debate. This puts much greater pressure on politicians – who do not have to be ideologically opposed to pure defined-contribution plans – to demonstrate their commitment to safe and adequate pensions by mandating investment return guarantees.

Pension privatisation in Germany in the 1990s and 2000s

This section presents the case study of the different stages in a political process that culminated in the adoption of the 2001 Riester reform. As it combined cuts in statutory pensions with a promotion of private defined-contribution pension plans, this reform is considered as a case of 'paradigmatic', institutional change (Häusermann 2010; Hinrichs and Kangas 2003; Jacobs 2011; Oelschläger 2009; Trampusch 2006a; Wehlau 2009; Wiß 2012). One crucial provision of the reform was the creation of new, individual, defined-contribution accounts that would supplement existing statutory and occupational pension schemes. To encourage the expansion of these so-called Riester plans, the Schröder government introduced tax deductions for high-income earners and state subsidies for low-income earners who voluntarily saved up to 4% of their gross wage in such accounts. To qualify for these incentives, the plans had to meet a number of regulatory criteria, including the provision of a nominal guarantee on all the contributions paid into the plans.

The reform also promoted the development of occupational provision. While occupational pensions were traditionally set up and financed by employers on a unilateral basis, the reform gave employees a legally enforceable *right* to obtain the creation of such plans by their employer, provided that workers themselves would contribute part of their salary (*Entgeltumwandlung* – of max. 4% of their gross salary) to it. It also created a new type of defined-contribution occupational schemes (called *Pensionsfonds*) that, like Riester plans, offered a mandatory nominal guarantee.

In studying the 2001 Riester reform, we provide a 'moving picture' rather than a 'snapshot' view of the reform process (Pierson 2004). We study longer spells of time that can capture how an issue is put on the political agenda. This is particularly useful for understanding the preferences of different interest groups and politicians' motivations in supporting change (Hacker et al. 2015). Thus, contrary to most existing accounts of the reform, whose focus is on debates that occurred after 1998, i.e., after the Schröder government was formed (cf. Häusermann 2010; Hinrichs and Kangas 2003; Jacobs 2011; Trampusch 2006a; Wehlau 2009; Wiß 2012; for an exception, see Oelschläger 2009), our analysis already starts in 1995 when defined-contribution plans were put on Germany's political agenda. In addition to using existing literature, we reconstructed actors' positions and the sequence of reforms through an analysis of quality German newspapers (including *FAZ – Frankfurter Allgemeine Zeitung, Handelsblatt* and *SZ – Süddeutsche Zeitung*) and newswires stored in the Factiva news database. We triangulated this empirical evidence with an analysis of policy papers published at the time, of minutes of parliamentary debates and of 13 interviews conducted with former ministers, civil servants and representatives of interest groups.[2]

This empirical section is structured in three parts. Firstly, we show how, in the mid-1990s, a coalition of – largely Frankfurt-based – banks, mutual funds and stock exchange professionals started advocating the introduction of 'pure' equity-oriented defined-contribution schemes. Their case for reform revolved primarily around strengthening German equity markets. Secondly, although life insurance companies criticised these proposals and called for minimum return guarantees, centre-right and centre-left politicians were initially very responsive to arguments about equity market development. The rise of a low-salience, financial regulation image of pensions was symbolised by the creation of a 'pure' defined-contribution – but not tax-incentivised – vehicle called *Altersvorsorge-Sondervermögen* by the centre-right Kohl government through the Third Capital Market Promotion Law in 1998. Thirdly, as the centre-left, Schröder government, elected in 1998, promoted fully-funded defined-contribution plans together with a retrenchment of public pensions, mobilisation from trade unions against retrenchment helped to reinstate defined-contribution pensions as a high-salience social policy issue and pushed Walter Riester to introduce mandatory nominal return guarantees relatively late in the reform process.

Frankfurt financiers' push for more equity culture in Germany

The debate on the introduction of defined-contribution pensions in Germany erupted in late 1995 when Deutsche Bank Research – the *de facto* think tank of Deutsche Bank AG – published a paper entitled: 'From pension reserves to pension funds [Pensionsfonds]: An opportunity for the German financial market' (Nürk and Schrader 1995). At the time, stricter international accounting rules pushed large German companies to report the liabilities associated with their book reserve pension schemes, to back these liabilities with correspondent assets and to shift their management to external funds (Clark 2003). DB Research's paper called for regulatory and tax changes that would make the externalisation of book reserves more attractive. It recommended the establishment of Anglo-Saxon-style, equity-oriented 'pension funds' ('Pensionsfonds') as a new vehicle for occupational pensions. The paper argued that the preservation of book reserves created major 'liquidity and financing risks' for companies and that, even if such schemes had helped large German firms to fund themselves, the involvement of equity markets could improve the allocation of capital (Nürk and Schrader 1995: 28).

The paper was commissioned by Deutsche Bank's chief economist, Norbert Walter, and by Rolf-Ernst Breuer, a managing director of Deutsche Bank and chairman of the Frankfurt stock exchange group, Deutsche Börse AG (interview with a former DB Research employee, 19.05.2016). Together with other stock exchange professionals (Mattern et al. 1997; von Rosen 1997), Breuer regularly argued that the lack of equity-oriented, domestic pension funds was 'one of the reasons why Germany has no equity culture' (FAZ 1994), and that it constituted 'one of the most serious' problems affecting the competitiveness of German capital markets (Reuters 1994).

Simultaneously with the publication of DB Research's paper, the Frankfurt-based German Investment Funds Association (BVI – Bundesverband deutscher Investment-Gesellschaften) proposed creating an equity-oriented defined-contribution vehicle – dubbed 'Pensions-Sondervermögen' – that could be used both for occupational and personal pension plans (Laux 1995). Such funds would be attractive because 'hardly any other type of investment [could] yield similarly high returns' (Passow 1996).

The Deutsche Bank's and the BVI's proposals provoked a negative response by the Association of German Insurers (GDV – Gesamtverband der Deutschen Versicherungswirtschaft),[3] which argued that life insurance products were 'more than a financial investment', since they offered a guaranteed interest rate and a lifetime annuity at retirement (SZ 1996). As the trade association of occupational pensions (aba – Arbeitsgemeinschaft für betriebliche Altersversorgung e. V.) has put it, the Deutsche Bank's and BVI's proposals also caused 'anger' among employers and managers of traditional occupational pensions (aba 2013: 29). The aba and the Confederation of German Employers' Associations (BDA – Bundesvereinigung der Deutschen Arbeitgeberverbände) strove to explain that book reserves were both a solid vehicle for retirement provision and an important tool for companies' internal funding.

Yet, not all employers were hostile to these proposals. For example, Karl-Hermann Baumann, chief financial officer of Siemens AG, argued that his own group had considered externalising the management of its book reserves, but was unable to do it because this was not the 'most tax-efficient option' (SZ 1997a). Baumann was in fact a member of the executive committee of the Aktionskreis Finanzplatz e.V.. This interest group – founded by Deutsche Börse AG – also lobbied for the introduction of 'Pensionsfonds' (interview with a former official of Aktionsfreis Finanzplatz e.V., 15.01.2016). Its aim was to promote Frankfurt as an international financial centre. Board members included top executives of banks, investment funds, but also representatives of large non-financial companies (Bayer AG, Deutsche Telekom AG and Hoechst AG), the business press (Börsen-Zeitung and Handelsblatt) and politicians, such as Petra Roth, Christian Democratic (CDU) mayor of Frankfurt am Main, and Hans Eichel, the Social Democratic Prime Minister of the state of Hesse, where Frankfurt is located (Aktionskreis Finanzplatz e.V. 1997: 19–20).

Cross-party support for strengthening equity culture

While the Social Democratic Party (SPD) ferociously rejected the retrenchment of statutory pensions, enacted in 1997 by the Kohl government through the so-called Blüm II reform (e.g., Häusermann 2010: 137–8), parties' positions were, at the time, much less polarised on the issue of private retirement savings where a low-salience, financial regulation, image became temporarily dominant. In early 1996, the SPD's parliamentary group submitted a motion entitled: 'Strengthening German capital markets, promoting equity savings and improving venture capital' (SPD Bundestagsfraktion 1996). It proposed creating 'provident savings' products (Vorsorge Sparen), heavily invested in equities, and argued that this would help improve German companies' access to equity financing and introduce real competition between insurance companies and mutual funds in retirement savings. The motion explicitly referred to a concept of 'personal equity savings plan' (Persönlicher Aktien-Sparplan) advanced by the Deutsches Aktieninstitut, a think tank closely associated with the Frankfurt financial centre. In 1997, Hans Eichel, the Social Democratic Prime Minister of the German state of Hesse, announced that his administration would sponsor a bill in the Bundesrat – the upper house of the German parliament – to make the introduction of tax incentives for 'Pensionsfonds' possible (SZ 1997b).

Germany's liberal party, the FDP, also showed enthusiasm for proposals to develop equity-oriented defined-contribution pensions. In late 1995, it announced that it would seek the federal state's fiscal support for the BVI's 'Pensions-Sondervermögen' (FAZ 1995) and justified this by the need to promote 'equity culture' in Germany (e.g., von Rosen 1997: 13–14). The Pensions-Sondervermögen was eventually introduced as 'Altersvorsorge-Sondervermögen' by an FDP-CDU-CSU coalition through the Third Capital Market Promotion Law, passed in February 1998. Christian Democratic Chancellor, Helmut Kohl, argued that the law would 'strengthen the German financial centre' and 'strengthen the position of equities ... [in] pension savings' (Kohl 1997; see also Bundesregierung 1997: 2). The product's name was changed during the legislative process at the behest of the Bundesrat. Life insurance companies had contended from the beginning that 'Pensions-Sondervermögen' would lead to 'conceptual confusion' because it did not offer the safety guarantees – minimum return guarantees and annuity payments – that characterise a 'real' pension product (FAZ 1997a).

The 'Pensionsfonds' concept was considered too unripe to be included in the Third Capital Market Promotion Law. As pointed out by CDU and FDP politicians (FAZ 1997b), the Association of German Banks (BdB – Bundesverband deutscher Banken) had not yet managed to work out an official position on the issue. It would only publish such a document in 1999 (BdB 1999). The Federal Ministry of Finance emphasised that the debate about Pensionsfonds was a 'multidimensional subject area' with major fiscal implications (FAZ 1998). In order to work out a compromise on the issue, the Ministry set up a working group, gathering representatives of all segments of the financial services industry (insurance companies, banks, mutual funds, Deutsche Börse) and employers as part of a 'Forum Finanzplatz'. The working group published its report mid-1998 and recommended that Pensionsfonds should offer a 0% nominal guarantee on contributions (BMF 1998).

High-salience social policy image overrides low-salience financial regulation image

Despite the working group's recommendations, banks, mutual funds and stock exchange professionals never stopped trying to persuade politicians to create pure, equity-oriented, defined-contribution schemes (BdB 1999; Bräuninger and Wolgast 2000; BVI 2000; Wehlau 2009: 283–90). Yet, despite a cross-party consensus on the need to strengthen German's equity culture, the Riester reform – which was enacted in May 2001 – required providers of personal Riester products *and* occupational Pensionsfonds to guarantee capital preservation of contributions at retirement. This provision was, in fact, suggested relatively late in debates over the reform – in May 2000. It meant that insurance companies – which invested a small part of their assets in equity markets – would dominate the new market for Riester plans.

Insurers' calls for the introduction of guarantees in defined-contribution plans gained momentum after the centre-left Schröder government's decision to link the introduction of such plans with cuts in statutory pensions led organised labour to scrutinise all reform proposals and, in the process, to develop a stance on the regulation of pension funds. Largely because of a lack of technical expertise on pension fund regulation, trade unions had not been actively involved in the low-salient discussions over the 'pure' defined-contribution 'Pensionsfonds' and 'Pensions-Sondervermögen' concepts (Interview with former official of IG Metall, 16.02.2016). Yet, in the mid-1990s, Walter Riester – the vice-chairman and head of the industrial relations department of Germany's largest trade union, the IG Metall – started believing that pension privatisation could help contain non-wage labour costs in German manufacturing companies (cf. Riester 2004: 63–70). As his views fit with the SPD's 1998 election manifesto pledge to base the German pension system on four different 'pillars' (SPD 1998: 38–40), he was nominated Minister of Labour and Social Affairs in the Schröder government.

Between the end of 1998 and spring 2000, Riester developed several reform proposals, ranging from the creation of collectively-negotiated sector-wide occupational plans (called 'Tariffonds') to compulsory personal pension accounts, but all proposals were shelved because of – among other things – the opposition of the more traditionalist wing of the trade union movement and of the social policy wing of the SPD parliamentary group to the cuts in statutory pensions that would accompany the promotion of private plans (Jacobs 2011: 230–236; Wiß 2012: 153–6).

In this context, the regulation of defined-contribution plans became increasingly politicised. A blueprint for reform presented by Walter Riester in June 1999 briefly stated that there would be 'freedom of choice for investments made as part of occupational pension plans' (SZ 1999), which suggested that pure defined-contribution plans would be allowed. Unions did not yet express a firm stance at that stage. But, as it was clear that Walter Riester was planning to propose a new reform proposal in spring 2000, infighting within the IG Metall over the issue became evident. While the union's leader – Klaus Zwickel – argued that workers should be more inclined to hold equities since investing on the stock exchange had become a 'popular movement' (Handelsblatt 2000), the leader of the union's social policy wing, Horst Schmitthenner, retorted that 'social security' could not be 'built on a casino' (Spiegel Online 2000).

It is following this public confrontation that, in May 2000, – as part a new reform proposal that combined cuts in public pensions with the creation of tax subsidies for *voluntary* savings in personal pension plans – Riester proposed for the first time to force pension providers to guarantee the nominal value of all contributions paid into pension plans. Riester argued that 'highly speculative equity funds' were not suitable because private retirement savings had to 'partly replace' statutory pensions (Der Spiegel 2000).

This was a significant U-turn since, at Deutsche Börse's annual reception, held in January 2000, Chancellor Gerhard Schröder still insisted that the development of defined-contribution pensions offered 'an opportunity to... decrease the costs of equity capital' (Schröder 2001). The banking (BdB) and investment fund (BVI) lobbies repeatedly emphasised that the nominal guarantee would harm pension plans' returns and the German financial centre (see e.g., Der Spiegel 2001). Green and CDU parliamentarians called for pension funds to invest more in equities and were happy to lift the guarantee requirement (Berliner Zeitung 2000; Die Tageszeitung 2001). But banks' and mutual funds' arguments became inoperative with the government, as a high-salience social policy image of the reform process had now overtaken a low-salience, financial regulation one.

The Schröder government made nevertheless two concessions in response to lobbying by mutual funds and banks. Firstly, it agreed to change the formula for calculating the guarantee. The nominal amount of contributions to be guaranteed would not be updated every year during the accumulation phase, but would instead only be calculated at retirement, thereby avoiding the creation of a compound interest effect (interview with a former representative of BVI, 14.01.2016). Secondly, in late 2000, Finance Minister Hans Eichel agreed to add the 'Pensionsfonds' as a fifth vehicle for occupational provision (SZ 2000). On the day the Riester reform was finally enacted by the Bundesrat, a press release, issued by the Labour Ministry, stated that Pensionsfonds would 'strengthen Germany as a financial centre' and that 'freedom in the allocation of assets' would give them 'the opportunity to... generate higher returns' (BMA-Pressestelle 2001). Yet, here too, the government imposed a nominal return guarantee.

Conclusion

The study of – seemingly technical – regulations such as minimum return guarantees sheds light on important political dynamics and macro implications of the twin processes of financialisation and pension privatisation. These are contested processes: Business and financial market actors do not systematically win the day. Rather, as illustrated by the case study of the 2001 Riester reform in Germany, politicians' choices as to pension plan regulation are influenced by the political dynamics of reform that they themselves create. When banks, mutual funds, stock exchange professionals and large non-financial firms started to challenge the existing monopoly of the high-salient social policy image of pensions by calling for the introduction of 'pure', equity-oriented, defined-contribution schemes in the mid-1990s, their arguments about how such plans would boost equity market development won over large swathes of the centre-left and the centre-right. In 1998, the centre-right Kohl government opened the possibility for financial firms to offer such plans – albeit without tax incentives. At the time, the legislative change was politically viable, as it was introduced as part of a reform package focusing on the development of domestic capital markets. The Schröder government subsequently tried to create a Nixon-goes-to-China moment in German social policy reform by appointing a high-ranking union leader, Walter Riester, as Social Affairs Minister and by combining the development of defined-contribution plans with retrenchment. Yet this made political dynamics move from an informal, quiet policy venue to a higher-salient arena and made the attempt to use defined-contribution plans as an instrument for the expansion of equity investments falter.

Pension funds are typically seen as a driver of financialisation processes, whereby the financial industry has increasingly become the lead sector in Western economies and led other industries to adopt shareholder value (Engelen 2003; van der Zwan 2014). In the 1990s and early 2000s, new capital market regulations led large German companies to partly dissolve the networks of interlocking directorates and ownership ties that bound them together and to embrace shareholder value (Beyer and Höpner 2003; Streeck and Höpner 2003). In Germany, it is largely the same coalition of actors – large banks, stock exchange professionals and liberal-minded, centre-left or centre-right, politicians – that pushed for this restructuring of corporate governance practices (e.g., Cioffi and Höpner 2006; Lütz 1998) and, as demonstrated in this article, for an expansion of equity-oriented defined-contribution pension plans.

Yet the clash between the quiet politics of equity market development and the high-salience politics of social policy led to unintended consequences. As public pensions were cut, private pension products were regulated in a way that disappointed many financial market actors. In 2002, life insurance contracts attracted 90% of all savers (BMAS 2017). At the time, life insurance companies invested as much as 66.4% of their assets in fixed-income securities, only 3.2% in listed stocks and 22.9% in special funds that held both equities and fixed-income securities (Maurer 2004: 112). Such a bias in favour of fixed-income instruments continued characterising the German pension fund industry well into the 2010s, even despite the European Central Bank's low interest rate policy and, consequently, the low returns offered by many countries' sovereign bonds (e.g., BaFin 2016: 213–4). German pension funds' very low equity holdings have also meant that these funds have not been able to play an active role in the further promotion of shareholder value. On the whole, reforms introduced in the 1990s and early 2000s resulted in a half-hearted liberalisation of Germany' financial and corporate governance systems and the preservation of important elements of the stakeholder orientation of the German political economy (Jackson and Thelen 2015; Lütz 2005).

Our theoretical framework helps us shed light on developments in other temporal and national contexts. In Germany, a new Act on the Strengthening of Occupational Pensions, passed in 2017, introduced a 'pure' defined-contribution vehicle (Wiß 2019). It is noteworthy that this act only regulated occupational pensions and was passed in a context where political debates have focused on the need to increase, rather than to cut, the generosity of – statutory and occupational – pensions. In other countries, the first tax incentives for 'pure' defined-contribution pension plans were also typically created through acts that regulated the private pension industry[4] or the taxation[5] of savings, before retrenchment was on the political agenda. By contrast, East European countries that created mandatory personal pension plans – while radically cutting public provision – typically introduced return guarantees either in the form of an absolute minimum return (e.g., Hungary, Romania and Slovakia) or in relation to an industry average (e.g., Bulgaria, Croatia and Poland).

Seemingly technical regulations such as minimum return guarantees are pervasive not just in pension reforms (see also Anderson 2019; Wiß 2019), but, in reality, in most areas of financial regulation. Analysing the politics behind cross-national variation in such regulations should be an important task for students of comparative public policy and political economy for two reasons. Firstly, such regulations create winners and losers among providers of different types of savings products. Secondly and relatedly, by channelling people's savings towards specific types of products, such regulations also help channel those savings towards different types of investments: When savings are invested in equities as opposed to, say, sovereign bonds or bank accounts, it is very different types of actors – e.g., large vs. small companies or states – that benefit from those investments. Eventually, the presence or absence of such regulations shapes varieties of financialisation across countries. While many such regulations are hammered out in quiet meetings between politicians and business leaders, there are a number of policy fields – e.g., housing and education – where quiet politics of financial regulation can clash with the more noisy politics of social policy. Given the major socio-economic implications of such policy areas, there is undoubtedly a need for more research on the regulatory politics underpinning different national welfare-finance nexuses.

Notes

1. This number does not take into account equities held by insurance companies or mutual funds that manage retirement products.
2. The interviews were semi-structured and lasted between 30 min and 2 h. We also used policy documents, speeches and newspaper articles.
3. Interview with a former official of the Gesamtverband der Deutschen Versicherungswirtschaft – GDV, 12.02.2016
4. e.g. creation of 'individual retirement accounts' through the 1974 Employee Retirement Income Security Act in the United States; Law 8/1987 on the Regulation of Pension Plans and Funds in Spain; 1989 Decree-Law establishing retirement savings plans in Portugal.
5. e.g. 1986 fiscal law creating 'pension savings products' in Belgium; 1987 Law on Savings in France.

Acknowledgements

We are grateful to our interviewees for their time and to the editors of JEPP and the reviewers for helping to improve the argument.

Disclosure statement

No potential conflict of interest was reported by the authors.

Funding

This work was supported by the German Federal Ministry of Education and Research (BMBF) under [grant number 01UF1508].

References

Aba. (2013) *75 Jahre aba: Ein historischer Rückblick*, Berlin: Arbeitsgemeinschaft für betriebliche Altersversorgung e. V. (aba).

Aktionskreis Finanzplatz e.V. (1997) *Finanzplatz Deutschland: The Natural Choice*, Frankfurt a. M.: Aktionskreis Finanzplatz e.V.

Anderson, K. (2019) 'Financialisation meets collectivisation: occupational pensions in Denmark, the Netherlands and Sweden', *Journal of European Public Policy*. https://doi.org/10.1080/13501763.2019.1574309.

Anderson, K.M. and Meyer, T. (2003) 'Social democracy, unions, and pension politics in Germany and Sweden', *Journal of Public Policy* 23(1): 23–54.

Antolín, P., Payet, S., Whitehouse, E.R. and Yermo, J. (2011) 'The role of guarantees in defined contribution pensions', in *OECD Working Papers on Finance, Insurance and Private Pensions, No. 11*, Paris: OECD Publishing. doi:10.1787/5kg52k5b0v9s-en.

BaFin. (2016) *Jahresbericht der Bundesanstalt für Finanzdienstleistungsaufsicht 2015*, Bonn und Frankfurt a. M.: Bundesanstalt für Finanzdienstleistungsaufsicht.

Baumgartner, F.R. and Jones, B.D. (1993) *Agendas and Instability in American Politics*, Chicago: Chicago University Press.

BdB. (1999) *Betriebs-Pensionsfonds. Neue Impulse für die Betriebliche Altersversorgung*, Berlin: Bundesverband deutscher Banken.

Berliner Zeitung. (2000) 'Grüne unzufrieden mit Riesters Vorsorge-Konzept – Scheel', 20 October.

Beyer, J. and Höpner, M. (2003) 'The disintegration of organised capitalism: German corporate governance in the 1990s', *West European Politics* 26(4): 179–98.

BMA-Pressestelle. (2001) 'Bundesrat beschließt Rentenreform - Förderung der zusätzlichen Altersvorsorge kommt', available at http://www.beck.de/cms/main?sessionid=3BBE5EEF9D16437398A466E310328788&docid=19875&docClass=NEWS&site=Beck%20Aktuell&from=HP.0110.

BMAS. (2017) 'Statistik zur privaten Altersvorsorge', available at http://www.bmas.de/DE/Themen/Rente/Zusaetzliche-Altersvorsorge/statistik-zusaetzliche-altersvorsorge.html.

BMF. (1998) *Bericht des Arbeitskreises "Betriebliche Pensionsfonds" im Auftrag des "Forums Finanzplatz beim Bundersministerium der Finanzen"*, Bonn: Bundesministerium der Finanzen.

Bräuninger, D. and Wolgast, M. (2000) 'Reform der Altersvorsorge – Fehlentscheidungen vermeiden', *Aktuelle Themen* Nr. 177, 28.08.2000, Frankfurt a. M.: Deutsche Bank Research, available at https://www.dbresearch.de/PROD/DBR_INTERNET_DE-PROD/PROD0000000000017330/Reform_der_Altersvorsorge_-_Fehlentscheidungen_ver.pdf.

Bridgen, P. and Meyer, T. (2005) 'When do benevolent capitalists change their mind? Explaining the retrenchment of defined-benefit pensions in Britain', *Social Policy & Administration* 39(7): 764–85.

Bundesregierung. (1997) *Gesetzentwurf der Bundesregierung. Entwurf eines Gesetzes zur weitereun Fortenwicklung des Finanzplatzes Deutschland (Drittes Flnanzmarktförderungsgesetz)*. Bonn: Bundesrat. Drucksache 605/97 vom 15.08.97, available at http://dipbt.bundestag.de/doc/brd/1997/D605+97.pdf.

BVI. (2000) *BVI-Vorstandssprecher fordert echte Wahlmöglichkeit zwischen Investmentfonds und Versicherungen*, 29.09.2000, Frankfurt a. M.: Bundesverband Deutscher Investment-Gesellschaften e.V, available at http://www.verbaende.com/

news.php/BVI-Vorstandssprecher-fordert-echte-Wahlmoeglichkeit-zwischen-Investmentfonds-und-Versicherungen?m=2875.

Cioffi, J.W. and Höpner, M. (2006) 'The political paradox of finance capitalism: Interests, preferences, and center-left party politics in corporate governance reform', *Politics & Society* 34(4): 463–502.

Clark, G.L. (2003) *European Pensions and Global Finance*, Oxford: Oxford University Press.

Culpepper, P.D. (2011) *Quiet Politics and Business Power: Corporate Control in Europe and Japan*, Cambridge: Cambridge University Press.

Davis, E.P. (1995) *Pension Funds: Retirement-Income Security and Capital Markets. An International Perspective*, Oxford: Clarendon Press.

Der Spiegel. (2000) 'Aufmarsch der Lobbyisten', 31 July.

Der Spiegel. (2001) 'Riesters Reformruine', 12 February.

Die Tageszeitung. (2001) 'Künftig helfen Aktien statt Kinder', 2 January.

Dixon, A. and Monk, A. (2009) 'The power of finance: accounting harmonization's effect on pension provision', *Journal of Economic Geography* 9(5): 619–39.

Ebbinghaus, B. (ed) (2011) *The Varieties of Pension Governance: Pension Privatization in Europe*, Oxford: Oxford University Press.

Ebbinghaus, B. (2015) 'The privatization and marketization of pensions in Europe: a double transformation facing the crisis', *European Policy Analysis* 1(1): 56–73.

EIOPA. (2011) *Risk Mitigation Mechanisms for DC Related Risks*, Frankfurt a. M.: European Insurance and Occupational Pensions Authority. available at https://eiopa.europa.eu/Publications/Reports/Report-on-risk-mitigation-mechanisms-for-DC-related-risks.pdf.

Engelen, E. (2003) 'The logic of funding: European pension restructuring and the dangers of financialisation', *Environment and Planning A* 35(8): 1357–72.

Esping-Andersen, G. (1990) *The Three Worlds of Welfare Capitalism*, Cambridge: Polity Press.

Estévez-Abe, M. (2001) 'The forgotten link: the financial regulation of Japanese pension funds in comparative perspective', in B. Ebbinghaus and P. Manow (eds.), *Comparing Welfare Capitalism: Social Policy and Political Economy in Europe, Japan and the USA*, London: Routledge, pp. 190–214.

FAZ. (1994) 'In Deutschland gibt es keine Aktienkultur', 10 March.

FAZ. (1995) 'FDP: Private Vorsorge stärken', 15 September.

FAZ. (1997a) 'Lebensversicherer kämpfen weiter gegen Pläne zur Besteuerung', 4 June.

FAZ. (1997b) 'Koalition denkt über echte Pensionsfonds nach', 13 November.

FAZ. (1998) 'Arbeitskreis soll Pensionsfonds prüfen', 15 January.

Hacker, J.S. (2004) 'Privatizing risk without privatizing the welfare state: the hidden politics of social policy retrenchment in the United States', *American Political Science Review* 98: 243–60.

Hacker, J.S. (2006) *The Great Risk Shift*, New York: Oxford University Press.

Hacker, J.S., Pierson, P. and Thelen, K. (2015) 'Drift and conversion: hidden faces of institutional change', in J. Mahoney and K. Thelen (eds.), *Advances in Comparative-Historical Analysis*, Cambridge: Cambridge University Press, pp. 180–208.

Hall, P.A. and Soskice, D. (eds) (2001) *Varieties of Capitalism: The Institutional Foundations of Comparative Advantage*, Oxford: Oxford University Press.

Handelsblatt. (2000) 'Ein großer Wurf für die IG Metall', 14 April.

Häusermann, S. (2010) *The Politics of Welfare State Reform in Continental Europe: Modernization in Hard Times*, New York: Cambridge University Press.

Hinrichs, K. and Kangas, O. (2003) 'When is a change big enough to be a system shift? Small system-shifting changes in German and Finnish pension policies', *Social Policy & Administration* 37(6): 573–91.

Huber, E. and Stephens, J.D. (2001). *Development and Crisis of the Welfare State: Parties and Policies in Global Markets*, Chicago: Chicago University Press.

Jackson, G. and Thelen, K. (2015) 'Stability and change in CMEs: corporate governance and industrial relations in Germany and Denmark', in P. Beramendi, S. Häusermann, H. Kitschelt, and H.-P. Kriesi (eds.), *The Politics of Advanced Capitalism*, New York: Cambridge University Press, pp. 305–29.

Jacobs, A.M. (2011) *Governing for the Long Term*, New York, NY: Cambridge University Press.

Kohl, H. (1997) 'Deutsche Wirtschaft weiter im Aufwind – Rede des Bundeskanzlers in Leipzig', 3 November, available at https://www.bundesregierung.de/Content/DE/Bulletin/1990-1999/1997/86-97_Kohl_2.html.

Langley, P. (2008) *The Everyday Life of Global Finance: Saving and Borrowing in Anglo-America*, Oxford: Oxford University Press.

Laux, M. (1995) 'Fonds für Vermögensbildung und Altersvorsorge', *Börsen-Zeitung*, 25 November.

Lazonick, W. and O'Sullivan, M. (2000) 'Maximizing shareholder value: a new ideology for corporate governance', *Economy and Society* 29(1): 13–35.

Leimgruber, M. (2008) *Solidarity without the State? Business and the Shaping of the Swiss Welfare State, 1890–2000*, Cambridge: Cambridge University Press.

Lütz, S. (1998) 'The revival of the nation-state? Stock exchange regulation in an era of globalized financial markets', *Journal of European Public Policy* 5(1): 153–68.

Lütz, S. (2005) 'The finance sector in transition: A motor for economic reform?' *German Politics* 14(2): 140–56.

Mabbett, D. (2012) 'The ghost in the machine: Pension risks and regulatory responses in the United States and the United Kingdom', *Politics & Society* 40(1): 107–29.

Mattern, F., Seifert, W.G., Streit, C.C. and Voth, H.-J. (1997) *Aktie, Arbeit, Aufschwung. Wie der Finanzplatz Wirtschaft und Gesellschaft wieder in Schwung bring*, Frankfurt a. M.: Campus Verlag.

Maurer, R. (2004) 'Institutional investors in Germany: Insurance companies and investment funds', in J.P. Krahnen and R.H. Schmidt (eds.), *The German Financial System*, Oxford: Oxford University Press, pp. 106–38.

McCarthy, M.A., Sorsa, V.-P. and van der Zwan, N. (2016) 'Investment preferences and patient capital: financing, governance, and regulation in pension fund capitalism', *Socio-Economic Review* 14(4): 751–69.

Meyer, T. and Bridgen, P. (2012) 'Business, regulation and welfare politics in liberal capitalism', *Policy & Politics* 40(3): 387–403.

Naczyk, M. (2013) 'Agents of privatization? Business groups and the rise of pension funds in continental Europe', *Socio-Economic Review* 11(3): 441–69.

Naczyk, M. (2016) 'Creating French-style pension funds: Business, labour and the battle over patient capital', *Journal of European Social Policy* 26(3): 205–18.

Naczyk, M. and Seeleib-Kaiser, M. (2015) 'Solidarity against all odds: organized labor and the privatization of pensions in the age of dualization', *Politics & Society* 43(3): 361–84.

Nürk, B. and Schrader, A. (1995) *Von der Pensionsrückstellung zum Pensionsfonds: Eine Chance für den deutschen Finanzmarkt*, Frankfurt a. M.: Deutsche Bank Research, available at https://www.dbresearch.de/PROD/DBR_INTERNET_DE-PROD/PROD0000000000017120/Von_der_Pensionsrückstellung_zum_Pensionsfonds.PDF.

Oelschläger, A. (2009) *Vom Pensions-Sondervermögen zur Riester-Rente: Einleitung des Paradigmenwechsels in der Alterssicherung unter der Regierung Kohl?, ZeS-Arbeitspapier, Nr 02/2009*, Bremen: Zentrum für Sozialpolitik, Universität Bremen.
Orenstein, M.A. (2013) 'Pension privatization: evolution of a paradigm', *Governance* 26 (2): 259–81.
Passow, R. (1996) 'Vermögensaufbau mit Aktienfonds - Plädoyer für die Zulassung von Pensions-Sondervermögen', *Börsen-Zeitung*, 9 November.
Pierson, P. (1994) *Dismantling the Welfare State? Reagan, Thatcher, and the Politics of Retrenchment*, New York: Cambridge University Press.
Pierson, P. (ed) (2001) *The New Politics of the Welfare State*, Oxford: Oxford University Press.
Pierson, P. (2004) *Politics in Time: History, Institutions, and Social Analysis*, Princeton: Princeton University Press.
Quaglia, L. (2011) 'The Politics of insurance regulation and supervision reform in the European Union', *Comparative European Politics* 9(1): 100–22.
Reuters (1994) 'Breuer sieht "Barrieren" gegen die Aktie', 4 July.
Riester, W. (2004) *Mut zur Wirklichkeit*, Düsseldorf: Droste.
Schröder, G. (2001) 'Rede von Bundeskanzler Gerhard Schröder beim XVII. Deutschen Bankentag am 4. April 2001 in Berlin', available at https://www.bundesregierung.de/Content/DE/Bulletin/2001_2007/2001/26-2_Schröder.html.
SPD. (1998) *Arbeit, Innovation und Gerechtigkeit. SPD-Programm für die Bundestagswahl 1998*, Bonn: Vorstand der SPD.
SPD Bundestagsfraktion. (1996) *Antrag der Fraktion der SPD. Stärkung des Kapitalmarktes Deutschland, Förderung des Aktiensparens und Verbesserung der Risikokapitalversorgung*, Bonn: Deutscher Bundestag. Drucksache 13/3783 vom 09.02.96, available at http://dipbt.bundestag.de/doc/btd/13/037/1303784.pdf.
Spiegel Online. (2000) 'Zwickel unter Beschuss - Führungsstreit in der IG Metall', 24 April.
Streeck, W. (2009) *Re-Forming Capitalism: Institutional Change in the German Political Economy*, Oxford: Oxford University Press.
Streeck, W. and Höpner, M. (eds) (2003) *Alle Macht dem Markt? Fallstudien zur Abwicklung der Deutschland AG*, Frankfurt a. M.: Campus Verlag.
SZ. (1996) 'Kampf um die Private Altersvorsorge', 15 May.
SZ. (1997a) 'Pensionsfonds – Neuer Weg zur Betriebsrente', 3 January.
SZ. (1997b) 'Land Hessen für verstärkte private Altersversorgung', 3 April.
SZ. (1999) 'Private Zusatzrente im Visier', 26 June.
SZ. (2000) 'Eichel: Zulassung von Pensionsfonds denkbar', 6 December.
Trampusch, C. (2006a) 'Sequenzorientierte Policy-Analyse: Warum die Rentenreform von Walter Riester nicht an Reformblockaden scheiterte', *Berliner Journal für Soziologie* 16: 55–76.
Trampusch, C. (2006b) 'Industrial relations and welfare states: the different dynamics of retrenchment in Germany and the Netherlands', *Journal of European Social Policy* 16 (2): 121–33.
Trampusch, C. (2018) 'A state-centred explanation of the finance-pension nexus: New Zealand's pension reforms as a typical case', *Social Policy & Administration* 52(1): 343–64.
van der Zwan, N. (2014) 'Making sense of financialization', *Socio-Economic Review* 12(1): 99–129.
von Rosen, R. (1997) *Chancen-Gemeinschaft. Deutschland braucht die Aktie*, München: Wirtschaftsverlag Langen Müller / Herbig.

Wehlau, D. (2009) *Lobbyismus und Rentenreform. Der Einfluss der Finanzdienstleistungsbranche auf die Teil-Privatisierung der Alterssicherung*, Wiesbaden: VS Verlag.

Wiß, T. (2012) *Der Wandel der Alterssicherung in Deutschland: Die Rolle der Sozialpartner*, Wiesbaden: VS Verlag.

Wiß, T. (2015) 'Pension fund vulnerability to the financial market crisis: The role of trade unions', *European Journal of Industrial Relations* 21(2): 131–47.

Wiß, T. (2019) 'Reinforcement of pension financialisation as a response to financial crises in Germany, the Netherlands and the United Kingdom', *Journal of European Public Policy*. https://doi.org/10.1080/13501763.2019.1574870.

EU Pension policy and financialisation: purpose without power?

Waltraud Schelkle

ABSTRACT
This article asks whether the EU's pension policy promotes and achieves financialisation of old age security. Financialisation in this context means financial market integration that, in conjunction with pension reforms in member states, creates a market-based mode of governance for old age security. After an overview of how significant private pension funds have become in the EU, the article takes a most-likely case study of financialisation, the Pan-European Pension Product (PEPP), to see how successful the EU's pension policy proved to be in establishing the PEPP. The findings suggest that EU policymaking in pensions tries to instrumentalise financial market integration for pension provision but this does not necessarily lead to financialisation of old age security. Market integration is a multi-faceted process of creating, emulating and correcting markets that obstructs a single-minded policy thrust like financialisation.

Financialisation and EU pension policy

An early meaning of financialisation portrayed it as an accumulation regime that replaces industrial capitalism and the national models which had evolved with it (van der Zwan 2014: 101–2). The imperative of capitalist activity becomes to privilege financial over real investment by maximising the financially measurable and tradeable shareholder value of corporations. An element of this is that governments are expected 'to promote an "equity culture" in the belief that it will enhance the ability of its own nationals to compete internationally' (Dore 2008: 1098). While the focus is on nation-states, in particular the US, European integration could also be portrayed as a handmaiden of financialisation (Engelen 2003: 1359; Pochet 2003: 50). It can transform national accumulation regimes by opening up new business opportunities for transnational financial firms (Hassel et al. 2019): after all, market integration happens by harmonising national legislation and regulation that ensures the freedom of capital and financial services. The latest idea of a Capital Markets Union (CMU) is a project with a financialising potential.

The proposition of financialisation is both objectionable and tempting when it comes to old age security, which is the theme of this special issue. Pensions are a sensitive area for the EU, because old age security is a prerogative of national welfare states which can be closed off for competition, to be Europeanised only at the margins (Schelkle 2013). Institutions, eg national tax treatment of pension savings and their stakeholders, middle class voters or organised labour market parties, have often proved formidable hurdles to European integration of pension provisions. But there are also strong incentives to make financial market integration and an 'equity culture' serve old age security. If private finance would offer attractive pension products, it could help to solve two problems that the EU Commission has long emphasised: first, it might reduce governments' expensive obligation to secure living standards in old age and, second, it might diversify longevity risks and thereby stabilise the returns on pension savings across member states. This makes financialising initiatives an attractive proposition to the Commission, member state executives, and sometimes even social partners.

But how sustained and ultimately successful are attempts at promoting financialisation in European integration? The literature has noted that financialisation is often a state-sponsored process (Boyer 2000; Krippner 2011: 2; Natali 2018: 459). Financial sector interests are likely to support pension financialisation through market integration. However, and this is key to my analysis and argument, market integration combines market making with regulation. Most of the financialisation literature suggests that regulation will not stop financialisation from progressing regardless (Berry 2016; Engelen 2003). The theoretical background to this is that Classical Political Economy sees big business (here: cross-border finance) and politics as prone to collusion in self-serving ways. However, state actors, including supranational technocrats, may pursue their own agenda when promoting market integration and stabilisation, here: financialised governance of old age security. Keynesian political economy has explained this role of the state in a long and inclusive list of scholarly work, explicitly so in Weir and Skocpol (1985) and Hall (1989). State-sponsored market integration typically entails a good deal of social regulation of markets to satisfy concerns of various constituencies but also to protect the public purse against exposure (Schelkle 2012; Tuytens 2018). This agenda can even be supported by parts of the financial sector, for their own reasons: integrative measures can create unwanted competition and certain market failures pose existential threats to some but not others. This heterogeneity of financial interests, combined with policymakers' sensibilities for market failure, render financialisation of pensions a much less straightforward proposition than the financialisation literature has it.

Market integration can mean at least three different things that do not serve financial interests uniformly: first, the creation of cross-border markets invariably leads to some domestic business losing out; second, the emulation of market principles like competition can undermine business opportunities created by state-guaranteed property rights; and, third, market correction may eliminate exploitative or discriminatory practices on which business once thrived. The next section outlines in more detail how the European Commission pursues all three of these elements with respect to cross-border markets for pensions and follows this up in the case study of a Pan European Pension Product (PEPP). This unpacking of what market integration entails helps us to understand how European integration may, but does not have to, lead to financialisation of old age security. It is an empirical question. My working hypothesis is that EU-sponsored financial market integration for pensions does not lead to pension financialisation in the sense that the accumulation of pensions rights becomes financialised (Boyer 2000) or a risk-return calculus and individual responsibility will become priorities (Langley 2008: 70) relative to social policy and insurance concerns; even some financial actors may express such concerns, possibly for self-serving, anti-competitive reasons.

The next section describes the theoretical approach for analysing financialisation in the Keynesian tradition of political economy and relates it to the relevant literature. It is followed by a brief look at the evidence for a trend towards financialisation in the sense of pension privatisation in EU member states. Next, the article takes up a most likely case study of financialisation, the creation of an EU-standardised personal pension plan, which was a financial sector initiative that the Commission turned into an attempt at positive integration of pension markets. The conclusions discuss whether the EU is a purposeful agent of pension financialisation and which the most important limitations are on its power to act in this way.

The concept of pension financialisation

The literature on accumulation and growth regimes (Aglietta 2000: 156–8; Engelen 2003) considered whether the ageing of rich countries is the structural force behind a self-fulfilling dynamic of rising demand for financial assets and rising asset prices, generating financial cycles and establishing the central bank as 'the linchpin of the whole financial structure' (Aglietta 2000: 156). The notion of 'pension fund capitalism' (Clark 2000) studied the investment behaviour of private pension funds given that they may exercise an increasing role in corporate governance of non-financial firms. Financial sociologists and IPE scholars of the 'everyday life of global finance' (Langley 2008: ch.4) considered whether an increasing share of privately funded pensions and a variable rate of return (Defined Contribution, DC) – instead of pensions that come with a promised benefit (Defined Benefit, DB) – would turn citizens from insurance-seeking savers into yield-craving investors.

In this article, I will argue that financial expansion and cross-border integration is necessary but not sufficient for the diagnosis of financialisation. I propose a theoretical framework that can make sense of the already existing comparative evidence that shows symptoms of pension financialisation in very different welfare states, while others fail to show such symptoms despite the rise of finance; hence, time-honoured regime typologies will not do.[1] This framework is based in the Keynesian tradition of political economy, which is opposed to historical determinism and interested in policy choices, in contrast to the original financialisation literature in a classical (Marxist) tradition (van der Zwan 2014: 101–2). Keynesian political economy has as its central tenet that financial markets are the gatekeepers to investment and employment in capitalist economies. Notwithstanding this pivotal role of financial markets, the Keynesian tradition also maintains that financial markets are prone to failures and, occasionally, to systemic failure, as in the Great Depression. Finance needs the visible hand of government to stabilise markets although the necessity does not guarantee that the hand is always willing and able to help. This insight made Keynes, the economist, also a political economist, for instance in his newspaper articles on 'the economic consequences of Mr Churchill' in 1925. Ideas, enshrined in existing institutions, can have a more or less retarding effect on policy change but they also make state action more than the result of societal pressures (Widmaier 2016: 10–11). This allows 'the role of the state enlightened by Keynesian reason [to be] that of a great "reconciler" of individual and collective interests', to use Mann's (2016: 124) ironic but insightful characterisation. Keynesian political economists, from Weir and Skocpol (1985) to Eichengreen (2007), have shown that even conservative administrations adopted ever more responsibilities and business-friendly governments refrained from endorsing laissez faire, especially when faced with disastrous market failure.

We can take these insights further by asking what role state actors like the EU Commission and business play in the rise of finance. In contrast to the Keynesian optimism that state intervention and activism tend to be desirable and feasible, the financialisation literature has pointed out early on that state-sponsorship was implicated in bringing about a problematic dominance of financial-commercial over socio-economic considerations (Krippner 2011). In a similar vein, this article disentangles the meaning of European market integration to find out how actors interested in integration promote financialisation but also why they may fail to do so (Grahl and Teague 2005: 1008–10).

There is, first, the creation of (cross-border) markets for pension savings and longevity insurance where there were none before. Financial regulation of pension provision, such as harmonised standards for prudential supervision, is one main instrument for creating cross-border markets as providers can then use the licence in the home state as a passport to markets in other member states. A parallel EU standard, in addition to national regimes, can also create a new transnational market. But market opportunities for some often come at the cost of others, for instance pitch banks against insurers with regulatory compromises limiting the opportunities for both.

Secondly, the emulation of market principles in occupational and public schemes serves to foster integration of very different systems. The (ex)portability of pension rights can be seen as the emulation of market principles in statutory pensions, facilitating mobility of workers competing for jobs in other member states. The emphasis on fiscal sustainability in an ageing society can also be seen as a market emulating thrust since it tries to instil a hard budget constraint on public finances, analogous to constraints faced by commercial providers. This emulation of market principles can contribute to financialisation in the third sense of the individualisation of risks. But it can also undermine business opportunities in member states, notably where demand for private pension plans is propped up by tax-subsidies, inhibiting the expansion of other pension plans.

Finally, in line with established evidence on market liberalisation (Vogel 1996), regulation tends to be introduced over time to correct failing markets, typically in the wake of some scandal or investigative media reporting. In fact, we should expect tight regulation especially in markets for social services because member states already treat this as a sphere where market correction is required. Discrimination due to asymmetric information, on grounds of nationality and gender, is a relevant example for market failure in insurance generally and pensions specifically. While market correction can help insurance markets for longevity to function and provide established firms a competitive advantage, it can also rein them in if they thrived mainly on excessive fees and risk-shifting to ignorant customers.

Two questions arise: first, what exactly are the drivers of financialisation? Van der Zwan (2014: 106) notes that the forces behind financialisation as an accumulation regime are often left in the abstract. One of the few exceptions, Krippner's historical-sociological study of the US, identified state officials dealing with policy dilemmas (Krippner 2011: 22), a finding that is perfectly in line with Keynesian political economy. This article examines whether the EU Commission was indeed the key driver, and considers its relationship to organised financial interests. Second, how contentious were apparent changes in the governance of old age security? While market creation and emulation is always popular with business, market correction should be contested by business although not in principle since regulation is an element of competition (Vogel 1996). The Keynesian vantage point leads me to expect that political concerns about market failure that cause political embarrassment and impose adverse distributional outcomes on core constituencies can easily derail a one-dimensional drive towards pension financialisation, however attractive the latter may appear at first.

Financialisation and national pension systems

Member states' pension systems developed under a complex set of influences of which EU pension policy is but one. Engelen (2003: 1357–8) claimed that private funding of old age security could come to rival public provisions. The most recent available OECD data on the significance of private pensions among 22 EU member states shows that Denmark and the Netherlands have accumulated private pension funds worth double their GDP, followed in some distance by the UK, Sweden and Finland (OECD 2017: Tables 8.1 and 8.4). With the exception of the UK, one would not expect these political economies to be the paragons of Anglo-American pension financialisation. Member states also vary considerably in terms of coverage.

The level of public and private gross payouts[2] suggests that only the Netherlands, Sweden and the UK qualify as having financialised pension systems. Private funds contribute a sizeable share to old age security only in these three countries, i.e., between more than half (Netherlands) and more than a third (Sweden) of all benefit-expenditure (OECD 2017: Tables 7.3 and 7.4). The fact that these three countries represent very different welfare state configurations supports to some extent the claim of financialisation scholars that it can be a common, transnational trend.

The relative immaturity of private funds could be responsible for the low number of 'financialised' countries, especially in Central and Eastern European countries. A better way may therefore be to look at relative growth of public and private benefits. The most recent data for 2000–2013, during which new member states had time to build up private funds, shows that out of the 22 EU members for which the OECD (2017) provides data, six experienced financialisation (Austria, the Czech Republic, Germany, the Netherlands, the Slovak Republic, and Sweden) in the sense that private pension payouts rose faster than public pensions. Only Germany reduced spending on public pensions and built up, from a very low level, a private layer. But another six member states show the opposite, increasing public spending while private pension benefit–expenditure fell (e.g., Denmark, from 2.4% of GDP in 2000 to 1.0% in 2013). It should be noted that a small drop in payouts looks large, given low levels of private pensions in most countries (eg a decline in France from 0.3% of GDP in 2000 to 0.2% in 2013 amounts to a decrease by one third).[3] The OECD (2017: 144) notes that, on average, private pension benefits are stable since around 2000, after they increased from 1.0% of GDP in 1990 to 1.5%. This includes occupational and personal pensions.

A cross-border market for personal pensions[4]

This section looks at an initiative by European banks and the European Commission to lend personal pensions a helping hand. The focus on these actors stacks the cards against my working hypothesis: the financialisation literature suggests that they should be the most single-minded promoters of financialisation. My conceptual framework outlined above suggested that market integration does not mean a single direction of travel towards financialisation. So when would market integration in practice mean financialisation? The case study does not speak to financialisation as shareholder value maximisation in corporate governance. But financialisation in the other two meanings is potentially observable. A financialised regime of *pension accumulation* would manifest itself in (a) markets for Pan-European personal pensions being created through regulatory competition among national regimes; (b) market principles being emulated by fiscally prudent support for annuities markets; and (c) markets being corrected only through low prudential standards. Financialisation as *socialisation of individual investors* would be indicated by (d) market creation that consists of a shift from DB to DC pensions, (e) market emulation through unlimited plan options, and (f) market correction only through low standards of consumer protection. The guiding principle of the assessment is that rule-based integration contributes to financialised pension accumulation if it replaces a public policy logic with a commercial logic (eg competition rather than wide equitable risk-pooling, lifelong income through annuities markets rather than pay-as-you-go pensions) and projects individuals as active investors calculating risk and return (of a DC pension) who can make choices over EU-wide offers.

The plan to create a standardised EU-wide personal pension scheme, the PEPP started out, in the mid-2000s, as an initiative by the European Financial Services Round Table (EFR), which is an organisation of currently 23 CEOs of the biggest banks and insurers in Europe. The EFR asked for an EU regime parallel to the then 25 national legal regimes that governed personal pensions. A parallel regime requires the Commission to abandon the usual harmonisation approach. The EFR initially did not get 'much applause from Brussels' as Nijssen (2006), the former global head of pensions at ING Group, put it in an online journal of the pension industry. He summarises the EFR's motivation straightforwardly:

> The EFR rightly states that arranging pan-European pensions by harmonising the national legislation of 25 EU countries is virtually a mission impossible. So why not take a short cut by having an EU-wide "26th regime" framework with only a limited number of basic principles that are acceptable to all member states?

About a year later, on 8 May 2007, the (Ecofin) Council of Economic and Finance ministers ended with conclusions on 'Ageing and financial markets' that invited the EFR to specify their proposal. This encouraging response was not necessarily expected since the significance of private pensions in member states is negligible for many, as we have seen above. The EFR report in June reframed the issue of an EU-wide pension scheme and sounded as if written by the ministers themselves: responding to the 'demographic challenge' meant that entitlements of tomorrow's pensioners will be reduced and a 'pensions gap' would arise that personal (and occupational) pensions could fill (EFR 2007: 4). This pensions gap rationale would later be echoed by the Commission when it asked EIOPA[5] to advise on the PEPP (EIOPA 2014: 4–5). The original EFR proposal for an expedited legislative process for Single Market legislation on pensions was only the last of six reasons for why a PEPP is needed. We can see in this the mirror image of the well-known state-sponsorship of financialisation, ie organised financial interests adapting to and sponsoring a public agenda.

The EFR report analysed the differences in personal pension legislation in five different countries (Czech Republic, France, Germany, Italy and the Netherlands) to identify obstacles to an EU-wide scheme. At several points, the authors deny that different tax treatments would constitute a major impediment. Tax harmonisation is anathema to most member states and any attempt in this direction would have killed the proposal.[6] On the subject of tax subsidies to old-age provisions, the report resorts to the principle of non-discrimination, ie 'any Member State may limit the tax deductibility or tax incentives given to contributions to a Pan-European pension plan, as long as these limitations do not constitute unequal treatment in comparison with other pension plans'. (EFR 2007: 35) It also proposed a minimum of old age security, in the form of nominal value protection: '[t]he provider has to offer at least an option in which the value of the plan at the retirement is not less than all the contributions paid minus expenses (including the cost of the additional risks covered)'. (EFR 2007: 18, 33) The deduction of expenses would make this a weak form of nominal guarantee, and EIOPA as well as the European Parliament later wanted to cap these expenses or have the principal guaranteed before the deduction of fees (European Parliament 2018: A63). Such guarantees create a default risk for insurers because they create nominally fixed obligations while the corresponding assets have a variable nominal value. The EFR report thus conceded the need for consumer protection which comes at a risk for the pension provider. It is an ambiguous (protective and risky) move in terms of financialisation.

Fast forward to 2011–12, when the Commission launched a White Paper on 'safe, sustainable and adequate pensions'. This was obviously against the background of massively increased public debt in the wake of the financial crisis but also considerable risks to pension funds, which had lost up to 25% of their value at the bottom of the stock market crash (Laboul 2011). At a public event organised by EIOPA, a Commission official gave four reasons for the initiative on behalf of three DGs (EIOPA 2014: 4): first, care for the old age security of migrants, the number of which had increased from 2.1% of the labour force in 2005–3.1% in 2012; second, adapt regulation in line with 'the general shift towards individual responsibility for securing retirement income (DB to DC)'; third, address various market failures so that governance and risk management are dealt with adequately in all member states; and fourth, compensate low or declining replacement rates of public and occupational schemes (the 'pensions gap').

A central claim of the Commission was that these multiple objectives would be served by market integration. Given the background of a financial crisis, this claim was hardly self-evident. Furthermore, it was argued that, for pensions, the best strategy for integration would be to create a so-called 2nd regime product: in other words, to set out common standards for a scheme with a European 'kitemark' that would be acceptable in all member states and fully transferable across borders. This was in line with the original EFR proposal of a parallel regime and strongly supported by the financial services sector (EFR 2007, 2011) and by EIOPA, the financial supervisor for pension funds. The latter argued that 'a 2nd regime product instead of a Directive harmonising European standards is the best solution to keep the costs low, by avoiding legal uncertainty and gold-plating by Member States'. (EIOPA 2016: 67) The Commission may not have been enthusiastic at first, yet the PEPP follows the EU approach in occupational pensions. IORPs standardised an organisational form, ie cross-border providers of occupational pensions. Both IORPs and PEPPs are designed to complete the Single Market for longevity insurance, with the capacity to pool risks across member states even if all citizens were immobile. One can see in this approach an attempt at introducing a financialised regime of pension accumulation in that it puts competitive pressure on national regulation, a concern that was later expressed by PensionsEurope (2018: 9, 11).[7]

EIOPA's vision for the PEPP stressed the importance of counteracting market inefficiencies and failure on the supply side: scale economies and competition had to be increased so as to raise financial returns; products made trustworthy; transparency and information requirements raised (EIOPA 2014: 6). Given cognitive biases on the consumer side, EIOPA advocated a 'caveat venditor' (sellers beware) principle, as had been suggested for auto-enrolment to occupational pensions in the UK (EIOPA 2016: 69–70). If something goes wrong, pension providers have to prove that they fulfilled their obligations rather than the client-savers having to prove that they were not made aware of the risks. Clearly, EIOPA did not see individuals as investors who could be left to their own devices.

Insurers were not enamoured by this approach. Insurance Europe (2016) argued that the proposals did not take the specificity of pension products sufficiently into account; the PEPP was more like an ordinary savings product than a pension. It criticised provisions that would allow consumers to switch frequently and the proposed information requirements which were the same as for investment products, covering the rate of return, but not tax treatment, the payout phase, and the biometric risks. Last but not least, the organised insurers criticised that the EU proposal did not insist on an option that would deliver a life-long income, notably annuities (Insurance Europe 2016: 5). In other words, the insurance association insisted that a pensions product is different from individual savings accounts insofar it provides insurance for longevity and possibly survivors. By neglecting these differences, the Commission proposal took the path of pension financialisation.

But the lobby group of European insurers also objected to the prescription of a default option that guarantees the capital paid in and wanted instead an unlimited number of investment options; nor did the insurers association support any cap on costs and charges (Insurance Europe 2016: 6, 7). In other words, Insurance Europe would have liked a proposal that would strengthen the insurance industry's competitive advantage as Europe's major personal pensions and annuities provider vis-à-vis other financial institutions, while giving insurers maximum commercial flexibility. This was in contrast to PensionsEurope (2018: 14), which supported limited investment options, taking their long-term impact on 'environmental, social and governance factors' into account instead of problematising them as a commercial constraint.

The final proposal for a PEPP was published by the Commission in June 2017. The European Parliament discussed hundreds of amendments; and the Council gave a mandate for negotiation with the Parliament on 19 June 2018.[8] Senior officials in the Commission stress that this was supported by three Directorates, for Social Affairs, the Internal Market and Competition. The emphasis shifted to the contribution that such a pension product could make to the CMU. The Commission had been emboldened by a Council resolution of 28 June 2016, five days after the Brexit referendum, to pursue CMU, originally a pet project of the UK government. Taking this cue from the Council, the PEPP became a vehicle for facilitating long-term investment in the depressed EU economy. It would presumably do so by reducing the need for maturity transformation through matching long-term savings, by reducing their costs through standardisation, and by helping 'them pool contributions from different national markets' (Commission 2017a: 3). This vision was directly opposed by PensionsEurope (2018: 7): 'PEPPs cannot be considered as pure investment products, as they are connected with social policy in general and pension policy in particular, both prerogatives of the Member States'. The Council position paper for the final negotiations would reflect this prerogative by requesting that PEPPs be authorised nationally rather than supranationally (Council 2018: para's 14, 56).

The proposal includes a mandatory safe option, with nominal value protection, among a maximum of five investment options. The Commission's version is not inflation-indexed. As the European Federation of Investors and Financial Services Users notes in its contribution to the consultation: 2% inflation over 40 years wipes out 55% of the value of pension savings (Better Finance 2017). The European Parliament (2018: A130) requires a safe option to be inflation-indexed and include fees. Even so, a 'safe' default option arguably rules out a pure DC scheme.

The Commission proposal contains detailed information requirements and, in Article 48, caps on the costs of switching providers to 1.5% of the balance to be switched (Commission 2017a: 8, 13). This figure is much higher than any explicit switching fees prevailing in member states (OECD 2017: 161) and the European Parliament has sought to lower it to 0.5% (EP 2018: A152). The proposal enumerates all the types of providers it wants to encourage to take up PEPP, insurers being only one of them (Commission 2017a: 3). It stresses that self-employed and even unemployed citizens can thus save for their retirement. The Commission adopted the approach of the regulator, EIOPA, with its financial-supervisory attention to market failure. The proposals are oriented to correcting asymmetric information and misperception on the consumer side, and lack of competition and transparency of terms and conditions on the supply side.[9]

However, the proposal contains very little on decumulation. It does not prescribe an option that provides for lifelong income and leaves the regulation of payout options to member states' national legislation (Articles 51–2). To prescribe more would have entered the contested area of social policy and tax harmonisation which the Commission shied away from. Annuities markets are under-developed in most member states because they depend on underpinning from government.[10] Governments must share in the longevity risk because private insurers have the same problems as pension policymakers in estimating the continuous rise in life expectancy. But if private annuity providers get it wrong, as they have in the past, they may go bust. Governments can support annuities markets by, for instance, issuing more long-term bonds. But these are costly in public debt management terms as investors demand higher yields (Stewart 2007: 7). Moreover, governments are reluctant to share longevity risks with private insurers as they are already overexposed to these risks through their public pension systems. Last but not least, governments need to make annuities attractive, eg through tax incentives, or mandatory, as there is otherwise an adverse selection problem: predominantly socio-economic groups with a long life expectancy choose annuities (Stewart 2007: 9). But enforcing annuities in this way would expose governments to the critique that they force people with health conditions or shorter life expectancy, typically correlated with lower income, into unfavourable insurance contracts that benefit disproportionately the worried well. One of the most controversial requests of the European Parliament (2018: A34, Art.52(2)) is therefore that the 'basic option' should contain a mandatory fixed annuity of 35%. This element of pension financialisation – providing a life-long income through financial markets – is at cross-purposes with the risk appetite of governments. This prevents the development of more complete markets for old age security.

One grave limitation of attempts to create a cross-border pension product is the lack of provision for a safety net for failing pension providers. A pension provider's default is arguably a remote possibility, but a severe stock market crash that diminishes the value of assets, when a large share of obligations consist of the safe (nominally guaranteed) investment option have made this a quantifiable probability. Article 49 concerns only the protection of savers in the case of financial losses short of the PEPP provider's default. Chapter IX on supervision does not say anything about default of a large cross-border pension provider, except that EIOPA would have some conciliation role if national supervisors cannot agree (Article 56).

The PEPP proposal shares this blind spot with the CMU initiative that assumes stock market investors can bear their losses, even though the experience of the financial crisis in 2007–9 suggests otherwise. Regulations had to be suspended at the height of the crisis so that pension providers did not become technically insolvent: the crash of asset prices pushed their reserve holdings below statutory levels and made returns plummet (OECD 2015).

This omission is rather striking. From the perspective of Keynesian Political Economy, whereby state actors have some autonomy in undertaking welfare-enhancing market regulation, the best explanation is ideational (Hall 1989; Tuytens 2018). The Commission remains attached to a pre-crisis paradigm of financial regulation. The proposal asks for investment of pension savings according to the relatively low standard of the 'prudent person rule' (Article 33). The responsibility of supervising compliance with these stipulations lies with national supervisory authorities and the prudent person rule makes it very hard to avoid a race to the bottom as it can mean different things in different jurisdictions (Haverland 2007). The European Parliament has not challenged this low standard of prudential supervision, although it has stipulated considerably more protection for 'PEPP savers', notably that the conditions in the 'basic' option for 'the accumulation phase [...] shall be no less favourable than applicable national rules' (European Parliament 2018: Art.40). Although it is hard to see how to operationalise this amendment, it is a clear signal against a permissive interpretation of prudential principles.

We can thus conclude this section on the PEPP by noting that the proposal has changed its thrust quite a bit over the lifetime of its gestation. The following overview (Table 1) summarises the findings.

The summary shows elements of financialisation in the design of the PEPP but overall more counter-evidence. First of all, rules that would have allowed

Table 1. Findings of the PEPP case study.

Meanings of financialisation Elements of market integration	Accumulation regime	Individual socialisation
Creation	(a) ✓ Regulatory competition through parallel EU regime: 2nd regime	(d) [X] Shift from DB to DC pension: safe option with [vague] nominal guarantee
Emulation	(b) X Fiscally prudent support for annuities markets: no support granted by member states	(e) X Unlimited plan options: five options
Correction	(c) ✓ Low prudential standards: prudent person rule	(f) X Limited consumer protection: caveat venditor principle

Note: ✓ stands for a positive finding of financialisation, X for a negative finding.

for a relatively financialised accumulation regime (parallel transnational regime, low standard of prudent person rule) were undermined by rules for consumer protection that cater to individuals as risk-averse savers (no pure DC but an option with a weak nominal guarantee, limited options, caveat venditor principle); the amendments of the European Parliament will make this protective thrust even more pronounced. Furthermore, even within the provisions for a financialised accumulation regime, market emulation did not work in favour of market creation because support for annuities markets was not to be had in fiscally prudent terms. The trilogue negotiations are likely to accommodate the Council position by introducing more national prerogatives because PEPPs are part of social law; in return, the European Parliament is likely to introduce more stringent consumer protection. My erstwhile conclusion is that the financial industry, especially the initiating banks, will not show much interest in offering the PEPP.

Conclusion: purpose without power?

The evidence provided above suggests that there is no sign of a pervasive shift to private pension funding in EU member states. The rise of pension finance in the 1990s has levelled off in 2000, pension assets and coverage rates in most EU member states do not suggest relevance and salience. Public pensions have also continued to rise (OECD 2017: 143–4). But the Council responded encouragingly to an initiative by organised interests in European banking for an EU-wide personal pension product which, after initial reluctance, three important Directorates in the Commission dutifully supported. The article traced the evolution of this proposal to its fruition in 2017 and the onset of the legislative process up to September 2018.

Even this most likely case for pension financialisation does not find it. The relevant literature interprets limited evidence as a matter of time: the accumulation of private pension claims and the shift to DC schemes will make financialisation ever more prevalent (Engelen 2003: 1369–70; Langley 2008: 87;

Natali 2018: 459–60). My theoretical framework, applied to an admittedly small case study, leads me to a principled objection to such projections. It can be formulated in contrast to Posner and Véron (2010) who see 'power without purpose' in the EU's approach to financial regulation. I see a purpose, financial market integration, which is so multi-faceted, however, that it does not translate into straightforward financialisation. And the power of the EU is rather limited because, contrary to what the financialisation literature says, finance as a 'power resource' is divided, here: between banks, insurers and pension funds. The pushback tends to come from national state actors using this division.

The EU has a pension policy that reaches all three layers of old age security (public, occupational, personal) through rules-driven market integration (Anderson 2015: ch.4; Schelkle 2013). But they are subject to differentiated regulation, as Keynesian political economy would lead one to expect. Such differentiation could be observed in our case study. The initial emphasis of an EU-wide personal pension plan was on market creation, through a parallel regime that promised a short-cut around regulatory harmonisation. As preparations progressed, the mandatory reports by the pension regulator EIOPA added a heavy dose of market correction that made the entire policy proposal much less attractive for banks and insurers. The European Parliament and, interestingly, PensionsEurope pushes further in that direction. Finally, the real or perceived budget constraints of member states, an element of market emulation that EU fiscal surveillance keenly pursues, ruled out the extension of tax subsidies to the new Pan-European plan as well as public support for attractive features like a market-based provision of life-long income.

Even if market integration would point in one direction, the lack of power is another obstacle to financialisation as a policy agenda. The main stakeholders of a financialised EU pension policy look for market opportunities, first and foremost, rather than for a stabilising market infrastructure. The CEOs sitting around the EFR clearly saw an untapped source of business for their members and lost interest as ever more market correction made it into the proposal. The critical response of the European insurance association indicated that they noticed the opening up of competition in a market segment where their members dominated. But even though the organised insurers raised valid points against pension financialisation in the original proposal of the banking lobby, their own intervention came across as self-serving and opportunistic. The lack of legitimate supporting interests limits the power of the EU to instrumentalise financial markets for social policy purposes. The Council, supported by PensionsEurope (2018), requested more control over this process exactly because social policy is a national competence which in turn constrains the Commission in its available instruments. The EU's exclusively regulatory power is ultimately limited power because the Commission cannot engage in fiscal sponsorship of pension financialisation through tax incentives (Commission 2017b) or safety nets.

Financial interests can still exert influence, of course. The mixed evidence shown in the summary above could be read in this way. Naczyk (2013: 445) reviews a number of studies, which show that private insurers have historically always lobbied in favour of containing public pensions. While the evidence from the OECD (2017) suggests that they have not been very effective in this respect, the insurance elements of the PEPP indicate that they may be heard in other respects. But the financial industry did not speak with one voice. This observation expands on the argument of Naczyk (2013): he finds that 'capital' is not of one mind when it comes to pension privatisation, employers can be ambivalent while financial firms support it. The PEPP case study suggests that financial firms disagree once we get to the details of pension privatisation and the compromises can neutralise some of their influence.

More research is needed on how finance actually exerts influence, in comparison with other collective actors (Natali 2018). Even the most painstaking research on the US (Krippner 2011: ch.3; Langley 2008: ch.4) is about the unintended consequence of policy changes that empowered finance, not about how finance used its power in bringing about financialising policy changes. If financial market integration is to be harnessed for old age security, the EU may have to cultivate institutionally a network of diverse stakeholders (European Parliament 2018: A147). But again, the representation of diverse interests would work against financialisation becoming the sole logic governing pension funding. Neither purpose nor power make the EU a force for pension financialisation.

Notes

1. In addition to the contributions in this issue, Belfrage (2008: 290) finds that Swedish households have not turned from passive savers to active investors; Mabbett (2012) shows that savers have to be 'nudged' to join private pension schemes in Anglo-America; and Natali (2018: 459–60) notes varying degrees of financialisation in Italy, the Netherlands and the UK.
2. Gross means before taxes on benefits and without tax subsidies for pension savings because neither is comparable across countries (OECD 2017: 144).
3. The other four member states for 'de-financialisation' were Belgium, Finland, Italy, and the UK (OECD 2017: Tables 7.3 and 7.4).
4. I am grateful for background interviews with Per Eckefeldt and Luigi Giamboni (DG Ecfin), on 4 July 2017. They are not responsible for any misunderstandings and the following is strictly my interpretation.
5. EIOPA is the European Insurance and Occupational Pensions Authority, a regulatory agency created for the Single Market in financial services.
6. Similarly, labour and social law have seriously obstructed the proliferation of pan-European occupational pension funds, IORPs (Guardiancich 2011: 24–5).

7. PensionsEurope represents national associations of occupational and personal funded pension providers.
8. Rust (2018). The Council had to overcome divisions regarding the question whether IORPs should be allowed to offer PEPPs; the compromise was that those who can offer personal pensions under national law should also be allowed to offer PEPPs. The Economic and Monetary Affairs Committee of the European Parliament finalised its position in September 2018 and the trilogue negotiations were to start around the time of writing.
9. However, biometric risks, such as survivor benefits, can be covered by a PEPP which favours insurance providers (Commission 2017a: 13, Art.42).
10. The only OECD countries that have developed annuities markets are Australia, Canada, Switzerland, the US and the UK (Stewart 2007: 3n). The UK market collapsed after 2015 when compulsory annuitisation of tax-subsidised pension savings was abolished.

Disclosure statement

No potential conflict of interest was reported by the author.

Funding

This research was funded by the German Federal Ministry of Education and Research, BMBF (Bundesministerium für Bildung und Forschung). [grant number 01UF1508].

References

Aglietta, M. (2000) 'Shareholder value and corporate governance: some tricky questions', *Economy and Society* 29(1): 146–59.
Anderson, K.M. (2015) *Social Policy in the European Union*, Basingstoke: Palgrave MacMillan.
Belfrage, C. (2008) 'Towards 'universal financialisation' in Sweden?', *Contemporary Politics* 14(3): 277–96.
Berry, C. (2016) 'Austerity, ageing and the financialisation of pensions policy in the UK', *British Politics* 11(1): 2–25.
Better Finance (2017) *Feedback from: better finance*. Available at https://ec.europa.eu/info/law/better-regulation/initiatives/com-2017-343/feedback/F6960_en.
Boyer, R. (2000) 'Is a finance-led growth regime a viable alternative to Fordism? A preliminary analysis', *Economy and Society* 29(1): 111–45.
Clark, G.L. (2000) *Pension Fund Capitalism*, New York: Oxford University Press.
Commission (2017a) *Proposal for a Regulation of the European Parliament and of the Council on a pan-European Personal Pension Product (PEPP). (29.6.2017) COM(2017) 343 Final*, Brussels: European Commission.

Commission (2017b) *Commission Recommendation of 29.6.2017 on the Tax Treatment of Personal Pension Products, Including the Pan-European Personal Pension Product. C (2017) 4393 Final*, Brussels: European Commission.

Council (2018) *Regulation on Pan-European Pension Product – Mandate for Negotiations with the European Parliament. 9975/18. 16 June 2018*, Brussels: Council of the European Union.

Dore, R. (2008) 'Financialization of the global economy', *Industrial and Corporate Change* 17(6): 1097–112.

EFR (2007) *Pan-European Pension Plans. From Concept to Action. (June)* Brussels: European Financial Services Roundtable.

EFR (2011) *EFRP Position Paper. 2011/0296 (4 May)*, Brussels: European Federation for Retirement Provision. Available at http://www.pensionsEurope.eu/system/files/2012%20-%20EFRP%20Position%20Paper%20%20MiFID%20II_MiFIR%20-%20final%20-%202012-05-04.pdf

Eichengreen, B.J. (2007) *The European Economy Since 1945: Coordinated Capitalism and Beyond*, Princeton: Princeton University Press.

EIOPA (2014) *Towards an EU Single Market for Personal Pensions. An EIOPA Preliminary Report to COM. EIOPA_BoS_14/029*, Frankfurt a.M.: European Insurance and Occupational Pensions Authority.

EIOPA (2016) *EIOPA's Advice on the Development of an EU Single Market for Personal Pension Products (PPP). EIOPA-16/457*, Frankfurt a.M.: European Insurance and Occupational Pensions Authority.

Engelen, E. (2003) 'The logic of funding European pension restructuring and the dangers of financialisation', *Environment and Planning A* 35(8): 1357–72.

European Parliament (2018) Report on the proposal for a regulation of the European Parliament and of the Council on a Pan-European Personal Pension Product (PEPP), A8-0278/2018. 6 September. Brussels: Committee on Economic and Monetary Afffairs.

Grahl, J. and Teague, P. (2005) 'Problems of financial integration in the EU', *Journal of European Public Policy* 12(6): 1005–21.

Guardiancich, I. (2011) 'Pan-European pension funds: current situation and future prospects', *International Social Security Review* 64(1): 15–36.

Hall, P.A. (1989) *The Political Power of Economic Ideas: Keynesianism Across Nations*, Princeton, NJ: Princeton University Press.

Hassel, A., Naczyk, M. and Wiß, T. (2019) 'The political economy of pension financialisation: public policy response to the crisis', *Journal of European Public Policy* [= SI Paper, Details to be Added by Editors/Producer].

Haverland, M. (2007) 'When the welfare state meets the regulatory state: EU occupational pension policy', *Journal of European Public Policy* 14(6): 886–904.

Insurance Europe (2016) *Insurance Europe's Comments on Pan-European Personal Pension Products. PERS-.SAV-16-026*, Brussels: Insurance Europe aisbl

Krippner, G. R. (2011) *Capitalizing on Crisis: the Political Origins of the Rise of Finance*, Cambridge, MA and London, England: Harvard University Press.

Laboul, A. (2011) 'Pension fund assets climb back to pre-crisis levels but full recovery still uncertain', *Pension Markets in Focus* (July), issue 8, OECD.

Langley, P. (2008) *The Everyday Life of Global Finance: Saving and Borrowing in Anglo-America*, Oxford and New York: Oxford University Press.

Mabbett, D. (2012) 'The ghost in the machine: pension risks and regulatory responses in the United States and the United Kingdom', *Politics & Society* 40(1): 107–29.

Mann, G. (2016) 'Keynes resurrected? Saving civilization, again and again', *Dialogues in Human Geography* 6(2): 119–34.
Naczyk, M. (2013) 'Agents of privatization? Business groups and the rise of pension funds in Continental Europe', *Socio-Economic Review* 11(3): 441–69.
Natali, D. (2018) 'Occupational pensions in Europe: Trojan horse of financialization?', *Social Policy & Administration* 52(2): 449–62.
Nijssen, J. (2006) 'Push to break down barriers', *IPE magazine* (May).
OECD (2015) 'Can pension funds and life insurance companies keep their promises?', *OECD Business and Finance Outlook 2015*. Paris: OECD Publishing, pp. 111–47.
OECD (2017) *Pensions at a Glance* 2017, Paris: OECD Publishing.
PensionsEurope (2018) Position paper on the pan-European Personal Pension Product (PEPP). 26 January 2018. www.pensionsEurope.eu
Pochet, P. (2003) 'Pensions: The European Debate', in G.L. Clark and N. Whiteside (eds.), *Pension Security in the 21st Century*, Oxford and New York: Oxford University Press, pp. 44–63.
Posner, E. and Veron, N. (2010) 'The EU and financial regulation: power without purpose?', *Journal of European Public Policy* 17(3): 400–15.
Rust, S. (2018) EU council reaches compromise proposal on PEPP. IPE news, 20 June 2018.
Schelkle, W. (2012) 'A crisis of what? Mortgage credit markets and the social policy of promoting homeownership in the United States and in Europe', *Politics & Society* 40 (1): 59–80.
Schelkle, W. (2013) 'The political economy of regulating longevity insurance in the EU', in U. Neergard, E. Szyszczak, J.W. van de Gronden, and M. Krajewski (eds.), *The Role of Social Services of General Interest in EU Law*, The Hague: TMC Asser Press, pp. 433–57.
Stewart, F. (2007) 'Policy Issues for Developing Annuities Markets', *OECD Working Paper on Insurance and Private Pensions*, Paris: OECD.
Tuytens, P. (2018) 'The political economy of private pension provision', Unpublished PhD thesis, LSE.
van der Zwan, N. (2014) 'Making sense of financialization', *Socio-Economic Review* 12(1): 99–129.
Vogel, S. (1996) *Freer Markets, More Rules: Regulatory Reform in Advanced Industrial Societies*, Ithaca: Cornell University Press.
Weir, M. and Skocpol, T. (1985) 'State structures and the possibilities for 'Keynesian' responses to the great Depression in Sweden, Britain and the United States', in P. B. Evans, D. Rueschemeyer and T. Skocpol (eds.), *Bringing the State Back in*, Cambridge: Cambridge University Press, pp. 107–63.
Widmaier, W.W. (2016) *Economic Ideas in Political Time: The Rise and Fall of Economic Orders From the Progressive Era to the Global Financial Crisis*, Cambridge: Cambridge University Press.

Financialisation meets collectivisation: occupational pensions in Denmark, the Netherlands and Sweden

Karen M. Anderson

ABSTRACT
This paper analyses three cases where unions and employers have embraced financialisation in occupational pension provision. The widespread use of funded occupational pensions in Denmark, the Netherlands and Sweden is rooted in social partner agreement that collectively organised, capital funded pensions can be harnessed to generate secure income. External funding (legal separation of pension reserves from the employer) and administration were key elements in strategies to provide secure occupational pensions. The introduction of funded occupational pensions took place in the context of meagre and/or incomplete statutory provision and before the expansion of generous basic pension coverage starting in the 1930s. This sequencing had a 'crowding in' effect, because well-paid workers sought collective solutions to their pension gap. Over time, these arrangements came to encompass nearly the entire labour market. Unions and employers have developed distinctive strategies for limiting investment risks, limiting the involvement of private financial actors, and ensuring that the interests of plan participants and investment managers are aligned.

Introduction

What explains the high levels of financialisation in the occupational pension schemes of Denmark, the Netherlands, and Sweden? Dutch and Danish occupational pension assets exceed 100% of GDP and approach 60% of GDP in Sweden. These high levels of financialisation are surprising when we consider the dominant approaches to the study of the 'finance-welfare nexus' that emphasise the risks associated with the growing financialisation of welfare. As pension financialisation increases, retirement income is increasingly financed by income from financial assets rather than payroll contributions and taxes. This development generates distributional and political dilemmas: retirees face 'cohort risk' (lower pension income because of falling financial asset prices at the time of retirement); pension savers may lose a substantial share of their pension savings in a downturn; retirement income becomes more unequal; and commercial financial actors use their growing political clout to ensure light regulation (Burtless 2012; Langley 2006; Mabbett 2012) .

The comparative political economy (CPE) literature has long recognised that occupational pension schemes (whether they are capital-funded or not) can perform several functions. Employers may offer them to recruit and bind employers to the firm, whereas workers are more likely to view occupational pensions as deferred wages. Varieties of Capitalism (VoC) scholars argue that employers in coordinated market economies (CMEs) negotiate occupational pensions with unions to facilitate the acquisition of sector- or firm-specific skills (cf. Mares 2003). However, the CPE literature is relatively silent on the drivers of occupational pension financialisation, although there is a growing literature on 'pension fund capitalism' that analyses its non-market features (Clark 2003; Wiß 2015), especially in providing 'patient capital' to firms (Estevez-Abe 2001; McCarthy *et al.* 2016). The CPE literature thus points to the importance of funded occupational pensions in CMEs, but provides an incomplete account of institutional origins and maintenance (cf. Thelen 2004).

This paper draws on the CPE and financialisation literature to develop a novel understanding of the origins and development of funded occupational pension schemes in three small CMEs: Denmark, the Netherlands and Sweden. The paper argues, first, that external funding (legal separation of pension reserves from the employer) and administration were key elements in strategies to provide secure occupational pensions. In Sweden and Denmark, white collar unions in the private sector took the lead in demanding external funding and administration of occupational pensions in the early twentieth century. Workers demanded external funding to protect pensions from employer insolvency and guarantee portability. In the Netherlands, several high-profile cases of insolvency in the 1930s galvanised support among workers, employers and the state to require external funding and administration.

Second, the paper argues that in all three countries, the introduction of funded occupational pensions took place in the context of meagre and/or incomplete statutory provision and before the introduction of generous basic pension coverage starting in the 1930s. This sequencing had a 'crowding in' effect, because well-paid workers sought capital-funded, collective solutions to their pension gap. These arrangements gradually encompassed nearly the entire labour market, including public sector and manual workers. Despite initial resistance, employers accepted external funding and administration as central elements of negotiated pensions. Similarly, unions continue to support collectively organised funded pensions because they offer more generous benefits than book reserves or direct employer provision and contribute to wage moderation. In other words, employers and unions embrace a particular form of pension financialisation: collective schemes that are anchored in wage bargaining and underpinned by strong state regulation (Morgan and Orloff 2017). For employers and unions, the potential risks of financial market volatility are weighed against the benefits of secure, portable pensions.

These arguments contribute to the CPE and financialisation literatures in two ways. First, the analysis demonstrates that there is a subset of CMEs that relies on autonomous, funded occupational pension schemes as central components of employers' industrial relations strategies. Besides providing investment capital, funded occupational pensions in Denmark, the Netherlands and Sweden are vehicles for providing secure occupational pensions. Second, the paper shows that occupational pension financialisation does not lead inexorably to negative consequences for workers. From the start, the embrace of funded pensions was about using financial products to hold pension savings in reserve, separate from employers. As financial markets have become more complex and global, occupational schemes have adjusted their investment strategies to changing regulatory and market conditions. This does not mean that funded pensions are immune to market volatility, however, as the recent Dutch experience shows.

The next section surveys the CPE and financialisation literature on occupational pensions. Subsequent sections develop my arguments about why organised labour and employers chose externally managed capital reserves for occupational pensions and how their evolving preferences and negotiations shaped subsequent development. The final section briefly discusses the implications of the analysis for the CPE literature.

Financialisation and occupational pension provision

According to the CPE literature, occupational pension provision may serve several purposes. For workers, occupational pensions provide an important supplement to statutory benefits (Trampusch 2006). For employers, occupational pensions reward staff for loyal service, binding them to the firm. VoC scholars build on these insights, arguing that occupational pensions are important elements in the production strategies of firms in CMEs. As deferred wages, occupational pensions are part of the wage/insurance package that encourages workers to invest in firm- and sector-specific skills (Estevez-Abe et al. 2001).

Capital-funded occupational pensions are also a potential source of 'patient capital' (Estevez-Abe 2001). For example, Swedish state-run pension funds financed housing construction in the 1960s and 1970s (Pontusson 1994). Similarly, Japanese pension capital provided long-term credit to the economy (Estevez-Abe 2001).

Both employers and unions have a strong interest in affordable, secure pensions. Rising occupational pension contributions can lead to wage bargaining conflict, because the scope for pay increases will be (partially) absorbed by pension costs. The security of occupational pension benefits is also crucial, because of their status as deferred wages. If occupational pension plans do not deliver promised benefits, workers are likely to demand higher wages. The deterioration of occupational benefits may also unleash conflict within unions between inactive (retired) and active (employeed) plan participants.

Employer and union preferences for secure occupational pensions turn on their relationship to statutory benefits. There is scholarly consensus that comprehensive, generous earnings-related public pension provision crowds out non-state provision except for highly paid employees. Conversely, basic state provision creates a pension gap for middle and high income workers, creating incentives in CMEs for negotiated pensions (Ebbinghaus and Gronwald 2011). We should thus expect the emergence and expansion of collectively negotiated pensions in political economies where statutory pension provision was insufficient to meet the needs of organised labour.

Even if workers engage in collective action for negotiated pensions, why would they prefer an externally managed scheme based on capital funding? Where employers offered pension provision as part of the employment contract, why would they consent to external financing and administration (legal separation of pension reserves from the employer)? These two dimensions of pension scheme design – the mode of financing (capital funding v. direct provision) and the location of administration (internal or external to the firm) dominated discussions around early negotiated pension schemes. In the early twentieth century, many employers offered pensions to recruit, reward and discipline staff, and they typically chose internal financing and administration so they could control rules for eligibility, vesting, and benefits. This approach also meant that employers controlled any capital set aside to finance pension payments. Employers could draw on internal pension reserves to finance investment or to cover losses, and if an employer went bankrupt, creditors often had priority over pension beneficiaries. If national regulation existed at all, it did little to protect employees' accrued pension rights.

The emergence of labour organisations, especially for salaried employees, made this approach more difficult to sustain. In the small CMEs, concerns about the portability and security of private sector pensions in the context of meagre statutory provision created strong incentives for employees to advocate financing and administration structures that provided the best protection available. Like manual workers, salaried workers were entirely dependent on their income from labour, so sickness, disability and old age were existential threats. However, the higher income levels of the growing cadre of salaried employees meant early statutory pension provision offered insufficient income replacement. Moreover, the growing class of white collar workers in early twentieth century capitalism was increasingly mobile, making vesting and portability important concerns. Most salaried employees lost their accrued pension rights when they changed employers or were laid off.

Early white collar workers' organisations thus faced the question of how to design workplace pensions so that pension rights would be secure, vested, and portable. The premium reserve model, a staple of the growing insurance industry, offered a solution. In a premium reserve, customers pay actuarially calculated premiums into a reserve fund, which is invested on capital markets. The premium reserve then pays a life-long annuity at retirement. Salaried employees' organisations also had good reasons to insist that the premium reserve (or pension fund) rest on external financing and administration so that employers could not control pension reserves. This structure would also strengthen the conceptualisation of pensions as deferred wages, rather than gratifications offered at employer discretion. Employees would have a legal right to the stream of income financed by their accrued pension savings, and they could change employers without fear of losing accrued rights.

To summarise, early organisations representing white collar workers had good reasons to prefer capital funding and the external administration of pension reserves because they viewed this approach as the most viable way to achieve secure pensions. External management of pension reserves was considered essential because it would ensure that pension reserves could be used for one purpose only: paying employee pensions; employers would not be able to finance investment or shortfalls by borrowing pension reserves, and pension assets would be protected if an employer became insolvent. The external financing and administration of pension reserves would also facilitate portability, which employers would also benefit from.

The liberalisation and expansion of financial markets since the 1970s has substantially altered the context within which funded occupational pensions operate. The post-war period saw the expansion of occupational pension coverage in the affluent democracies. Where funding prevailed, assets expanded rapidly, especially after financial liberalisation. The asset mix also shifted from primarily fixed-income investments and real estate to riskier investments like equities. At the end of 2016, pension assets in the OECD totalled $ 38 trillion (OECD 2017). Danish, Swedish and Dutch pension assets measured as per cent of GDP are very high (209% of GDP in Denmark, 180% of GDP in the Netherlands, and 80% of GDP in Sweden), well above the levels we would expect for CMEs. Pension assets as per cent of GDP in both France and Germany are less than ten per cent of GDP (all figures for 2016).

Why would employers and unions in the small CMEs continue to support capital-funded occupational pensions? The financialisation literature does not offer a clear answer to this question. Financialisation is defined here as the extent to which the financial resources that fund some activity are derived from financial transactions rather than from the income generated by activity in the 'real economy": the industrial, commodity and service sectors (Krippner 2005; Van der Zwan 2014).

Much of the recent financialisation literature emphasises the risks associated with pension financialisation, but it also provides insights into the meso-level characteristics that mitigate these risks. Burtless (2012) compares the workings of private and public pensions schemes, arguing that public schemes are superior in covering risk. He also identifies the attributes of private schemes that would make them more robust (mandatory participation; matching/subsidization; mandatory annuitization; financial knowledge). All of these features require some state intervention in the regulatory sphere. A growing literature examines the conditions that contribute to solidarity in capital-funded pension schemes. Clark (2003) acknowledges the potential for capital-funded pension schemes to provide adequate retirement income based on collective risk-sharing, pointing to the important role of collective bargaining in securing good pension outcomes in, for example, the Netherlands. Leimgruber's (2008) study of the development of Swiss funded pensions reaches similar conclusions. The close integration of the first and second pillar, compulsory second pillar membership, and collective risk-sharing, make the Swiss system fairly flexible and stable.

Taken together, these contributions argue that it is possible to design capital-funded occupational pensions so that they generate secure income and promote solidarity. But why did labour market actors choose funding in the first place? And how and why did the state support these choices? The next section addresses this question by tracing the emergence of collectively organised, prefunded pensions in Denmark, the Netherlands and Sweden and discusses their recent performance.

The choice for external funding

The case studies that follow are based on a most different case study design (Gerring 2006). The three countries have similar values on the key independent (employer-white collar union cooperation) and dependent variables (the choice for capital funding and external administration of assets) and variation across a range of potential explanatory variables such as economic structure, the organisation of labour relations, the political power of the left, and the extent of statutory provision.

Sweden, Denmark and the Netherlands are cases of early financialisation in the sense that most private occupational pensions have been based on external funding and administration rather than direct provision (employers pay pensions out of current revenues) or book reserves. Public sector occupational schemes in Denmark and Sweden were tax-financed, but they introduced funding after WWII. The Dutch civil service pension fund, ABP, has always been funded, but often ran deficits in the 1950s and 1960s (Van der Zwan 2017).

The introduction of (quasi-) universal, flat-rate pensions early in the twentieth century (Sweden 1913; Denmark 1922; Netherlands 1919) reduced poverty, but their limited income replacement created a problem for the growing number of private sector salaried employees, so employee organisations and employers took steps to fill this gap. White collar unions were strong enough to ensure that occupational pensions were negotiated collectively – a clear break from employer voluntarism. The inclusion of workplace pensions in collective contracts increased in tandem with the expansion of collective bargaining. In the Netherlands, 1949 legislation allowed the Social Affairs Minister to declare a sectoral pension scheme binding on all employers. Collective labour market institutions were strong enough in Sweden in Denmark to obviate this kind of legislation.

Improvements in the coverage and generosity of basic pensions after World War II reduced the size of the pension gap for most households, relieving some of the pressure on occupational pensions. In Sweden and Denmark, the generosity of basic pensions was significantly improved in the latter half of the 1930s with the removal of income tests for most households. Sweden removed all income tests in 1946, and Denmark removed most of them in the 1950s. In the Netherlands, 'emergency' basic pensions were introduced in 1947 and institutionalised in 1957.

Denmark

In the early twentieth century, pension policy covered two groups: the extremely poor and privileged civil servants. 1891 legislation introduced means-tested tax-financed old age pensions (basic pensions would not become universal until 1922), and higher civil servants had state-financed coverage. Salaried employees in the metalworking sector, organised in the Association of Salaried Employees (FVJ) faced a pension gap, and they struck one of the first collective pension deals with employers (organised in the Association of Manufacturers). The new scheme, *Pensionskassen for Værkstedsfunktionærer i Jernet (PVJ)*, was established in 1900, and it broke new ground by introducing parity employer/employee contributions and bipartite administration of pension capital external to participating firms (Due and Madsen 2003: 25).

As enterprise size increased in the early 1900s, growing numbers of salaried staff, (including skilled craftsmen) began to question the prevailing model of company-based pensions, because pension reserves were held within the firm, and pensions were not portable. Salaried staff thus faced considerable pension losses when they changed employers, faced redundancy, or if an employer faced financial difficulties. Employers also began to change their thinking about occupational pension design. Many small and medium size enterprises (SMEs) could not afford their own schemes, making it difficult to recruit qualified managers and foremen. Large enterprises had also grown more dependent on a mobile cadre of salaried staff, and many began to view internally financed and managed company schemes as an obstacle to mobility (Thorsen 1967: 11–13).

The establishment of the Pension Insurance Agency (*Pensionforsikringsanstalten, PFA*) in 1917 was a decisive step on the path to collective, externally managed capital-funded pension provision in the private sector. Thorsen's (1967: 1–28) reconstruction of the decision-making around the establishment of the PFA provides insight into the actor preferences that shaped the design of the PFA. The peak organisation for managers and foremen in the private sector, FdF (*Fællesrepræsentationen for danske Funktionærforeninger*), pushed for benefits similar to civil servant pensions (final salary, defined benefit), and they also wanted portability (for the reasons discussed above). FdF considered existing private sector pension schemes to be insecure, because employers controlled financing and vesting. Fd's pension committee proposed a national pension fund for managers and foremen inspired by the railway sector's pension scheme for technical staff, but with a crucial innovation: tripartite administration (employers, employees, the state). In June 1916, FdF contacted the Confederation of Danish Employers (DA), requesting cooperation in setting such a scheme up.

DA had already begun to study the pension issue, setting up its own committee to formulate a proposal in 1915. Employers were willing to improve pension security but there was no consensus about the organisational form (employer voluntarism v. external financing and management) or whether membership should be restricted to DA members. There were two initital proposals: an employer-controlled pension agency based on collective, voluntary insurance or a pension agency based on individual funded accounts. DA decided on collective insurance open to all employers in industry and commerce in order to increase risk-sharing across firms and facilitate portability (Thorsen 1967: 17–18).

DA now tried to reach agreement with the organisation representing firms in industry and commerce (*Engageringskontoret for Handel og Industri*); the parties established a joint pension committee to work out a proposal. Portability was a central issue, and the negotiators agreed that the new pension agency should not be linked to a specific branch organisation. The parties agreed to establish a pension agency based on collective insurance open to all private employers based on pension insurance (similar to a premium reserve). The PFA was set up in 1917 as a stock-based corporation (*aktieselskab*) but functioned as a mutual insurance company (for details, see Thorsen 1967: 22), with employers and employees sharing administration (stockholders were also represented but had little influence).

The development of the insurance sector supported the shift to funded pensions managed by independent entities. In 1917, life insurance companies got the right to offer pension insurance (annuities), and firms began to transfer their pension schemes to these vehicles (Østrup 2009). Legislation adopted in 1935 would also prove crucial for the development of occupational pensions. The 1935 Law on the Supervision of Pension Funds *(Lov nr. 183 af 11. maj 1935 om Tilsyn med Pensionskasse)* required private employers to fully fund pension commitments in a recognised life insurance company, or an independent pension fund under public supervision. Capital could not be held within the firm as shares or a loan (see Feldbæk, Løkke and Jeppesen 2007: 269).

The expansion of externally funded and managed occupational pension schemes created pressure to extend these design principles to the public sector. Until the late 1950s, civil servants were tenured and received earnings-related, tax-financed pensions. In order to recruit new tenured civil servants at higher salaries, government offered new recruits employee status, with collectively negotiated wages and portable, funded pensions. Sectoral pension schemes in the private sector also grew significantly. The first sectoral fund, for engineers, was founded in 1953. By the end of the 1950s, the role of unions in bargaining and administration was firmly established (Due and Madsen 2003).

Political stalemate prevented progress on negotiated pensions for manual workers until 1991 (Due and Madsen 2003). Legislation adopted in 1956 and 1964 raised the universal, flat-rate statutory pension (*folkepension*) considerably, giving many manual workers adequate retirement income. However, as manual workers' wages increased, so did calls to extend occupational pensions to all workers. After years of political stalemate, the social partners took the first steps toward comprehensive second pillar coverage based on external funding and administration in 1989. The process was largely complete by 1993 in terms of coverage and by early 2000 in terms of achieving full contribution rates. Today, the coverage rate of occupational pensions is more than 90%, up from about 33% in the late 1970s.

The Netherlands

As in Sweden and Denmark, many private sector workers faced inadequate pension provision in the early 1900s, and even those with workplace-based pensions could not be sure that they would receive promised benefits. Conflicts about the regulation of private sector pensions played out in industrial relations, but unlike Sweden and Denmark, the Dutch state played an important role because of its active involvement in labour relations. Dutch corporatism institutionalised the interests of employers and unions in policymaking, thereby preventing excessive state influence (Cox 1993: 7). Confessionally-based unions and employers organisations were especially eager to keep the state out of social provision. Unions and employers thus enjoyed a privileged role in policymaking, often helping to draft legislation on occupational pensions.

Early private sector pensions were voluntary employer plans to reward service and loyalty. Growing labour organisation changed this, as unions increasingly negotiated wages and working conditions with employers. Occupational pensions soon became incorporated into employment contracts (Tulfer 1997: 12–13); by 1918, there were 738 schemes in the private sector (Tulfer 1997: 13–14). As in other countries, workplace pensions were intended to provide a decent standard of living for salaried employees and other valued staff. Statutory provision was minimal; voluntary statutory provision for manual workers was not adopted until 1919, and even then, many workers lacked pensions. Even if labour organisations influenced the design of these early schemes, however, vesting was unusual. Pensions were neither secure not portable.

In the early twentieth century, most workplace schemes were employer-financed, relying on book reserves, direct provision or annual employer contributions; these schemes would not be regulated until the 1950s. However, 1908 legislation (*Koninklijk Besluit, 31 maart 1908*) introduced requirements for schemes that included employee contributions: employee participation in administration; limits on allowable investment categories (including investments in the sponsoring firm); external administration of assets; and moderate vesting rules (employees leaving a company after at least one year of service had the right to a refund of all contributions). The goal of the legislation was to protect workers' pension savings, but it would soon prove inadequate because most pension schemes were employer-financed (Tulfer 1997: 14).

Improvements in the legal status of employment contracts, the growth of collective labour organisations, and the spread of collective agreements contributed to the expansion of occupational pension funds. 1928 legislation strengthened provisions adopted in 1907 on collective agreements, which increasingly included clauses about participation in sectoral pension funds. In 1937 legislation requiring participation in a collective agreement was introduced and was extended to sectoral pension funds in 1949 (Anderson 2011). The first sectoral scheme was established in 1917 in the dairy sector, followed by one in the mining sector in 1918 (Tulfer 1997: 15).

The 1935 bankruptcy of Royal Dutch Lloyd exposed the weakness of prevailing regulation. Lloyd employees and pensioners lost all of their pension claims in the bankruptcy proceedings because the scheme was employer-financed and thus not subject to the 1908 regulations. The government responded in 1936 with a legislative proposal to improve pension security: employers or groups of employers providing pensions would be required to contract with insurance companies or use the statutory pension insurance programme. Employers and unions in the Labour Council (*Hooge Raad der Arbeid*), the bipartite body advising the government on socio-economic policy, agreed with the goals of the legislation, but rejected the insurance requirement. The overwhelming majority of the Council argued that this would lead to massive plan closures because a majority of plans was either directly provided (i.e., out of current revenues), or financed by annual employer contributions or investments in the firm itself (Hooge Raad 1937: 3). The Council then formulated its own proposal, which the government later used as the basis for legislation (World War II slowed down the legislative process, so it was not complete until 1951). The legislation, the 1952 Pension Act (PSW, *Pensioen- en spaarfondsenwet*) required employers with official (written) pension plans to ensure that capital assets be sufficient to cover pension obligations. To achieve this, pension funds should contract with a life insurance company or administer a fund to achieve the same result. Funds would be required to report to the Insurance Chamber every five years, and company pension funds could only cover 10% of liabilities with debt certificates. The law gave pension funds 25 years to complete the transition to full external funding.

The PSW was a milestone in occupational pension provision because it confirmed the principles of external funding and vesting. Employers were not required to offer pensions (unless party to a binding collective agreement), but if they did, contributions and assets would be protected against employer insolvency. Pension rights could not be cashed out, and employees got the right to take their pension rights with them to a new employer. Pension funds were also required to have a responsible financial and actuarial structure (Nijhof 2009; Van der Zwan 2017).

The underdevelopment of statutory provision and the threat of legislation in the 1950s shaped union and employer preferences concerning occupational pension regulation. Estimates vary, but occupational pension coverage appears to have increased from one third in 1950 to 70% in 1958 (Oude Nijhuis 2013: 90). Employers prioritised the continued development of occupational pensions (rather than the expansion of statutory provision), because they wanted to keep the internal investment opportunities that these schemes offered, and they wanted to continue using occupational pension plans to promote wage moderation in the context of growing state involvement in wage policy (as was common in the 1940s and 1950s; Oude

Nijhuis 2013: 88–89). Unions supported the PSW because it would make occupational pensions more secure (Oude Nijhuis 2013: 90–91).

The coverage of occupational pensions expanded rapidly in the post-war period, as did statutory provision. 1957 legislation introduced the universal basic pension (AOW; a temporary measure had been in place since 1947), and occupational schemes quickly adjusted their schemes to statutory provision. The growth of collective bargaining encouraged the expansion of sectoral occupational pension funds, but the law allowed labour market actors to choose between a trust model and an insurance model. Unions and employers overwhelmingly opted for the former, cementing the status of defined benefit pension funds organised as trusts as the main vehicle for occupational pension schemes (Tulfer 1997). By 2000, about 90% of wage-earners participated in negotiated occupational schemes, and these have developed into an important supplement to the statutory basic pension, providing about half of pension income in 2016.

Until the late 1980s, external funding meant investments in fixed-income assets, like government and corporate bonds, loans, and mortgages (i.e., patient capital; see McCarthy et al. 2016). By the 1990s, the globalisation of financial markets meant that stock markets offered attractive returns, and employers and unions began to embrace these investment opportunities. Unions were initially resistant to investments in equities, but soon came to support this because of the promise of higher returns necessary to finance final salary, DB plans (McCarthy et al. 2016: 761).

Sweden

As in Denmark, salaried employees in the private sector faced a large pension gap in the first decades of the 1900s because of inadequate public provision. 1913 legislation introduced meagre universal old-age pension coverage, but it provided insufficient benefits for salaried employees. However, the 1913 law also included a voluntary, workplace-based, contributory supplementary pension based on vesting (*oantastbarhet*) and capital funding. Individuals using the voluntary scheme controlled their pension savings, and employers were forbidden from using the capital reserves. The principles of vesting and external capital-funding set an important precedent for subsequent occupational pension policy (Harrysson 2000).

Employer voluntarism dominated the lightly regulated, existing occupational pension schemes of the early 1900s. As the number of salaried employees in the private sector grew, many formed unions, and pensions were a key issue. Salaried employees and some experts began to view occupational pensions as a deferred wage with the status of a property right, rather than a discretionary payment for loyal service (Harrysson 2000; SOU 1938: no. 18). Some employers were not averse to this approach.

For salaried employees in industry, pensions caused particular concern, and they organised a union (*Svenska Brukstjänstemannaföreningen, SBF*) in 1909 to pursue a solution. SBF soon realised its members could not finance pensions on their own, so it turned to employers in the Swedish Industrial Association (*Svenska Industriförbundet*, SIF). Key among SBF's demands was that pensions be vested and secure, allowing portability in the growing SME sector. At the same time, leading figures in Chambers of Commerce were also trying to improve pension provision for salaried employees in commerce. In 1917 they joined SIF to establish SPP, (*Sveriges privatanställdas pensionskassa*) for salaried employees in industry, commerce, shipping and other sectors. Employers and salaried employees' organisations agreed on several key principles: vesting, capital funding, external administration of pension reserves, and employer/employee representation on the SPP board. Employers and employees shared contributions, and benefits were 60% of final salary (SPP 1942).

The establishment of SPP sparked debate about occupational pension design. The principle of vesting remained controversial in the 1920s, because many employers were reluctant to relinquish control over pension reserves and payments (Harrysson 2000: 71–72). Pension provision remained uneven, despite the establishment of SPP, and many employers offered pensions that were neither vested nor secure. Salaried employees would not win the right to bargain collectively until 1936, so their organisations had few resources to back up their pension demands. The establishment of *Pensionanstalten Sverige* (PS) by fifteen insurance companies in 1925 fed the determination of salaried employees to win vested, secure pensions. PS was an attempt to reassert partial employer control over occupational pensions because it was not based on vesting. Salaried employees' organisations protested this development (SOU 1929: no 3, 13), turning to the government for support. They also stepped up their organising efforts (see below).

In December 1926, organisations representing white collar workers outside SPP (foremen, railroad office staff, and bank personnel) jointly requested the government to legislate improvements in the security and vesting of their pensions to match what SPP was offering (SOU 1929: no 3, 33). The organisations pointed to recent cases of cancelled pension promises because of employer insolvency and employers (especially in banking) using pension reserves to pay creditors or facilitate mergers (SOU 1929: no. 3, 16–17).

Government-appointed experts produced a legislative draft in December 1927 based on vesting and secure funding, but employers unanimously rejected it, emphasising employer control over pension design, especially vesting. Government experts refused to let the issue rest and formulated a compromise proposal published in September 1928 (SOU 1929: no. 3). Nothing came of the compromise proposal, but the issue of vested, secure pensions would remain politically salient, largely because SPP had become the standard against which other workers' organisations judged their own pensions.

Eight associations representing white collar workers, several of which had pressed the government in 1926 to improve the security and vesting of pensions, joined to form the Central Organisation of Salaried Employees (*De anställdas centralorganisation*, DACO) in 1931, which won the right to bargain collectively in 1936. Several white collar unions had engaged in collective bargaining for decades, but these were largely sectors where strikebreakers were hard to find (i.e., journalists) or where labour was scarce (Kjellberg 2013). One of DACO's key issues was improving the security and vesting of occupational pensions.

SPP's merger with *Pensionsanstalten* (a private competitor) to become *Svenska Personal-Pensionskassan* (also SPP) in 1925 reinforced its organisation as a mutual insurance company. The state also stepped in to provide regulation in the context of uneven acceptance of vesting and external financing (Harrysson 2000: 8). The principles of vested, secured rights carried the day, and firms participating in SPP had to accept these rules. In the 1930s, the state supported this by adopting regulations to make pension reserves more secure (SOU 1937: no.13) and by abolishing the favourable tax treatment of some forms of internally-held pension provisions (Harrysson 2000). By 1926, 155 employers, many of them large industrial firms, used SPP to insure 5,397 salaried employees (SOU 1929: no 3, 14).

The introduction of local government pension schemes also contributed to the growth of vested, capital-funded pensions. State-level civil servants already had their own, tax-financed, pensions, but the basic pension introduced 1917 did not include civil servants, leaving local civil servants without coverage. In 1919, local governments established their own pension scheme and chose SPP to administer it. The new scheme, *Sveriges Kommunalanställdas Pensionskassa* (SKP) was up and running 1922, and like the nascent private sector schemes, it was based on secure, vested pensions defined as deferred wages. In the following decades, SKP expanded to include more and more local authorities (Grip 1994).

The implementation of the ATP reform in 1960 re-opened the issue of portable, secure pension schemes for private sector salaried employees because it introduced statutory, earnings-related pensions to the entire labour market. This meant that existing schemes for salaried employees would be transformed so that they supplemented generous statutory benefits. Before 1960, coverage for salaried employees was incomplete, and SPP was the most common provider, although some employers used book reserves. SAF, SIF and SALF (*Sveriges Arbetsledareförbund;* Swedish Supervisors' Union) agreed on the importance of creating a uniform, national system subject to collective bargaining. By now, however, some employers were sceptical of funding, especially since the ATP system would increase collective capital formation. SAF remained divided on the issue of funding, preferring to allow employers to choose between the premium reserve system (i.e., SPP) and some form of internal financing (book reserves). Agreement on financing was particularly difficult, because there was no organisation capable of administering pensions based on book reserves. Unions and employers struck a deal that included the choice between the premium reserve and a firm-level pension trust based on book reserves. The new scheme, ITP (*Industrins tilläggspension*), would top up the ATP benefits to 65% for the salary below the ATP ceiling, and 32.5% for the salary up to two times the amount paid by ATP. To guarantee vested pension rights, trusts would be required to purchase credit insurance to guarantee the value of accumulated pension rights in case of insolvency (Larsson 2009). SAF, SIF, and SALF agreed to establish a mutual insurance company for this purpose, FPG (*Försäkringsbolaget Pensionsgaranti, Ömsesidigt*). Another new organisation, the Pension Registration Institute (*Pensionsregisreringsinstitut, PRI*) would administer the ITP system (record contributions, calculate and pay benefits). In the fall of 1960, all SAF members approved the proposal, and the deal applied to about 200,000 white collar workers (SOU 1961: no. 14, 36).

In line with the development of ITP, SAF and the Trade Union Confederation (*Landsorganisation, LO*) agreed in June 1971 to introduce contractual pensions in 1972. The issue of financing was difficult, as many employers and unions preferred to retain the book reserve arrangements already in place in many schemes. The parties agreed on the necessity of capital-funded pensions but compromised on how to achieve this. Firms would pay cash premiums to a SAF-LO owned, mutual insurance company (AMF). Firms could also opt to pay their premiums with interest-bearing debt certificates (*räntebärande revers*), but these would have to guaranteed by credit insurance in a different division of AMF. All pension benefits would be vested (AMF 1973: 3–5).

By the late 1970s, employers' concerns about the growing cost of defined benefit (DB) plans for salaried employees led to industrial conflict. Employers and unions agreed to a partial transition to funded, defined contribution (DC) plans. The new scheme, ITPK (administered by SPP) would pay benefits based on fund performance, complementing DB ITP benefits. Employers and unions agreed on the next significant changes in the late 1980s and 1990s: individual investment choice in ITPK and the gradual transition from DB to DC (those born after 1979 have DC). LO and SAF negotiated an even more far-reaching shift for private sector blue-collar workers in 1996, when STP (a DB scheme) was replaced with the SAF-LO pension plan. The new plan is DC and gives participants full investment choice. Public sector employers and unions also negotiated the gradual transition from DB to DC schemes with individual investment choice in the 1990s and 2000s.

From patient to impatient capital

The liberalisation of financial regulation in the OECD since the 1970s and the globalisation of financial markets have meant that many capital-funded pension schemes increasingly rely on short-term investments in shares and private equity (see Wiß 2019). By the 1990s, Danish, Swedish and Dutch occupational pension schemes had substantial investments in international equities. This shift had to be reconciled with key union/employer goals: stable, secure pension benefits; stable non-wage labour costs; and collective risk-sharing. Rather than open pension markets completely to financial service providers and global markets, unions and employers have retained collective governance, so that pensions are standardised across firms and sectors, and employers cannot compete for workers on the basis of pension benefits. Bipartite administration of pension funds ensures that pension design represents a deal acceptable to both parties, and statutory regulation supports collective governance (cf. Naczyk and Hassel 2019).

In Sweden, bipartite administration keeps administrative costs low and ensures that private sector DC plans offer participants high quality investment vehicles (by restricting entry to funds with low fees and superior performance). The majority of private-sector negotiated pension schemes operate much like the DC premium pension that was introduced in 2000 as part of the 1998 statutory pension reform (Anderson and Immergut 2007). Public sector schemes follow a similar model (these plans are shifting from DB to DC; for details, see Anderson 2015).

The Danish occupational pension sector, like the Swedish, covers more than 90% of the labour market and is regulated according to national and EU insurance law. The large number of schemes means there is greater differentiation than in Sweden, moderating the extent of collective risk-sharing. As in Sweden, the expansion of the occupational pension sector prompted institutional innovation: the three largest sectoral schemes were established after 1991: *PensionDanmark* for manual workers in the public and private sector; *IndustriensPension* for private sector industrial workers; and *PKA* for workers in health and social care. Each is non-profit and jointly managed by employers and unions.

The political settlement underpinning the Swedish and Danish systems is stable, but the same cannot be said for the Netherlands. Dutch occupational pensions are DB and highly popular, but demographic and economic challenges have created strong reform pressures. Unions and employers supported the shift to equities and other forms of impatient capital in the 1980s and 1990s because they viewed this a viable strategy for financing increasingly expensive final salary DB benefits (McCarthy *et al.* 2016). Pension fund losses in the 2001 dot.com bubble forced a shift from final salary to average salary schemes in 2005, and the 2008 financial crisis resulted in large contribution increases, benefit freezes and even modest cuts in many schemes (Anderson 2017). Pension funds recovered fairly quickly from both crises, but low interest rates and increasingly life expectancy have increased the cost of accumulated pension liabilities, pulling down many funds' coverage ratios. Neither the government nor the social partners has been able to agree on the parameters of a new system, but there has been no retreat from the principles of capital-funding, external administration, and portability. Instead, reform debates focus on how to shift to a collective DC system.

Conclusion

This paper offers a new understanding of the origins and development of capital-funded occupational pension in CMEs. The paper argues that labour's embrace of occupational pension financialisation is rooted in concerns about pension security and portability. Salaried employees joined with employers to establish jointly owned, non-profit organisations legally separate from employers to manage and invest pension capital. Capital funding was not the goal of this arrangement, but rather a means to achieving other goals. Despite enormous pension reserves, commercial pension providers have not made large inroads into the occupational pension market. Where they are active, as in Denmark and Sweden, they compete against non-profit providers, and they face the very considerable bargaining power of bipartite pension schemes that demand high quality pension products with low management fees.

Unions and employers in all three countries continue to support funding in the context of financial liberalisation because it delivers stable labour costs and good pension outcomes. Indeed, employers and unions share an interest in harnessing financial markets to generate investment returns that finance good pensions. This is somewhat less true in the Netherlands, as stakeholders continue to debate the contours of a new system. There is, however, no consensus among Dutch stakeholders that capital funding should be abandoned. Instead, current reform debates centre on how to shift from DB to some form of collective DC and to improve governance, especially concerning risk management and investment policy (De Deken 2017; Frijns et al. 2010).

The analysis presented here has two implications for the CPE literature. First, socially embedded occupational pension markets are potential elements of the household consumption growth regime identified by Baccaro and Pontusson (2016). By exploiting the opportunities of global financial markets, financialised pension provision is an important driver of household income. Buoyant financial markets result in higher pension incomes, but the converse is also true, especially in DB systems like the Netherlands. Second, the paper's emphasis on historical sequencing and the importance of employer-union cooperation and non-profit financial companies points to promising research avenues as occupational pension financialisation develops in other countries.

Disclosure statement

No potential conflict of interest was reported by the author.

References

AMF (1973) Arbetsmarknadsförsäkringar, pensionsförsäkringsaktiebolag. Kompletterende bestämmelser rörande åligganden för arbetsgivaren.

Anderson, K. M. (2011) 'The Netherlands: Adapting a multipillar system to economic and demographic change', in B. Ebbinghaus (ed.), *Varieties of Pension Governance: Pension Privatization in Europe*, Oxford: Oxford University Press, pp. 292–317.

Anderson, K. M. (2015) *Occupational Pensions in Sweden*, Berlin: Friedrich Ebert Stiftung.

Anderson, Karen M. (2017) 'Anpassung der Alterssicherungssysteme an das veränderte Marktumfeld. Ein internationaler Vergleich', *Deutsche Rentenversicherung* 72(4): 440–456.

Anderson, Karen M. and Immergut, Ellen M. (2007) 'Sweden: after social democratic hegemony', in Ellen M. Immergut, Karen M. Anderson and Isabelle Schulze (eds), *The Handbook of West European Pension Politics*, Oxford: Oxford University Press, pp. 349–395.

Baccaro, L. and Pontusson, J. (2016) 'Rethinking comparative political economy: the growth model perspective', *Politics and Society* 44(2): 175–207.

Burtless, G. (2012) 'Can improved options for private saving offer a plausible substitute for public pensions?', *Politics & Society* 40(1): 81–105.

Clark, G. (2003) *European Pensions and Global Finance*, Oxford: Oxford University Press.

Cox, R.H. (1993) *The Development of the Dutch Welfare State*, Pittsburgh: University of Pittsburgh Press.

De Deken, J. (2017) 'The Netherlands. The challenges posed by the unintended universal financialization of retirement provision', in D. Natali (ed.), *The New Pension Mix in Europe*, Brussels: Peter Lang, pp. 151–82.

Due, J. and Madsen, J.S. (2003) *Fra magtkamp til konsensus. Arbejdsmarkedspensionerne og den danske model*, Copenhagen: DJØF Publishing.

Ebbinghaus, B. and Gronwald, M. (2011) 'The changing public-private mix in Europe: from path dependence to path departure', in B. Ebbinghaus (ed.), *Varieties of Pension Governance: Pension Privatization in Europe*, Oxford: Oxford University Press, pp. 23–55.

Estevez-Abe, M. (2001) 'The forgotten link: the financial regulation of Japanese pension funds in comparative perspective', in B. Ebbinghaus and P. Manow (eds) *Comparing Welfare Capitalism*, London: Routledge, pp. 190–216.

Estevez-Abe, M., Iversen, T., & Soskice, D. (2001) 'Social protection and the formation of skills: A reinterpretation of the welfare state', in P. A. Hall and D. Soskice (eds),

Varieties of Capitalism. The Institutional Foundations of Comparative Advantage, New York: Oxford University Press, pp. 145–83.
Feldbæk, O., Løkke, A. and Jeppesen, S. (2007) *Drømmen om tryghed. Tusind års dansk forsikring*, Ylling: Gads Forlag.
Frijns, J.M.G., Nijssen, J.A. and Scholtens, L.J.R. (2010) *Pensioen: "Onzekere zekerheid"*, Den Haag: Ministry of Social Affairs and Employment.
Gerring, John (2006) *Case Study Research*, Cambridge: Cambridge University Press.
Grip, G. (1994) *Från stor livförsäkring till folkförsäkring : en skrift med anledning av Folksam Livs verksamhet 1914-1994*, Stockholm: Folksam.
Harrysson, L. (2000) *Arbetsgivare och pensioner. Industriarbetsgivarna och tjänstepensioneringen i Sverige 1900-1948*, Hässleholm: Värpinge Ord & Text.
Hooge Raad (1937) *Advies van den Hoogen raad van Arbeid inzake een voorontwerp-personeelfondsenwet*, 's-Gravenhage: Algemeen Landsdrukkerij.
Kjellberg, A. (2013) 'Privattjänstemännens fackliga organisationsmiljö 1880-1930', *TAMREVY* 2: 4–13.
Krippner, G. (2005) 'The financialisation of the American Economy', *Socio-Economic Review* 3: 173–208.
Langley, Paul (2006) 'The Making of Investor Subjects in Anglo-American Pensions', *Environment and Planning D: Society and Space* 24(6): 919–934. http://doi.org/10.1068/d405t
Larsson, M. (2009) 'Pensionssystem i brytningstid - den svenska tjänstepensionsdebatten under 1950-talet', *Scandinavian Insurance Quarterly* 1: 45–60.
Leimgruber, M. (2008) *Solidarity without the State?*, Cambridge: Cambridge University Press.
Mabbett, D. (2012) 'The ghost in the machine: pension risks and regulatory responses in the United States and the United Kingdom', *Politics & Society* 40(1): 107–29.
Mares, I. (2003) *The Politics of Social Risk: Business and Welfare State Development*, Cambridge: Cambridge University Press.
McCarthy, M., Sorsa, V. and Van der Zwan, N. (2016) 'Investment preferences and patient capital: financing, governance and regulation in pension fund Capitalism', *Socio-Economic Review* 14(4): 751–69.
Morgan, K. J. and Orloff, A. S. (eds) (2017) *The Many Hands of the State: Theorizing Political Authority and Social Control*, Cambridge: Cambridge University Press.
Naczyk, M. and Hassel, A. (2019) 'Insuring individuals ... and politicians: financial services providers, stock market risk and the politics of private pension guarantees in Germany', *Journal of European Public Policy*. doi:10.1080/13501763.2019.1575455
Nijhof, E. (2009) 'Pensions and providence: Dutch employers and the creation of funded pension schemes', *Enterprise and Society* 10(2): 265–303.
OECD. (2017) *Pension Markets in Focus 2017*, Paris: OECD.
Østrup, F. (2009) 'Den finansielle globalisering: Påvirkningen af den danske model', in: *Globaliseringens udfordringer: Politiske og administrative processer under pres*, in M. Marcussen and K. Ronit (eds.), *Globaliseringens udfordringer*, København: Hans Reitzel, pp. 65–92.
Oude Nijhuis, D. (2013) *Labor Divided in the Postwar European Welfare State*, Oxford: Oxford University Press.
Pontusson, J. (1994) *The Limits of Social Democracy*, Ithaca: Cornell University Press.
Statens, Offentliga (1937) SOU no. 13.
Statens Offentliga Utredningar (1929) SOU no 3.
Statens Offentliga Utredningar (1938) SOU no 18.

Statens Offentliga Utredningar (1961) SOU no 14.
Svenska Personal-Pensionskassan (1942) *SPP 1917-1942. Minnesskrift över de första 25 åren*, Stockholm: P.A. Nordstedts & Söner.
Thelen, K. (2004) *How Institutions Evolve: The Political Economy of Skills in Germany, Britain, the United States, and Japan*, Cambridge: Cambridge University Press.
Thorsen, S. (1967) *Privatfunktionærernes Pensionforsikring 1917-1967*, Copenhagen: PFA.
Trampusch, C. (2006) 'Industrial relations and welfare states: the different dynamics of retrenchment in Germany and the Netherlands', *Journal of European Social Policy* 16 (2): 121–33.
Tulfer, P.M. (1997) *Pensioenen, fondsen en verzekeraars*, Kluwer: Deventer.
Van der Zwan, N. (2014) 'Making sense of financialization', *Socio-Economic Review* 12(1): 99–129.
Van der Zwan, N. (2017) 'Financialisation and the pension system: Lessons from the United States and the Netherlands', *Journal of Modern European History* 15(4): 554–78.
Wiß, T. (2015) 'Pension fund vulnerability to the financial market crisis: The role of trade unions', *European Journal of Industrial Relations* 21(2): 131–47.
Wiß, T. (2019) 'Reinforcement of pension financialisation as a response to financial crises in Germany, the Netherlands and the United Kingdom', *Journal of European Public Policy*. doi:10.1080/13501763.2019.1574870. *[= SI paper, details to be added by editors/producer]*.

Index

Note: **Bold** page numbers refer to tables; *italic* page numbers refer to figures and page numbers followed by "n" denote endnotes.

Altersvorsorge-Sondervermögen 104, 106
Anderson, K. M. 14, 135
Anglo-Saxon pension funds 100
Arbeitsgemeinschaft für betriebliche Altersversorgung (Aba) 46–7, 105
asset allocation 67; changing patterns of 69; pension fund 71; regulation's role 70; strategic 68, *72*
Asset Liability Management (ALM) 66–7
'asset only' investment strategy 12
Association of British Insurers (ABI) 47
auto-enrolment 4, 28, 30, 33n4
autonomous actors 82

bankruptcy (1935) of Royal Dutch Lloyd 145
Beveridgean systems 45
Beveridge multipillar model 41
bipartite administration 150
Bismarckian pension system 40, 45
Blyth, M. 22
Bridgen, P. 20. 31
Britain: dual transformation in 53; financialisation 52; pension systems 40; rebalancing multipillarism in 48–9
Bundesverband der deutschen Arbeitgeber (BDA) 46
Bundesverband Deutscher Industrie (BDI) 46
Bundesverband deutscher Investment-Gesellschaften (BVI) 105
Bundesverband Investment & Asset Management (BVI) 47
Bundesvereinigung der Deutschen Arbeitgeberverbände (BDA) 105
Burtless, G. 140

capital-funded occupational pensions 137
capital 13
Capital Markets Union (CMU) 118
Central Organisation of Salaried Employees *see De anställdas centralorganisation* (DACO)
changing investment norms 65–6
Clark, G. 140
Classical Political Economy 118
cohort risk 135–6
'collectivization of risks' 42–3
Commission proposal 127
comparative political economy (CPE) 136–7
complexity in financial products 81
Confederation of British Industry (CBI) 46
conservative-led coalition government 83
Conservative-Liberal coalition 49
Contractual Trust Arrangements (CTAs) 71
coordinated market economies (CMEs) 59, 136
countering financial interests for social purposes 79–80; electoral considerations, role of 87–8; organised interest groups, role of 89–90; state-centric approach 83–7; state intervention in financial welfare markets 81–2
cross-border market for personal pensions 123–9
cross-party support for strengthening equity culture 105–7
'crowding in' effect 136
Culpepper, P. D. 102
cutbacks in public pension benefits 13, 50

Danish Employers (DA) 142–3
Danish occupational pension sector 150
DB investment: changing patterns of asset allocation in 69; financial industry influence in 64–5
DC investment: changing patterns of asset allocation in 69; financial industry influence in 64–5, 22
de-financialisation 131n3
de-risking 61–3
De anställdas centralorganisation (DACO) 148
defined-contribution–pension plans 9–10
defined benefits (DB) 2, 21, 120; arrangement 62; indexation 28–9; schemes 48
defined contributions (DC) 21, 119; arrangement 62; pensions 5, 10, 13, 108; plans 107–8; principle 2; schemes 9, 45, 48
Denmark: external funding 141–3; occupational pension financialisation 14; private pension funds 122
Department for Work and Pensions (DWP) 87
Deutscher Beamtenbund (dbb) 46
Deutsche Rentenversicherung (DRV) 46
Deutscher Gewerkschaftsbund (DGB) 46
disembedding markets 22

Ebbinghaus, B. 12, 39, 45
Eichengreen, B. J. 120
employer: employer-sponsors 59–61; employer-white collar union cooperation 140; using financialised pensions 31; voluntarism 146
Engelen, E. 121
equity: culture 117; equity exposure 61
equity-oriented defined-contribution vehicle 105
equity-oriented 'pension funds' 104
EU pension policy and financialisation 117–19; cross-border market for personal pensions 123–9; financialisation and 122
European Federation of Investors and Financial Services Users 127
European Financial Services Round Table (EFR) 123–4
European Insurance and Occupational Pensions Authority (EIOPA) 131n5
European Union, pension financialisation in 13–14

external funding, choice for 140–1; Denmark 141–3; Netherlands, The 143–6; from patient to impatient capital 150–1; Sweden 146–9
external shocks 20

Fællesrepræsentationen for danske Funktionærforeninger (FdF) 142
finance-welfare nexus 135
financial-market based pension schemes 21
financial crises: case selection and vulnerability to 24–5; developments 25–6
financialisation 1–2, 4, 19, 40, 44–5, 52, 118; EU pension policy and 117–19; and national pension systems 122; and occupational pension provision 137–40; *see also* pension financialisation
financial market crisis (2007/08) 10
financial professionals 63–4
financial regulation 13; of pension provision 119–20
financial services provider 98–9, 101–2
Försäkringsbolaget Pensionsgaranti, Ömsesidigt (FPG) 149
Frankfurter Allgemeine Zeitung, Handelsblatt (FAZ) 103
Frankfurt financiers' push for more equity culture in Germany 104–5
FRS17 70
funded pensions 1, 58

Gelepithis, M. 12, 58
Germany: Bismarckian pension system 40; financialisation 52; fostering belated multipillarism in 50–1; Frankfurt financiers' push for more equity culture in 104–5; funding requirements 25; nominal funding ratios *26*; occupational pensions 24; pension policy 53; pension privatisation in 103–4; trajectory reforming 29–30
Gesamtverband der Deutschen Versicherungswirtschaft (GDV) 47, 105
'glidepaths' 69
global finance 30–1
governance of pension funds 28
government and pension financialisation 31
Grand Coalition (2018–) 51
Great Depression 120

INDEX

Hall, P. A. 22, 118
Hassel, A. 1, 13, 97
high-salience social policy image 107–9
Hylands, T. 31

individual choice within financialised pension products 21
individualization 44–5
Industrins tilläggspension (ITP) 149
Institute of Directors 46
institutional change 22–3
insurance companies' business model 101
investment consulting for pension funds 65
Investment Management Association (IMA) 89
investment professionals 12
IORPs database 125, 132n8

Jensen, C. 31
Joint Industry Code of Conduct 89

Keynesian political economy 120

labour and social law 131n6
labour organisations 138
labour relaxed regulations (2004) 84–5
Landsorganisation (LO) 149
Leimgruber, M. 140
liability-driven investment 66–8; crises reinforcing trend towards 68
Liberal Market Economy (LME) 59, 100
'lifestyling' 65, 69
Lipsmeyer, C. S. 31
low-salience financial regulation image 107–9

Mann, G. 120
market-correcting policies 10
market integration 119
marketisation 2, 43–4
market principles, emulation of 121
Meyer, T. 20, 31
Minimum Funding Requirement (MFR) 66, 70
Mixed Market Economies (MMEs) 60
multi-pillar model 2
multipillarisation 40; decomposing paradigm shift 43–5; overcoming status quo 45–8; paradigm shift toward 42; political economy of 41–3

multipillarism 41; fostering belated multipillarism in Germany 50–1; rebalancing in Britain 48–9
Myners Report 29
Myners review 64–5

Naczyk, M. 1, 13, 97, 131
Natali, D. 20
National Employment Savings Trust (NEST) 46, 85
National Pensioners' Convention (NPC) 46
national pension systems 122
Naumann, E. 45
Netherlands, The: external funding 143–6; funding ratios in 25; nominal funding ratios *26*; occupational pensions in 24, *27*; private pension funds 122; trajectory reforming 26–8
New Labour 49
Nijssen, J. 123
nudging 33n4, 49

occupational and personal process 2
occupational pension provision 137–40
occupational pensions: British post-war development 48; financialisation 137; in Netherlands 24
old-age pensions 2, 5
organised capital 46
organised labour 12, 42–3, 46, 100

Pan-European Pension Product (PEPP) 14, 119, 125–6, 128, **129**
paradigm shift 40; decomposing 43–5; in Germany 50–1; toward multipillarisation 42
path reinforcement 23
patient capital 9, 136, 137, 150
pay-as-you-go (PAYG) 21, 41–2, 58
Pensioen-en spaarfondsenwet (PSW) 145
pension accumulation 123
PensionDanmark 150
pension financialisation 2–4, 19, 21–2, 119–22; contributions to private pension plans *6*; correcting failures in private pension markets 9–11; and financialisation of economy 8–9; no convergence among OECD countries 4–8; in OECD countries 3; reversal of 22–3; special issue structure 11–14; spending on public/private pensions *6*; *see also* financialisation
Pension Fund Governance Act (2013) 28

pension fund investment strategies:
de-risking 61–3; employer-sponsors
and plan members 59–61; financial
professionals 63–4; UK 'de-risks' 64–9
pension funds 4, 8–9, 33n3, 66; assets
(2001–2015) 25; capitalism 60, 136;
governance 12, 22; governance of
28; investment consulting for 65; in
Netherlands 24; in OECD countries
3; real net investment rate of return 26;
regulation 11; trustees 63
pension policy 1, 102
pension privatisation 99–102; cross-
party support for strengthening
equity culture 105–7; Frankfurt
financiers' push for more equity
culture in Germany 104–5; in Germany
103–4; high-salience social policy
image 107–9
Pension Registration Institute *see*
Pensionsregisreringsinstitut (PRI)
Pensions-Sondervermögen 105–107, 68, 70, 80
Pensions Act (2004) 29
Pensions and Lifetime Savings
Association (PSLA) 46
PensionsEurope 126, 132n7
Pensionsfonds 33n1, 71, 107
pensions gap 125
Pensionskassen 33n1
*Pensionskassen for Værkstedsfunktionærer i
Jernet* (PVJ) 141
Pensionsregisreringsinstitut (PRI) 149
pension systems 1–2
permanent austerity 99
personal pension 49; cross-border
market for 123–9
Pierson, P. 42
plan members 59–61
political economy of multipillarisation
41–3; *see also* pension financialisation
population ageing 99
pre-funded defined-contribution
plans 2, 9
pre-funded private defined-contribution
pension plans 7, 10
pre-funded private pensions 11
price cap 89
private defined-contribution pension
plans 97–9
private pension markets, correcting
failures in 9–11
privatization 39, 43–5

public policy 39
'pure' defined-contribution plans
3, 98, 101–2
'pure' equity-oriented defined-
contribution schemes 104

real economy 140
regulatory flexibility 28
reinforcement of pension financialisation
20–1; employers 31; global finance
30–1; government 31; path
reinforcement 23; trade unions 32;
trajectory reforming 26–30; *see also*
pension financialisation
Riester' pension plans 13, 98

Schelkle, W. 13, 117
semi-obligatory financialisation 11
shareholder value 2, 5, 8, 100, 109, 110, 123
Skocpol, T. 118, 120
small and medium size enterprises
(SMEs) 142, 147
social advocacy groups 42, 45, 46, 49, 50
Social and Economic Council (SER) 27
social policy dimension 13
sovereign debt crisis 10, 11, 19, 25, 30, 32
state-centric approach 80, 83–4;
coalition government introducing
regulations 85–7; labour relaxed
regulations (2004) 84–5
state intervention in financial welfare
markets 81–2, 90
Süddeutsche Zeitung (SZ) 103
Svenska Brukstjänstemannaföreningen
(SBF) 147
Svenska Industriförbundet (SIF) 147
Svenska Personal-Pensionskassan 148
Sveriges Arbetsledareförbund (SALF) 148
*Sveriges Kommunalanställdas
Pensionskassa* (SKP) 148
Sveriges privatanställdas pensionskassa
(SPP) 147–8
Sweden: bipartite administration 150;
external funding 146–9
Swedish Industrial Association *see*
Svenska Industriförbundet (SIF)

Tariffonds 107
tax harmonisation 124, 127
the Pensions Regulator (tPR) 68
Third Capital Market Promotion Law
104, 106
Trades Union Congress (TUC) 46, 47

INDEX

trade union(s) 2, 8, 9, 12, 14, 32, 42, 100, 107
Trade Union Confederation 149
trajectory reforming: Germany 29–30; Netherlands, The 26–8; UK 28–9
Tuytens, P. 13, 78
twin processes 2, 39, 41, 43, 109
typically incremental process 2

UK 'de-risks' 64; changing investment norms 65–6; changing patterns of asset allocation in DB and DC investment 69; crises reinforcing trend towards liability-driven investment 68; financial industry influence in DC and DB investment 64–5; liability-driven investment 66–8

United Kingdom (UK); asset allocation in UK pension funds *61;* nominal funding ratios *26;* occupational pensions in *27;* pension fund investment 59; trajectory reforming 28–9

van der Zwan, N. 44, 121
van Kersbergen, K. 31
Varieties of Capitalism approach (VoC approach) 5, 136–7
Vis, B. 31

Weir, M. 118, 120
welfare-finance nexus 98, 100–1
welfare privatization 78–9
White collar unions 136, 141
Wiß, T. 1, 11, 19